COURTSHIP AND MARRIAGE
IN VICTORIAN ENGLAND

Recent Titles in
Victorian Life and Times

The Sporting Life: Victorian Sports and Games
Nancy Fix Anderson

Food and Cooking in Victorian England: A History
Andrea Broomfield

Health, Medicine, and Society in Victorian England
Mary Wilson Carpenter

Victorian Childhoods
Ginger S. Frost

Gone to the Shops: Shopping in Victorian England
Kelley Graham

Victorian Religion: Faith and Life in Britain
Julie Melnyk

Family Ties in Victorian England
Claudia Nelson

Victorian Technology: Invention, Innovation, and the Rise of the Machine
Herbert Sussman

COURTSHIP AND MARRIAGE IN VICTORIAN ENGLAND

Jennifer Phegley

VICTORIAN LIFE AND TIMES
Sally Mitchell, Series Editor

AN IMPRINT OF ABC-CLIO, LLC
Santa Barbara, California • Denver, Colorado • Oxford, England

Library of Congress Cataloging-in-Publication Data

Phegley, Jennifer.
  Courtship and marriage in Victorian England / Jennifer Phegley.
    p. cm. — (Victorian life and times)
  Includes bibliographical references and index.
  ISBN 978-0-313-37534-7 (hardcopy : alk. paper) — ISBN 978-0-313-37535-4 (ebook)
1. Marriage—England—History—19th century.   2. Courtship—England—History—19th century.   I. Title.
  HQ615.P49   2012
  306.73'4094209034—dc23   2011032184

ISBN: 978-0-313-37534-7
EISBN: 978-0-313-37535-4

16   15   14   13   12   1   2   3   4   5

This book is also available on the World Wide Web as an eBook.
Visit www.abc-clio.com for details.

Praeger
An Imprint of ABC-CLIO, LLC

ABC-CLIO, LLC
130 Cremona Drive, P.O. Box 1911
Santa Barbara, California 93116-1911

This book is printed on acid-free paper ∞

Manufactured in the United States of America

For images produced by ProQuest as part of *British Periodicals*, inquiries may be made to the following:

ProQuest
The Quorum
Barnwell Road
Cambridge
CB5 8SW UK
Tel: +44 (0) 1223 215512
Web page: http://www.proquest.co.uk/

This permission is granted for the use of the images in this book only. You should contact ProQuest if you plan to use these images in other contexts or to republish any other images from *British Periodicals*.

FOR SCOTT

CONTENTS

LIST OF ILLUSTRATIONS

SERIES FOREWORD

Although the 19th century has almost faded from living memory—most people who heard firsthand stories from grandparents who grew up before 1900 have adult grandchildren by now—impressions of the Victorian world continue to influence both popular culture and public debates. These impressions may well be vivid yet contradictory. Many people, for example, believe that Victorian society was safe, family centered, and stable because women could not work outside the home, although every census taken during the period records hundreds of thousands of female laborers in fields, factories, shops, and schools as well as more than a million domestic servants—often girls of 14 or 15—whose long and unregulated workdays created the comfortable leisured world we see in Merchant and Ivory films. Yet it is also true that there were women who had no household duties and desperately wished for some purpose in life but found that social expectations and family pressure absolutely prohibited their presence in the workplace.

The goal of books in the Victorian Life and Times series is to explain and enrich the simple pictures that show only a partial truth. Although the Victorian period in Great Britain is often portrayed as peaceful, comfortable, and traditional, it was actually a time of truly breathtaking change. In 1837, when 18-year-old Victoria became Queen, relatively few of England's people had ever traveled more than 10 miles from the place where they were born. Little more than half the population could read and write, children as young as five worked in factories and mines, and political power was entirely in the hands of a small minority of men who held property. By the time Queen Victoria died in 1901, railways provided fast and cheap transportation for both goods and people, telegraph messages sped to the far corners of the British Empire in minutes, education was compulsory, a man's religion (or lack of it) no longer barred him from sitting in Parliament, and women were not only wives and domestic

servants but also physicians, dentists, elected school board members, telephone operators, and university lecturers. Virtually every aspect of life
had been transformed either by technology or by the massive political and
legal reforms that reshaped Parliament, elections, universities, the army,
education, sanitation, public health, marriage, working conditions, trade
unions, and civil and criminal law.

The continuing popularity of Victoriana among decorators and collec-
tors, the strong market for historical novels and for mysteries set in the
age of Jack the Ripper and Sherlock Holmes, the new interest in books
by George Eliot and Charles Dickens and Wilkie Collins whenever one is
presented on television, and the desire of amateur genealogists to discover
the lives as well as the names of 19th-century British ancestors all reveal
the need for accurate information about the period's social history and
material culture. In the years since the first edition of my book *Daily Life
in Victorian England* was published in 1996, I have been contacted by many
people who want more detailed information about some area covered in
that overview. Each book in the Victorian Life and Times series will focus
on a single topic, describe changes during the period, and consider the differences between country and city, industrial life and rural life, and above
all, made by class, social position, religion, tradition, gender, and economics. Each book is an original work, illustrated with drawings and pictures
taken from Victorian sources, enriched by quotations from Victorian publications, based on current research, and written by a qualified scholar.
All of the authors have doctoral degrees and many years' experience in
teaching; they have been chosen not only for their academic qualifications
but also for their ability to write clearly and to explain complex ideas to
people without extensive background in the subject. Thus the books are
authoritative and dependable but written in straightforward language;
explanations are supplied whenever specialized terminology is used, and
a bibliography lists resources for further information.

The Internet has made it possible for people who cannot visit archives
and reference libraries to conduct serious family and historical research.
Careful hobbyists and scholars have scanned large numbers of primary
sources—19th-century cookbooks, advice manuals, maps, city directories,
magazines, sermons, church records, illustrated newspapers, guidebooks,
political cartoons, photographs, paintings, published investigations of
slum conditions and poor people's budgets, political essays, inventories
of scientists' correspondence, and many other materials formerly accessible only to academic historians. Yet the World Wide Web also contains
misleading documents and false information, even on educational sites
created by students and enthusiasts, who don't have the experience to
put material into useful contexts. So far as possible, therefore, the bibli-
ographies for books in the Victorian Life and Times series will also offer
guidance on using publicly available electronic resources.

Courtship shapes the plot both of Victorian fiction and of current paperback historical novels; the "Victorian wedding" remains a romantic ideal for many 21st-century brides. But how accurate are our stereotypes of 19th-century behavior and ceremony? In *Courtship and Marriage in Victorian England,* Jennifer Phegley demonstrates that although elaborate weddings were customary only for relatively few people in the highest social classes and that in those classes dating was virtually unknown, there were nevertheless respectable couples who lived together without matrimony as well as surprising 19th-century equivalents to Match.com.

A scholar of 19th-century literature and the author of several books, including *Educating the Proper Woman Reader* (2004), which examined the serialized fiction in widely read family magazines on both sides of the Atlantic, Phegley draws material from conduct books, etiquette guides, letter-writing manuals, newspaper "agony columns," law treatises, periodicals, memoirs, and novels to show how class, circumstances, and social expectations influenced courtship, marriage, and alternatives to marriage during the Victorian period. She also carefully delineates 19th-century alterations in the laws of marriage, divorce, and married women's rights, information essential to understanding changes during the century.

Sally Mitchell, Series Editor

ACKNOWLEDGMENTS

This book would not have been possible without the encouragement, guidance, and astonishing knowledge of Sally Mitchell, who invited me to write it in the first place. Andrea Broomfield convinced me to take on the project and generously responded to early drafts. In addition, her book in this series served as a model of how to go about combining original scholarship with an accessible overview of a topic. I thank Mariah Gumpert, as well, for being an incredibly helpful and understanding editor.

I had a great deal of assistance while researching this book. The University of Missouri–Kansas City Women's and Gender Studies program helped jump-start the project by awarding me a research grant. Kristin Huston and Kelly Mathews energetically tracked down 19th-century periodical articles on microfilm before our university had access to full-text digital databases, for which I am grateful. Thanks to Kitty Ledbetter for putting me in contact with Kathryn Powell, who spent hours copying conduct books from microfilm at the Texas State University Library, and Sarah McNeely, who provided copies of the *Englishwoman's Domestic Magazine* courtship advice column. The staff at the Yale University Library microfilm room were also very helpful.

The process of obtaining images and permissions was an organizational feat that could not have been pulled off without the assistance of an entire team of people. Special thanks to Katy Holyoak at the Royal Collection Picture Library, St. James's Palace, London; Pat Fox and Margaret Tenney at the Harry Ransom Humanities Research Center at the University of Texas at Austin; Amy Jones from the Department of Special Collections and Rare Books at the University of Missouri–Columbia; Scott Gipson, Stuart Hinds, Diane Hunter, and Chris LeBeau at Miller Nichols Library, University of Missouri–Kansas City; and Chris Cotton from ProQuest. The University of Missouri-Kansas City Women's and Gender Studies

Program and Department of English provided funding that helped pay for the image permissions.

Writing this book was even more challenging than researching it, given the abundance of primary sources and existing scholarship on the subject. Luckily, I had a wonderful network of supportive colleagues. Lynda Payne read portions of the manuscript, while Virginia Blanton, Rebecca Dingo, Miriam Forman-Brunell, Jennifer Frangos, Debbie Smith, and Lisa Tantonetti provided advice and encouragement. Collaborating with Lauren Obermark on a conference paper shaped my thinking about 19th-century love letters. Dana Tulodziecki held me to a strict writing schedule by meeting me regularly at local coffee shops, while Scott Ditzler supplied me with bottomless cups of hot tea and good humor to keep me going. I also have to thank my mom, Roxanne Coughlin, for her constant encouragement and my sister, Lindsay Coughlin Siehl, for introducing me to the pleasures and pains of contemporary wedding planning.

MARRIAGE LAW CHRONOLOGY

1753   **Lord Hardwicke's Marriage Act** standardized wedding ceremonies by requiring that they be conducted by ordained Anglican clergymen in official churches in one's parish of residence after the reading of the banns for three Sundays prior to the marriage. Alternatively, a marriage license could be obtained, though it was more expensive and required a four-week waiting period. The act was intended to prevent clandestine marriages, particularly among minors, by requiring parental consent for those less than 21 years of age.

1835   **Deceased Wife's Sister's Marriage Act** prohibited marriage between a widower and his sister-in-law. Based on ecclesiastical canon law opposing unions of familial affinity, this act made marriages that had previously been voidable only if challenged in court absolutely illegal.

1836   **Civil Marriage Act** recognized weddings performed in churches other than the Church of England if they were licensed for marriage and the ceremony was conducted in the presence of a civil registrar. It also allowed civil services to be conducted in the Office of the Registrar.

1839   **Custody of Infants Act** allowed a mother to petition for custody of children under seven years old in case of divorce, unless she had been guilty of adultery. A mother could also request periodic access to children over seven.

1856   **Lord Brougham's Marriage Act** was aimed at ending "Scots" marriages that evaded English marriage law. The act required one member of a marrying couple to reside in Scotland for three weeks prior to marriage in that country. This act also lowered fees for civil marriages and eliminated the requirement of a public announcement of intent to marry for civil weddings in England.

1857   **Matrimonial Causes Act (often called the Divorce Act)** allowed a wife to sue for divorce if her husband committed adultery and if it was compounded by desertion (for more than two years) or brutality or if his adultery was committed with a relative, a man, or an animal. A husband could seek a divorce based on adultery alone.

1870   **Married Women's Property Act** gave married women the right to their own earnings after marriage and to amounts of up to £200 that were gifts or inheritances.

1873   **Infant Custody Act** provided the possibility that a mother could obtain child custody even if she had committed adultery and increased the age of the eligible child from 7 to 16.

1878   **Amendment to the Matrimonial Causes Act** permitted a woman to seek a legal separation and maintenance order through a local magistrate if her husband was convicted of assaulting her. If the order was granted, neither party could legally remarry, as they could with a divorce.

1882   **Married Women's Property Act** gave every married woman sole possession of all earnings and inheritances, before or after marriage.

1886   **Guardianship of Infants Act** established that the welfare of the child should be considered in all custody decisions, eliminating the de facto right given to the father. It also granted the mother the right to guardianship after the death of the father or to joint custody with a guardian appointed by the father.

1886   **Maintenance in Case of Desertion Act** reinforced the 1878 Amendment to the Matrimonial Causes Act by expanding the possible causes of separation and maintenance to include desertion and neglect. In 1895, persistent cruelty was also added as a legitimate cause for formal separation, and the requirement of convicting and jailing the husband first was eliminated.

1907   **Repeal of the Deceased Wife's Sister's Marriage Act**

1918   **Voting Act** enfranchised all women over age 30.

1923   **Divorce Law Reform Bill** allowed women to divorce their husbands for adultery alone.

1928   **Equal Franchise Act** provided equal voting rights for all women over age 21.

1

Victorian Marriage: Love, Companionship, and the Law

The worst of all mockeries is a marriage without love: a yoking together, but not a union; bondage, without a bond; a multiplication of the burdens of life for both parties, without a mutual life interest.

—*Reynolds's Miscellany*, September 1848

My heart is capable (I feel it is) of a love to which *no* deprivation would be a sacrifice—a love which . . . would bear down all the restraints which *duty* and *expediency* might throw in the way. . . . But the all-perfect Mortal, who could inspire me with a love so extravagant, is nowhere to be found—exists nowhere but in the Romance of my own imagination!

—Jane Welsh, in a letter to her future husband, Thomas Carlyle

The Victorian period was an age of love. The best-remembered novels of the period—Charlotte Brontë's *Jane Eyre*, Charles Dickens's *David Copperfield*, and George Eliot's *Middlemarch* among them—hinge on the trials and triumphs of love and conclude with satisfying marriages of companionate souls. As Annie S. Swan wrote in her book on courtship and marriage in 1894, "it is beyond question that love, courtship, and marriage are words to conjure with in the garden of youth, and that a love-story has yet the power to charm even sober men and women of middle age, for whom romance is mistakenly supposedly over." Love, as the *Reynolds's Miscellany* epigraph suggests, was believed to be the strongest foundation for marriage and the best way to ensure happiness. According to John Maynard's

Matrimony: Or, What Marriage Life Is, and How to Make the Best of It (1866), marrying for anything other than love—even if urged to do so by one's parents or friends—was potentially disastrous: "In such cases, the beauty of marriage is destroyed, the fountain of life embittered, the pathway across time strewed with thorns, and overcast with clouds of gloom." Maynard thus implores women to remember that "gold is a paltry thing compared to love, that yielding to the unreasonable wishes of parents and friends will . . . be a life-long source of misery to you. Rather refuse the offers of a hundred men, than marry one you do not, cannot love." The virtues of love were not just for women, though *Reynolds's Miscellany* repeated a popular notion about men, women, and love in 1863: "There is no doubt that love is the great leading activity of a woman's life. Man has other things which divide his attention; the cares and anxieties of the world—the struggle for fame, or wealth, or power—press more closely upon him; but love is to a woman the grand reality." Yet, love was considered just as beneficial for men as for women. Even Samuel Stone Hall's *Bliss of Marriage, or How to Get a Rich Wife* (1858) lectured his gold-digging target audience about the benefits of love: "Love is the softener and polisher of the human mind; it transforms barbarians into men; its pleasures are refined and delicate; and even its pain and anxieties have something in them soothing and pleasuring."[1] All of this advice—and much more available in etiquette guides, magazines, and novels—pointed toward one recently entrenched ideal: that of the companionate marriage, a union based on love and mutual affection.

The companionate marriage had become a common aspiration by the dawn of the 19th century. Broadly speaking, prior to 1660, families were largely patriarchal and authoritarian, with marriages relying on parental decisions guided by the mutual benefits of social and economic exchange. Families slowly evolved over the course of the 17th and 18th centuries, becoming tighter-knit units based as much on affection as on social status or economics. Within these newly conceived families, the companionate marriage became the ideal, and love was seen as a crucial component of marriage. As a result, those who were marrying were given more control over choosing their own partners. Marriage was no longer simply a transaction between families facilitated by the heads of households; it was instead imagined as a union of companions who were supposed to emotionally enrich each other's lives. As Stephanie Coontz explains,

> the sentimentalization of married love in the Victorian period was a radical social experiment. The Victorians were the first people in history to try to make marriage the pivotal experience in people's lives and married love the principle focus of their emotions, obligations, and satisfactions. . . . Victorian marriage harbored all the hopes for romantic love, intimacy, personal fulfillment, and mutual happiness that were to be expressed more openly and urgently during the early twentieth century.

Jane Welsh's conception of romantic love—expressed in a letter to her future husband, the Victorian sage Thomas Carlyle—reflected popular sentiments that were transforming notions of the very purpose of matrimony.
For her, love could make any problem solvable and any burden bearable.
Unfortunately, as Coontz points out, "these hopes for love and intimacy
were continually frustrated by the rigidity of nineteenth-century gender
roles."[2] Jane Welsh was a clever, well-educated, wealthy heiress, but once
she married Carlyle, the fortuneless, crabby, intellectual author whose
status was inferior to her own, her ideals of love and companionship
were tamed by the realities of household drudgery and the difficulty of
intellectual equality between a husband and a wife. While Carlyle wrote
his philosophical and historical treatises, Jane was expected to minister to
his every need, including battling with the neighbors to keep their roost-
ers quiet so as not to disturb his sleep or his work. The Carlyle marriage
exemplifies the pitfalls of marrying for love and expecting companionship in a society in which men and women were assigned very different roles within the family and society and were treated very differently
under the law.

While most Victorians struggled with the contrast between the ideal
and the reality of marriage, one iconic couple stood as a beacon of companionate domesticity and a model for the nation: Queen Victoria and
Prince Albert. They were married on February 10, 1840, when both were
only 20 and Victoria had reigned as Queen for fewer than three years.
The couple faced many challenges, including the controversy surrounding Albert's German heritage and the Queen's volatile temper. Perhaps
the biggest challenge was the fact that as the nation's sovereign ruler, the
Queen was not subject to the laws and restrictions that burdened other
women. She was, therefore, not required to submit to her husband's will.
The Queen's autonomy made her marriage unique. Indeed, a cartoon depicting Victoria proposing to Albert uses the couple's gender role reversal
for comic effect (Figure 1.1). The title "Leap Year!" refers to the tradition
that a woman could propose to a man on February 29 of a leap year, which
only occurs every four years. Victoria proposed to Albert in October 1839,
which was not a leap year, but they were married the following February,
during a leap year. While the Queen made a grand effort to play up her
domesticity—she and Albert seemed to embody Victorian family values—
there was no getting around the fact that she had unrivaled power over
her husband and the nation.

Yet, Victoria and Albert were most likely in love and certainly companionable. She wrote in her journal soon after their wedding: "MY
DEAREST DEAREST DEAR Albert sat on a footstool by my side, and his
excessive love and affection gave me feelings of heavenly love and happiness I never could have hoped to have felt before! He clasped me in his
arms, and we kissed each other again and again! His beauty, his sweet-
ness and gentleness—really how can I ever be thankful enough to have

Figure 1.1. "Leap Year!" The Royal Collection, © 2011 Her Majesty Queen Elizabeth II.

such a *Husband*!" In this relationship, though, the roles were in many ways reversed. Victoria called Albert her "Angel," and he became the overseer and organizer of the home, while she attended to the business of the nation. Though the "Angel in the House" (named after Coventry Patmore's famous mid-century poem) was supposed to be a woman, Albert embodied the role perfectly. He made the Queen's household run more efficiently by cutting wasteful spending, rearranging the chain of command among the servants, and better coordinating activities, ultimately saving £25,000 a year, for which he was rewarded in the press with caricatures of himself counting scrub brushes. Eventually, Albert closely advised Victoria in politics and business, but she continued to carefully balance her public image as head of state with that of submissive wife, insisting that she was everything a wife was supposed to be (despite the fact that she dreaded getting pregnant and having babies, a key duty of a wife). Privately, Victoria admitted, "Our position is very different from any other married couple. A. is in my house and not I in his. . . . Dearest Angel Albert, God only knows how I love him. His position is difficult, heaven knows."[3] Gail Turley Houston argues that this confusion of gender roles "complicated the concepts of womanhood and sovereignty" while also revealing Albert to be "both the antithesis and the ideal of Victorian masculinity." This state of contradiction was something that the couple was remarkably successful at concealing at the same time that they "graphically embodied" it for the public.[4] Victoria and Albert were certainly an unusual model, but in many ways they took the new marital ideal toward its logical conclusion: that of a marriage of equals.

DEFINING THE COMPANIONATE MARRIAGE

The companionate marriage, as defined by Coventry Patmore in "The Angel in the House," was the highest form of pleasure on earth:

> Feasts satiate; stars distress with height;
> Friendship means well, but misses reach,
> And wearies in its best delight, . . .
> And to converse direct within Heaven
> Is oft a labour in the breast; . . .
> But truly my delight was more
> In her to whom I'm bound for aye
> Yesterday than the day before
> And more to-day than yesterday.

Patmore is known for his worship of the domestic goddess who selflessly serves her husband, but his vision of marriage was also reliant on the ideal of an equivalent meeting of souls. He writes of marriage as nature's "arithmetic of life," in which "the smallest unit is a pair."[5] Patmore distinguishes a marital union from a passing attraction and places mature love and friendship above passion. Today he is often criticized for perpetuating a sexist view of woman as completing the man (which was based on legal and biblical definitions of marriage), but his conception of wedded bliss is not far from that held by journalist and women's rights activist Annie Swan later in the century. Swan defines the companionate marriage as a relationship based primarily on "comradeship—a standing shoulder to shoulder, upholding each other through thick and thin, and above all keeping their inner sanctuary sacred from the world." Companionate marriage was, then, based not only on love but also on mutual loyalty, duty, and protection. Swan mapped out specific duties for both husbands and wives. A husband was expected to

1. love his wife "sincerely, ardently, supremely";
2. prove his love by creating a happy home;
3. provide a comfortable economic livelihood for his wife through industrious and temperate behavior; and
4. prepare for his wife's maintenance after his death.

Likewise, a wife was supposed to

1. love her husband above all others;
2. obey her husband "in all things not sinful";
3. keep herself "clean and neat" but not "extravagant in dress"; and
4. keep her house tidy and prepare meals on time.

Swan also outlined the mutual duties of married couples, indicating that the relationship was, ideally, a partnership. Together, husbands and wives were entreated to

1. bear and forbear with each other;
2. conceal each others' imperfections from the world; and
3. endeavor to increase each other's happiness.[6]

These high expectations focused on creating a home life that was a fortress against the corrupting forces of the outside world. Husband and wife were to work together to create a private realm of comfort and happiness. Women were, of course, expected to submit to the will of their husbands but to serve as their moral and spiritual guides, while men were expected to control their tempers and curtail their demands on their wives. While we can easily recognize the constraints imposed on women by their all-consuming role in the Victorian home, the rigorous refashioning of men's roles in domestic life are perhaps less obvious.

During the 18th century, men participated in a lively network of masculine activities outside of the home, frequenting public houses and men's clubs after work. Middle-class Victorian men, on the other hand, were expected to spend time in the evenings around the hearth reading and talking to their wives and children. John Tosh argues that

by elevating the claims of wife and mother far above other ties, domesticity undermined the tradition of a vigorous associational life with other men, and imposed a new constraint on men's participation in the public sphere. . . . Domesticity supposedly allowed workhorses and calculating machines to become men again, by exposing them to human rhythms and human affections. The very qualities which set the family apart from the prevailing social mores were what recommended it to middle-class men who were appalled by the disfigurement of industrialism, even as they struggled to profit from it.

Men, then, had to dramatically switch gears to fit into two worlds: that of the rough-and-tumble working world and that of the domestic sanctuary. Swan acknowledges that men had a great deal of work to do if they were to meet new expectations for domestic behavior: "It is without a doubt a more arduous task for a man to cultivate the unselfish spirit, because the training of the race for centuries has rather tended to the fostering of selfishness in him."[7] Men faced new and continuing challenges to conduct themselves appropriately in both the public and the private spheres.

The companionate marriage, while gesturing toward equality between the sexes, was in reality based on the attraction of opposites. Tosh argues it was "assumed that sharply distinguished roles could be deeply satisfying to both parties: to the husband on account of the emotional support he received from his wife, and to the wife because of the window on the wider world which his education and experience made available to her." According to A. James Hammerton, "the domestic idyll promised a conjugal utopia of mutual forbearance and respect, where husbands' and wives' understanding of each other's separate responsibilities and cares would guarantee marital harmony."[8] Both partners in the companionate marriage were subject to high—and unrealistic—expectations, but women, whose lives were confined to the domestic sphere, were under much greater pressure to make a happy home. The icon of angelic womanhood within the home is prolific conduct book author Sarah Stickney Ellis.

In *The Wives of England* (1843), Ellis insists that the truly companionate marriage is an obtainable ideal; indeed, her books are intended to facilitate its cultivation. Yet, Ellis warns young women that being a wife is hard work and entails much sacrifice. Though, like Patmore, she deems married love "the richest treasure which this earth affords," she explains her mission as a reality check on sentimental notions of married life:

> If . . . I have selected words of warning, in preference to those of an opposite nature, it has been because the tide of popular feeling, especially amongst young women, is already sufficiently strong in favour of matrimonial alliances. . . . This disproportion betwixt expectation and reality, arises from ignorance . . . of the human heart, of the actual circumstances of human life, of the operation of cause and effect in human affairs.

In the face of youthful and romantic notions of love, Ellis—who did not marry until the age of 38 and worried that her minister husband would not be able to handle her independence as an author—sought to awaken women to the potential challenges of marriage while emphasizing the elements of domestic life they could control. She notes that "perhaps there never yet was a woman of warm feelings, or man either, who had not, in early life, some vision of conjugal felicity, which after experience and knowledge of the world have failed to stamp with the impress of reality."[9] As Hammerton argues, Ellis's "austere prescriptions actually reflected women's heightened expectations of the quality of marital companionship, but, by contrast, her discouraging descriptions of marital experience mirrored the more realistic contradictions in a form of companionate marriage still based on separate spheres and patriarchal authority."[10] Ellis advises women to "be prepared for discovering faults in men, as they are for beholding spots in the sun, or clouds in the summer sky" but not to "love them less, because they cannot admire them more." Instead, she urges readers to remember that "strife of public affairs, and the competition of business . . . require a degree of concentrated effort in favour of self, and a powerful repulsion against others, which woman, happily for her, is seldom or never called upon to maintain." Wives, then, must tolerate their husbands' lack of domesticity and urge them toward the pleasures of home whenever possible since the involvement of men in the capitalist world of competition distorts their sympathetic faculties and increases their selfishness.

In Ellis's conception, wives are the antidote to the immoral realm of business and commerce. The role of the wife becomes greater than the role of any individual woman; she sees the wife as a symbol of the nation itself:

> Let us prove, for the benefit of succeeding generations, how much may be done for the happiness of our homes, and the good of our country, by being satisfied with the position in which Providence has placed us, and by endeavoring to adorn that position with the lasting embellishments which belong to an enlightened understanding, a well-regulated mind, and a benevolent, sincere, and faithful heart.[11]

While a married woman was expected to play the domestic goddess to an often unworthy husband, Ellis argues she should do her job to the best of her abilities regardless of her personal disappointment. Thus, Ellis becomes the icon of domesticity even while expressing dissatisfaction with its constraints. Ellis's willingness to articulate the ways in which marital ideals often failed to match reality is typically overlooked by 21st-century audiences, but it is probably what made her works so popular among her original readers.

The ideal of the companionate marriage may not have coincided with the reality of middle-class domestic life, but it jarred even more clumsily against a more combative style of marriage among the working classes. Marital violence occurred in all classes, but, according to Elizabeth Foyster, new conceptions of companionship allowed "middling and elite women to demand better conduct from their husbands. Marital conduct was rendered into an indicator of class superiority and difference." However, what was considered acceptable behavior was also changing among the working classes. Hammerton points out that "the fact that so many working men were aware of these prescriptions, but too often failed to live up to them, may have promoted a disturbing sense of guilt and some confusion over the nature of masculinity. . . . 'Manliness,' as middle-class men had been learning, was now to be tested not only among male peers but in the domestic sphere by more civilized behaviour toward women." Notions of domesticity clashed with the realities of working-class life as male breadwinning became central to definitions of masculinity but men continued to rely on the wages of their wives for the livelihood of their families. The disconnect between domestic ideology and the necessities of day-to-day survival certainly strained working-class family life and had the potential to increase marital volatility.[12] As expectations for happiness in marriage were raised for everyone, brutality and violence became less acceptable but remained pervasive.

Advice manuals such as *The Working Man's Wife* (1844) urged the adoption of the companionate ideal on the grounds it would improve the reputation of all working people, an argument also made by Chartists and other working-class activists. Echoing the arguments set forth by Ellis, this working-class marriage guide urged its readers to see themselves as representatives of the most civilized nation in the world and to behave accordingly. Even a working woman, the Religious Tract Society publication claims, could create a happy and harmonious home simply by making "the house tidy" and preparing meals before she left for work. On her return home from work, she would then be able to "cheer her husband by her presence, and to convince him that, even when duty calls her away, it is rendered pleasant by the thought that she is adding to the comforts of those dear to her at home." For working women, duty could and usually did lie outside the home, but it always beckoned back to the domestic realm. Anna Clark notes that although "the domestic ideal promised greater harmony, its stress on male dominance and female dependence contained within it the seeds of continuing family violence."[13]

The hope that partners would fulfill such lofty domestic roles—and the fact that they would likely fail—made it more difficult than ever to decide when and whom to marry. As Hammerton argues, "greater emotional expectations made marriage a much more hazardous venture for both parties" and "precepts for emotional compatibility elevated private behaviour to a matter of public importance and discussion on a quite unprecedented scale."[14] The weight of the choice of a partner was reinforced constantly in popular culture, and it was no secret that a bad decision could ruin one's life, or at least make it very unpleasant. The importance of knowing and loving one's partner before marriage is emphasized in a Valentine's Day article and illustration in the *Ladies' Treasury* in 1866 (Figure 1.2). The article insists that young ladies be allowed to choose husbands based on their own preferences and feelings, since if a woman is not attracted to a man,

> however handsome he may be in the eyes of others, he is no less an ogre to her. He is altogether deformed in her blind aversion. She sees in him only the exaggeration of repulsive ugliness such as our engraving represents. Other maidens, beautiful as herself, look on with approving, nay envious looks. Not one but would willingly change places with her. She alone feels the utter repugnance which death only can destroy. Be sure that if ever so small a dislike be felt before marriage, it will increase until the husband becomes in her eyes a monster. Then let not wealth or rank hide beneath a specious veil any moral deformity which would totally destroy all happiness, and perhaps end in crime and disgrace. Let not parents force their daughters to marry, however gilded the prospect.[15]

The illustration of a man admired by onlookers who appears to be a monster serves as a warning to parents that they should never arrange a marriage that is not desired by both partners and to young ladies that they should never marry based merely on the advice of others.

Even if allowed to choose one's own spouse, many worried that the initial passions would inevitably fade and might die out completely. As *Reynolds's Miscellany* quips, "marriage is like a roast leg of mutton on Sunday, served up cold on Monday, ditto with pickles on Tuesday, and hashed up on Wednesday." Similarly, the *Mirror* equates marriage to "a glass of soda water—very sparkling when it is first carried to the lips, but palpably tasting of acid before it is half swallowed." If marriage could go sour so quickly, even among profusely professed lovers, one had better be even more careful about deciding whom to marry. One unhappily married woman complained in the *London Reader* that

> I have had bad luck as a wife, for my husband and I have scarcely a taste in common. He wishes to live in the country, which I hate. I like the thermometer at 75 degrees, which he hates. He likes to have the children brought up at home instead of at school, which I hate. I like music, and wish to go to concerts, which he hates. He likes roast pork, which I hate, and I like minced veal, which he hates. There is but one thing we both like, and that is what we cannot both have, though we are always trying for it—the last word.

This frivolous (and likely fictional) woman confesses that her husband married her solely for her money, sentencing her to "ten years of purgatory."[16]

A FUTURE HUSBAND SEEN THROUGH THE MEDIUM OF REPUGNANCE.

Figure 1.2. "A Future Husband Seen through the Medium of Repugnance." *The Ladies' Treasury,* February 1, 1866, 80. Harry Ransom Humanities Research Center, University of Texas at Austin.

As if in response to such lamentations, the author of *The Working Man's Wife* declares that compatibility should be based not only on love or money but also on respect and generosity: "Some married people are not happy because they are always striving for their own way, and their own interest"; however, "if they had that true steady affection for each other which deserves the name of love, it would inspire such a regard for mutual comfort and respectability, as would induce them to wait patiently, and labour diligently, and save steadily, though at the expense of much self-denial, till they possessed the means of making each other comfortable."[17] Beyond love, then, true companionability and a willingness to sacrifice oneself for the good of the marriage partner were qualities more difficult to identify but no less crucial to marital happiness.

BEYOND THE COMPANIONATE IDEAL

Despite the importance of romantic love and companionship, Victorians were very practical people. It was an age of industry, efficiency, progress, and science. When it came to making a lifelong commitment, advice givers urged marriageable misses and misters to consider their choices in a clearheaded and logical way. If not, as Victorian fiction repeatedly shows, the consequences could be devastating. *Middlemarch* and *David Copperfield*, despite their ultimate happy endings, offer negative examples of marital choices in Dorothea Brooke's torturous union with Edward Casaubon and David's hapless marriage to Dora Spenlow. But it is Helen Lawrence's disastrous marriage to Arthur Huntingdon in Ann Brontë's *The Tenant of Wildfell Hall* that really stands out for its didactic intent to warn women about the consequences of making a bad martial decision. Helen's aunt teaches her the following unromantic rules of courtship, which Helen rebelliously ignores when she meets Arthur:

> Receive, coldly and dispassionately, every attention, till you have ascertained and duly considered the worth of the aspirant. . . . First study; then approve, then love. Let your eyes be blind to all external attractions, your ears deaf to all the fascinations of flattery and light discourse.—These are nothing—and worse than nothing—snares and wiles of the tempter, to lure the thoughtless to their own destruction. Principle is the first thing, after all; and next to that, good sense, respectability, and moderate wealth. If you should marry the handsomest, and most accomplished and superficially agreeable man in the world, you little know the misery that would overwhelm you, if, after all, you should find him to be a worthless reprobate, or even an impracticable fool. . . . Believe me, *matrimony is a serious thing*.

Arthur turns out to be violent, cruel, and unprincipled, but Helen marries him anyway. She writes in her diary, "If I had known him in the beginning, as thoroughly as I do now, I probably never should have loved him, and if I had loved him first, and then made the discovery, I fear I should have thought it my duty not to have married him. To be sure, I might have known him, for everyone was willing enough to tell me about him, and he himself was no accomplished hypocrite, but I was willfully blind."[18] Helen falls in love, defies all advice about how to evaluate a potential spouse, and suffers the consequences of a brutish husband.

The choice of a marriage partner, then, was supposed to be based on love, but also on considerations such as character. As the *London Reader* warned, "Do not marry a man who has only his love for you to recommend him. That is very fascinating but it does not make the man. If he is not otherwise what he should be, you will never be happy. The most perfect man that did not love you should never be your husband; but though marriage without love is terrible, love only will not do it." In *How to Be Happy though Married, Being a Handbook to Marriage by a Graduate in the University of Matrimony* (1885), Edward Hardy suggests that while romance is vital to making a happy match, "you would not like to live with a liar, with a thief, with a drunkard, for twenty or thirty years. . . . In their haste to be married many women are too easily satisfied with the characters of men who may offer themselves as husbands. They aim at matrimony in the abstract; not *the* man, but any man." Men, likewise, "should marry to obtain a friend and companion rather than a cook and housekeeper; but yet that girl is a prize indeed who has so well prepared herself for the business of wifehood as to be able to keep not only her husband company, but her house in good order." Similarly, an article in the *Critic* laments that

> some young men marry dimples, some ears; the mouth, too, is occasionally married, the chin not so often. Only the Other day, a young fellow fell head over heels and ears in love with a braid. . . . He was so far gone that he became engaged to this braid; . . . What do young men marry? Why, they marry these, and many other bits and scraps of a wife, instead of the true thing; and then, after the wedding, they are surprised to find that, although married, they have no wives.[19]

So, what—other than love, compatibility, or beauty—was marriage to be based on, and how was a suitable marriage partner to be found?

The erosion of parental power and the growth of choice led to a more structured system of formal courtship for the upper classes to ensure that the process of finding a spouse would still result in sound social and economic connections for families. The London Season—with its formal balls, dinners, garden parties, picnics, and other organized events—was restricted to certain families and served as a veritable marriage incubator for the upper classes. Pat Jalland contends that most marriages in upper-class families "involved love inspired by judgment rather than passion. . . . Even where the primary emphasis was placed on love between partners, it was generally felt that love would only last if compatibility existed in other respects also." For these women, "a marriage of social equals" was assumed to breed compatibility, though by the end of the century, alliances between the younger sons of landed aristocratic families and daughters of cash-rich middle-class families were widely accepted as a means of consolidating power and wealth.[20]

Marriage was still largely an economic decision. As the economy moved from communal agrarian modes of production toward waged manufacturing and commercial systems, the increasing separation of the home and the workplace precipitated the wider division between male and female domains. The resulting decrease in work opportunities for some working- and all middle-class women made marriage an economic necessity or, at least, the best means of improving their status. As a result of economic realities and social expectations, most Victorian women chose to marry. In 1871, nearly 90 percent of women between the ages of 45 and 49 were or had been married.[21]

Middle-class men were not expected to marry until they had sufficient means to support a wife and family; indeed, men were expected to have a year's income on hand, half of which was to be spent on furnishing a new home. The money required varied by class and social position, but advice manuals generally suggested an income of at least £300 per year as the entry point into middle-class living as this sum would likely allow the employment of three servants. An income of £1,000 or more could easily provide a horse and carriage with a groom in addition to the req- uisite household staff. Those earning only £100 to £300 per year could live modestly but respectably with one or two servants.[22] Patricia Branca insists, however, that "£300 was neither typical nor minimal, but rather the maximum income level of most middle-class families." Branca esti- mates that in 1867, 637,875 families earned between £100 and £300, while only 150,000 families earned over £300. Those earning incomes below £100 are estimated at 757,250.[23] Middle-class expectations, therefore, reached a wide range of people at lower income levels. New and far-reaching mari- tal expectations were likely at play in England's maintenance of one of the oldest average marriage ages in the world. Typically, women married between the ages of 23 and 26 and men between 25 and 30, with ages ris- ing as one rose in class status.[24]

For many men in the working classes—as for women of the middle classes—marriage was required to obtain financial stability. John Gillis notes that

> the three to four pounds saved by a housemaid were just enough to set up a petty cabinetmaker; a tailor could begin with as little as a single pound; and there were a host of other occupations equally de- pendent on another's contribution. It was not only what the woman brought to the arrangement, but her labor and housekeeping that made the difference between survival and destitution. In London, where the prosperity of most trades was seasonal, it was not at all unusual for families to be entirely dependent on women's work when the man's trade was slack.

Early in the century, then, workingwomen were in a position of power to command a husband. As the century wore on, however, the percentage of women working in factories for substantial wages declined. In 1851, 22 percent of female workers were employed in textile production; by 1911, the number had dropped to 16 percent. Likewise, the share of women in manufacturing declined from 43 percent to 37 percent during the same period. Women's positions in sales and domestic service increased, but these jobs allowed women less independence. By the end of the century, working-class women came to rely more on marriage than did their male counterparts. The upper working classes (especially those who worked as servants), like the middle and upper classes, delayed marriage in the hope that wives would not have to work.[25]

In *The Modern Marriage Market* (1898), Marie Corelli claimed that an overemphasis on the economics of marriage made it no better than slavery or prostitution. Interestingly, she based her harsh judgment of the state of matrimony on the ideal of companionate marriage, which she claims "is entirely lost in the scheming, the bargaining, and the pricing" of the marriage market. Marriage, she reminds readers, is

> a vow which declares that the man and woman concerned have discovered in each other his and her true mate,—that they feel life is alone valuable and worth living in each other's company,—that they are prepared to endure trouble, pain, sickness, death itself, provided they may only be together,—and that all the world is a mere grain of dust in worth as compared to the exalted passion which fills their souls and moves them to become one in flesh as well as one in spirit.[26]

In essence, Corelli argues for the place of love and mutual sacrifice as not just an ideal to hope for but as a requirement for a true marriage.

Like Corelli, others saw a preoccupation with money as corrupting. However, they geared their anxieties disproportionately toward women who were seen as increasingly approaching marriage in a business-like and even cross manner, choosing spouses based solely on status and wealth. An article in the *Anti-Teapot Review* in August 1867 articulates the view that courtship had "fallen to the lot of the weaker portion of humanity," who "as if to show skill over brute force" have adopted the worldliness of the marital decisions that would formerly have been made for them by their parents:

> It can hardly have escaped any one that courtship and matrimony are very different things from what they used to be, and that a great change has passed over them even within the last few years. . . . The ladies of the last century were a romantic, poetry-loving set; those of the present day are cool, calculating, and almost avaricious; and, it is to be feared, are daily becoming more so. . . . A love-marriage between two paupers is foolish, and evil enough in its consequences; but the thought of an intended bride directing the preparation of the marriage settlement, and squabbling for a larger jointure, is infinitely more revolting.[27]

There was certainly a backlash against women's ability to choose their own husbands, particularly among the upper classes, whose preoccupation with the events of the London Season put them on display as if in a shop window. More importantly, it was these women who had the ability to maintain control over their own money and property through marriage settlements that limited their husbands' control over their wealth. The *Anti-Teapot Review* seems to have been more fearful of women's potentially increasing power in marriage than of their economically motivated choice of a partner given that the women it complains about have their own money to bring to the marriage. Indeed, it is women's lack of poetry reading and romancing that strikes fear in the heart of the commentator. If women began to control their own money and were no longer captivated by silly romantic notions, the writer wonders what use men would be to them.

The perception of women's increased power in the marriage market—or marriage lottery, as it was often called—also inspired anxiety-ridden accounts of the state of courtship in the humor magazine *Punch*. "Love Making in 1891" depicts a woman in complete control of courtship as well as the legal and intellectual aspects of her budding relationship. To the frustration of her lover, her concerns are far from the romantic ideal:

> *Edwin.* Believe me, dearest—
>
> *Angelina.* Pardon me, EDWIN, but is that the best adjective you can use? The word "dearest" implies that I have cost you a great deal—have been very expensive. Now when I prepared our settlements with my Solicitor!—
>
> [Explains the Law of Real and Personal Property]
>
> *Edwin.* Thanks, darling, your lecture has been delightful. But see, the moonlight tinges the trees without—
>
> *Angelina.* Moonlight? I am glad you mentioned the moon. Do you know our planetary system is—
>
> [Exhaustively canvasses the whole system of modern astronomy]
>
> *Edwin.* Wonderful! But the nightingale has begun her sweet singing—[28]

While the hapless Edwin seeks in vain to kindle a romantic exchange, Angelina (certainly not the typical "Angel in the House") steers the conversation toward her marriage settlement and her scientific knowledge. This exaggerated depiction of the New Woman—who was overly educated and independent, even masculine—had become pervasive by the end of the century as women's educational and professional opportunities expanded. Angelina, then, represents the fear that women were truly becoming more like—or more equal to—men. No longer merely the Angel in the House, Angelina seeks to protect her own interests even within marriage. However, the shift toward greater equality in marriage partnerships could only be fully realized in a marriage of equals and equality would only come with changes in the law. Hammerton argues that the flood of discourse surrounding marriage helped move the public and the government toward the reform of laws pertaining to women, particularly child custody, divorce, and property ownership.[29] As a result, the Victorian era witnessed a drastic shift in perceptions of women's power in courtship, along with very gradual but important changes in women's legal status and rights.

WOMEN, MARRIAGE, AND THE LAW

At the beginning of the century, married women were considered *femmes covert*, completely "covered" or represented under the law by their husbands. English common law related to marriage was based on the concept that once married, women were under the legal protection and political representation of their husbands and therefore had no independent legal existence. William Blackstone's *Commentaries on the Laws of England* (1765–1769) clearly summarized the doctrine of coverture, stating that husband and wife were treated as one person, and that person was the husband. Everything a woman owned, inherited, or earned automatically belonged to her husband. She could not sign a contract or make a will. She had no legal standing in court and no right to the custody of her children. If a husband did not designate his wife as the legal guardian of their children prior to his death, the children would become wards of the court. A man's right to his children was absolute; even if he allowed his wife access to or custody of their children in the case of a separation, the decision was not legally enforced. Single women, on the other hand, maintained *femme sole* status, which allowed them legal rights to act in their own interests. However, the social stigma against old maids and widows made singlehood an undesirable state for many. The one act that would finally ensure legal equality for women by tearing down the notion of coverture was the right to vote, but this was not granted to all women over 21 until 1928.

While a commitment to the companionate marriage certainly helped break down the resistance to greater equality for women, Mary Shanley points out that those who sought to reform marriage laws "explicitly and forcefully challenged what they regarded as society's sentimentalization of family life." To expose companionate marriage as a fantasy, feminists asserted that the laws regulating marriage were "based on the premise that a wife owed obedience to her husband, and where she would not voluntarily follow his will the law would leave her no other option."[30] Caroline Norton, Barbara Bodichon, Frances Power Cobbe, and John Stuart Mill are just a few of the leaders who fought for marriage partnerships that were equal under the law as well as in conception and practice. As a result, by the end of the century, women had gained the rights to obtain child custody, to seek a divorce, to sign contracts, and to maintain their own property and earnings.

Child Custody Law

Caroline Norton's struggle to obtain independence from her abusive husband and to maintain custody of her children provides one powerful example of an individual seeking rights that would affect the entire nation. The 1827 marriage was rocky from the start. Caroline was the granddaughter of famous playwright Richard Brinsley Sheridan and associated with the upper echelons of society, but she had no marriage portion and was encouraged to marry into the nobility. George Norton, MP and younger son of Baron Grantley, aggressively pursued Caroline. While she was not interested in him at first, he seemed to be an excellent match, and her family urged her to marry him. Their happiness, if they had any, was short-lived. Caroline's family soon accused him of misrepresenting his wealth, relying on her family connections to obtain favors, and exploiting her literary talents for his own benefit. Karen Chase and Michael Levenson argue that

> part of the scandal of this failed marriage, and no doubt part of the fascination it attracted, came from this tableau of domestic reversal: the male breadwinner grown weak and ineffectual gives way to the energetic female. Within a wider economy that would resolve ever more thoroughly into separate spheres, the affront of the Nortons was precisely to invert the spheres. . . . There he lounged, that spoiled child of the aristocracy, desperate to preserve a life of ease and privilege; and there she labored, the professional writer, skillful in manipulating the new resources of publishing in order to earn a substantial income that would preserve the family's precarious gentility.[31]

The break in the marriage, however, was more directly precipitated by Norton's violent behavior toward his wife. This included an incident in which he tore a door off the hinges and threw his pregnant wife down a staircase. In 1835, after a period of separation, George seized their children and refused to allow Caroline to see them or even know where they were. Then, in 1836, he accused Caroline of adultery by suing her friend—and the nation's prime minister—Lord Melbourne for criminal conversation with his wife in the Court of Common Law. This was essentially a civil suit filed by a husband against another man alleging property damage (the corruption of his wife) and demanding that a fine be paid to him as compensation for his loss. A wife was not allowed to testify on her own behalf in such a suit, as she was not a party to the claim, though evidence would be presented against her. A successful criminal conversation case was required to seek a divorce with the right to remarry by private act of Parliament.

Prior to the 1857 Divorce Act, obtaining a divorce was difficult, expensive, and very rare. Ecclesiastical courts granted two kinds of divorce. Divorce from the bond of wedlock (divorce *a vinculo matrimonii*) was an annulment that allowed remarriage. This option was only available if the marriage was ruled invalid as a result of insufficient age, mental incompetence, sexual impotence, incest, or fraud. The more common form of divorce was separation from bed and board (divorce *a mensa et thoro*). This was granted primarily for adultery committed by a wife. To enable remarriage after such a divorce, a man could file a criminal conversation suit against his wife's alleged lover. If both an ecclesiastical divorce *a mensa et thoro* and a civil suit for criminal conversation were won, an act of Parliament was still necessary for a full divorce. This required a member of Parliament to sponsor a private bill of divorce, a rehearing of the evidence for the previous two trials, and a ruling on the distribution of money, property, and child custody should the act of Parliament pass.[32] The process of divorce indicates that it was, as Shanley explains, "punitive measure against an adulterous wife, and a way for a man to assure himself of legitimate offspring." Between 1827 and 1857, only three petitions for divorce were granted to women.[33]

George Norton lost his criminal conversation lawsuit and his bid for a divorce with the right to remarry was effectively ended. Both Lord Melbourne and Caroline were cleared of any wrongdoing. However, Caroline's reputation was sullied, and she became the subject of gossip and speculation in the press as well as in private circles. Furthermore, she still did not have access to her children. Thus, she seized the opportunity to take her case to the public, defending herself and all women from the law that prevented them from receiving custody of their children unless allowed by their husbands. Caroline Norton published two pamphlets protesting the state of child custody law following her husband's failed law suit: *Separation of Mother and Child by the Law of Custody of Infants Considered* (1837) and *A Plain Letter to the Lord Chancellor on the Infant Custody Bill* (1839). Both works provided emotional as well as factual appeals urging the Court of Chancery to overturn the law that automatically gave custody rights to fathers. Norton's pamphlets were influential, but her connections were crucial. Her powerful friends in Parliament were persuaded to sponsor legislation based on her complaints.

The passage of the 1839 Custody of Infants Act allowed a mother to petition for custody of children under the age of seven in case of divorce, unless she had been proven guilty of adultery. This was a victory, but the law did not go as far as Caroline wished, as it only protected women wealthy enough to bring a suit in the Court of Chancery. In 1873 the prohibition against granting custody to a woman who had committed adultery was removed; however, most mothers (whether adulterous or not) were still denied custody on the grounds that they could not financially provide for a child. The 1886 Guardianship of Infants Act finally established that the welfare of the child should be considered in custody cases, thereby striking a blow to the assumption that fathers would receive custody by default. It also granted rights of guardianship to the mother in case of the father's death and joint custody if the father had appointed a guardian other than the mother.

Divorce Law

The 1857 Matrimonial Causes Act (often called the Divorce Act) established a civil divorce court in London that could grant both judicial separations and divorces without the authority of the Church or Parliament. Criminal conversation suits would now be postdivorce proceedings, and monetary awards would be split among husband, wife, and children. The Divorce Act expanded the rights of women to seek divorce, but restricted the grounds on which a woman could build her case. A man could sue for divorce based on his wife's adultery alone, but a woman could only sue for divorce if her husband committed adultery compounded by desertion (for more than two years) or brutality, or if the adulterous sexual acts were committed with a relative, a man, or an animal. This legal double standard, inherited from the earlier ecclesiastical and Parliamentary divorce systems, prevailed until 1923. Within the first year of its passage, 253 petitions for divorce were filed; wives brought 97 of the cases. This was a shock to the judicial system as expectations had been that divorce proceedings would only rise from about 4 to about 20 per year.[34]

In a population of 40 million, however, the number of divorces granted each year was still statistically small.[35] Divorces remained rare and publicly humiliating. Suspicion and contempt were often directed at parties to divorce proceedings, though sympathy was also offered, especially in egregious circumstances. Because the new law barred divorce in cases where either conspiracy or collusion was proven, investigation by the court into the origins of the evidence was necessary to detect fabricated adultery cases that would free unhappy husbands and wives by mutual consent. Divorce proceedings were regularly covered in special columns in the newspapers and became popular fodder for gossip and entertainment. Queen Victoria complained that the newspaper reports of divorce cases were "of so scandalous a character that it makes it almost impossible for a paper to be trusted in the hands of a young lady or boy. None of the worst French novels from which careful parents would try to protect their children can be as bad."[36] The stories from the court reports gave rise to a distinct genre of literature in the 1860s: the sensation novel. Often equated with the corrupting French fiction the Queen despised, the plots of novels such as Wilkie Collins's *The Woman in White* (1860), Ellen Price Wood's *East Lynne* (1861), and Mary Elizabeth Braddon's *Lady Audley's Secret* (1862) and *Aurora Floyd* (1863) were driven by issues related to marriage law, property law, custody, and inheritance. Novelists avoided direct depictions of divorce cases, resorting instead to the even more dramatic plot device of the bigamous marriage. If audiences read only sensation fiction, they might have assumed that bigamy was a very common offense. A few bigamous unions were reported in the *Times* alongside divorce cases, fueling the craze for sensation novels that explored such relationships. Indeed, the *Times* was often as sensational as sensation fiction. Allen Horstman summarizes the following real-life sensations reported in the *Times*:

> Mrs. Woodward, daughter of a Worcester clergyman, sought a divorce in 1859. Mr. Woodward, a solicitor in Pershore, married her in 1847, but she discovered, after twelve years of marriage, that he led a double life. He continued an affair with the woman who kept his house before his marriage, setting her up with a house in Gloucester. In a scene resembling "French novels," he there passed weeks or even months at a time, posing as a commercial traveler, and fathering three children. Divorce Granted. . . .
>
> Naomi Vicars sought a divorce from James for his incestuous adultery. In 1831 James, a cotton spinner and son of a mill owner, had an illegitimate daughter, christened Mary Ann Vicars. He and Naomi, a widow, married six years later but he left her in 1852. Naomi soon found James living with Mary Ann, now 21, who was "frequently seen in her father's bedroom in her nightdress," Mary Ann had three children by James. Divorce Granted. . . .
>
> Dr. Beale, an MD in Paddington, married in 1852. Discovering his wife's adultery with a man they met at a tea party, he "immediately sent her to her mother's house" in 1855. Before 1857 he successfully sued the lover, a clerk in the railway booking office, in an action of crim. con., winning £100. He sought, in 1859, to terminate completely his connection with his wife with a divorce, something beyond his means before 1857[37]. . . .

Not only did the public devour newspaper columns and novels about divorce and bigamy, they also attended divorce proceedings, eagerly vying for the best seats in the crowded courtroom (Figure 1.3).

The spectacle of divorce permeated society, raising questions about the viability of the companionate marriage. Between 1896 and 1900, the number of divorce petitions filed nearly tripled to 675 from the 226 filed between 1861 and 1865.[38] The assumption that the new divorce court was completely out of the range of average people is undermined by the statistics. In the decade following the Divorce Act, members of the working class filed 23 percent to 31 percent of divorce cases, and members of the

Figure 1.3. "The New Court for Divorce and Matrimonial Causes, Westminster Hall." *Illustrated London News*, May 22, 1858, 504. Used by permission of the University of Missouri–Kansas City Libraries, Dr. Kenneth J. LaBudde Department of Special Collections.

lower middle class brought 19 percent to 23 percent of cases. Furthermore, women filed 40 percent to 45 percent of all cases. Throughout the century, rulings gradually shifted in favor of rights for wives, demanding that husbands exhibit behavior compatible with the companionate model of marriage.[39]

As a result of the distasteful publicity of the divorce scandal industry as well as the high cost of divorce proceedings, many sought to avoid the courts altogether by separating illegally and even taking new partners. This seemed to be the best solution for many working-class people who had little or no property to protect and who typically agreed to leave children in the custody of their mothers.[40] For them, divorce was attempted only in extreme cases. It was easier for working-class women to obtain a separation order than to navigate the divorce court, particularly for those who lived outside of London. The prospect of traveling to the London divorce court "built an economic fence that only the most determined working-class suitor could scale. An uncontested divorce case cost about the equivalent of thirty weeks' pay for the average male wage-earner" at the end of the century.[41] One effect of the sexual double standard, according to Horstman, was that while divorces came to outnumber separations four to one, women "sought separations instead of divorces ten times more often than men." A separation order did not permit remarriage, but it did allow women to protect their own money and property from their husbands.[42]

The 1878 Amendment to the Matrimonial Causes Act made judicial separation more accessible to working-class women by permitting local magistrates to grant legal separation and maintenance orders. First, however, a woman was required to charge her husband with aggravated assault in a police court and to receive a conviction. This was a useful substitute for the expensive and remote divorce court. However, many women were urged by local magistrates to reconcile with their husbands or were denied legal aid. For example, in the Preston police court in 1878, only 4 out of 55 women were granted legal orders for separation and maintenance, despite obtaining convictions for assault.[43]

The 1886 Married Women (Maintenance in Case of Desertion) Act helped reinforce the earlier law. Under this act, women were granted up to £2 per week by local magistrates if their husbands were found guilty of assault, desertion, or neglect. In 1895, the Summary Jurisdiction (Married Woman) Act added persistent cruelty to the offenses that would permit legal separation, making it easier to obtain and lifting the requirement of sending one's husband to jail first. The 1895 act also allowed husbands to pay maintenance directly to their deserted wives instead of requiring wives to rely on the parish to collect the money. Though referred to as "divorces for the poor," legal separations were not permanent—they lapsed if the parties reunited. Because financial survival was often difficult, many women who won separation orders eventually returned to their husbands. While access to divorce increased significantly, many remaining obstacles ensured that the English divorce rate was still the lowest in Europe at the end of the century.[44]

Married Women's Property Law

Laws regarding women's property were even slower to change than those granting child custody, divorce, or separation. Shanley argues that this was because "divorce simply gave legal recognition to de facto marital breakdown. A married woman's property law, on the other hand, would have recognized the existence of two separate wills within an *ongoing* marriage" and "very few Members of Parliament believed that two independent wills could exist in one household without inviting disaster."[45] The transformation of a woman from *femme sole* to *femme covert* on marriage was disproportionately harsh for those of the working and lower middle classes. These women typically brought a small dowry to their marriage in the form of money or household goods. They maintained no separate money or property and relied on their husbands for all their needs. Women of the upper middle classes and aristocracy, on the other hand, typically had a marriage settlement in addition to a dowry. A settlement placed substantial funds into a trust for her sole use, which could protect her against a rogue husband or provide for her in the case of her husband's death or bankruptcy.

A husband was bound to assume his wife's debts and was held liable for contracts made on her behalf. However, a woman's money and property could be safeguarded by the creation of a trust or settlement drawn up by her father and signed by the bridegroom. Under deeds of settlement, a woman could hold property and profits from trade, will property or money to others, sue others—including her husband—for violation of property rights, and receive gifts of property or money from her husband. However, in 1850, only about 1 in 10 women received a marriage settlement. According to Jalland, the husband's family often contributed to the settlement as well as the wife's. Sometimes the marriage portion or dowry was a part of the settlement, and sometimes it was considered a separate amount that was not specifically under the wife's control. Often, "the daughter's marriage portion was considered the equivalent of the annual allowance granted to sons at the age of twenty-one. It was customary for a certain sum to be granted to the daughter on marriage, according to her father's means and number of children, and then a larger sum would be inherited at the father's death." Among the upper classes, the amount of a settlement was typically between £15,000 and £50,000, invested at about 4 percent and yielding an annual interest of £600 to £2,000 per year.[46] In contrast, a working woman's dowry might include a few simple necessities such as the household linens or a sewing machine, and these things technically belonged to the husband on marriage.[47] Clearly there were vast differences among married women regarding their access to money and property.

In the 1850s and 1860s the women of the Langham Place Circle began agitating for changes in the laws related to women's property and marriage. Barbara Bodichon, a leading member of the group, published an important treatise outlining the state of the laws concerning women in 1854. *A Brief Summary in Plain Language of the Most Important Laws of England Concerning Women* characterizes women's status this way:

> A woman of twenty-one becomes an independent human creature, capable of holding and administering property to any amount; or, if she can earn money, she may appropriate her earnings freely to any purpose she thinks good. Her father has no power over her or her property. But if she unites herself to a man, the law immediately steps in, and she finds herself legislated for, and her condition of life suddenly and entirely changed. Whatever age she may be of, she is again considered an infant . . . she loses her separate existence, and is merged in that of her husband.[48]

Daughter of radical MP Benjamin Leigh Smith, Bodichon had a unique perspective on marriage law. She was an illegitimate child raised by her father, who left equal legacies to each of his children, whether male or female, legitimate or illegitimate. With an income of £300 a year for life once she reached the age of 21, Bodichon had rare financial security for her age and origins.[49] Like Caroline Norton, Bodichon's close relationship to several members of Parliament put her in an excellent position to write persuasively about the law. Her goal was to simply state the legal impediments faced by women, thereby making her case using facts that would have an overwhelming effect once assembled together. In 1856 she submitted to Parliament a petition advocating reforms in women's property laws. Signed by notable women such as poet Elizabeth Barrett Browning, novelist Elizabeth Gaskell, and economist and author Harriet Martineau, the petition aroused debate and contributed to the inclusion of some property protections for separated and divorced women in the 1857 Divorce Act.[50]

Frances Power Cobbe, continuing the crusade for reform, argued in "Criminals, Idiots, Women and Minors: Is the Classification Sound?" (reprinted as a pamphlet in 1869 from a *Fraser's* magazine article of December 1868) that taking away women's rights to own property on marriage was unjust as the only other class of people forced to give up such rights were convicted felons, minors, and those deemed mentally unfit. Cobbe first summarizes the ideal of companionate marriage in which the husband absorbs his wife's worldly belongings but "brings home his earnings, and places them in his wife's lap, bidding her spend them as she knows best for the supply of their homely board. . . . Thus they grow old in unbroken peace and love, the man's will having never once been disputed, the wife yielding alike from choice and from necessity to his superior sense and his legal authority." She then proceeds to argue that this ideal is not incompatible with women's control of their own property and money and that, indeed, more financial autonomy could benefit marital relations: "Is perfect love to be called out by perfect dependence? Does an empty purse necessarily imply a full heart? Is a generous-natured woman likely to be won, and not rather be alienated and galled, by being made to feel she has no choice but submission? Surely there is great fallacy in this direction." Cobbe concludes that "real unanimity is not produced between two parties by forbidding one of them to have any voice at all. The hard mechanical contrivance of the law for making husband and wife of one heart and mind is calculated to produce a precisely opposite result."[51] Cobbe's and Bodichon's efforts finally paid off with the Married Women's Property Act of 1870.

The 1870 act gave married women the right to their own earnings after marriage (but not any earnings prior to marriage, which would have belonged to the husband) and to amounts of up to £200 that came to them by gift or inheritance, so long as the money was in a Post Office Savings Bank or similar instrument. This was very helpful for working- or lower-middle-class women but did not cover the amount likely to be inherited by a middle-class woman. The Langham Place Circle and associated activists continued to push for more extensive reforms, which they finally achieved in 1882. Shanley calls the 1882 Married Women's Property Act "the single most important change in the legal status of women in the nineteenth century. . . . In enabling married women to act as independent legal personages, it not only gave them the legal capacity to act as autonomous economic agents, but struck a blow at the whole notion of coverture and the necessary subordination of woman's will to that of her husband."[52] The 1882 law gave every married woman sole possession of everything she earned or inherited, before or after marriage. This act came the closest of any marriage law reforms of the century to allowing the existence of marriages in which both partners were equal under the law.

CONCLUSION

Inevitably, those who resisted the companionate ideal as destructive to the institution of marriage may have been right. According to Coontz, instead of strengthening the emotional ties of family life as intended, the Victorian "focus on romantic love eventually undercut the doctrine of separate spheres for men and women and the ideal of female purity, putting new strains on the institution of marriage."[53] As a case in point, John Stuart Mill delivered a speech to Parliament in May 1867 in which he argued for the enfranchisement of women by pointing to the changing relationship between husbands and wives under the doctrine of companionate marriage:

Women and men are, for the first time in history, really each other's companions. Our traditions respecting the proper relations between them have descended from a time when their lives were apart—when they were separate in their thoughts, because they were separate equally in their serious occupations. In former days a man passed his life among men; all his friendships, all his real intimacies, were with men; with men alone did he consult on any serious business; the wife was either a plaything or an upper servant. All this, among the educated classes, is now changed. The man no longer gives his spare hours to violent exercises and boisterous conviviality with male associates; the two sexes now pass their lives together; the women of a man's family are his habitual society; the wife is his chief associate, his most confidential friend, and often his most trusted adviser.

While his colleagues took as gospel Mill's characterization of marriage, they did not accept the "logical" conclusion he drew from it: that men and women should be equal under the law.[54]

Yet, the dominant belief that companionate marriage required feminine submission rather than equality between the sexes was becoming untenable. As Chase and Levenson argue, the Victorian separate spheres ideology "began to generate its own undoing—that precisely in the extreme character of its separation between the sexes, it trained women for an independence." Mill's denunciation of his own rights in a letter written in March 1851 prior to marrying Harriet Taylor was certainly a harbinger of things to come. Mill rejects the "odious powers" a husband has over his wife under existing marriage laws and makes a "solemn promise never in any case or under any circumstances to use them." He instead provides his wife with "the same absolute freedom of action . . . as if no such marriage had taken place." As Phyllis Rose explains, "The Mills were embarked upon a great experiment, something new in the history of relations between men and women—a true marriage of equals." The fact that, as Rose sees it, Harriet actually called the shots and John submitted to her will, making the partnership a mere reversal of the standard marriage, is beside the point.[55] Oddly, the Mills, like Queen Victoria and Prince Albert, embodied the companionate marriage, a marriage based on love, physical and intellectual compatibility, and true respect for each other's individuality. However, these unusual couples were in the position to flaunt the laws to achieve what they saw as the true Victorian ideal of marriage.

During the Victorian period the aspiration to achieve companionate marriage based on mutual affection, respect, and love was pervasive. While economic and social status remained important to the choice of a spouse, romantic notions were, at least rhetorically, more important than ever before. Parental and familial control over matrimonial affairs took a backseat to courtship between individuals. The strengthening of martial expectations for compatibility were challenged from the start by the increasing importance of separate spheres ideologies that kept men in the public and women in the private realm. Furthermore, the complete dominance of husbands over their wives according to the law challenged the notion of mutual companionship. A gradual shift in the laws throughout the century began to make these new marital ideals more tenable as women gained greater control over their children, their money and property, and their right to legally dissolve the bonds of matrimony in extreme cases. These legal and cultural changes, however, did not alleviate the contradictory messages about marriage. Instead, they increased the calls for more radical reform of the institution to allow the achievement of a truly companionate ideal.

In the chapters that follow, I will explore traditional and nontraditional courtship practices, the details of wedding and honeymoon planning, and the growth of late-century challenges to marriage as an institution. Chapter 2 surveys courtship etiquette books to discover how Victorians were advised to choose a spouse, where and when they were expected to court, how they were supposed to communicate with a lover in person and in writing, and how they were guided to respond to a proposal. From unchaperoned working-class home visits and countryside strolls to highly regulated middle-class balls and lawn parties to the aristocratic London Season, this chapter examines matchmaking in all of its traditional manifestations by focusing on conduct literature and love letter writing manuals. Regardless of their presentation of largely unattainable goals, these books promoted the idea that readers could control their lives and their social status.

While courtship etiquette books for all classes were available in abundance and advice about proper behavior with members of the opposite sex was easily accessible, most conventional advice failed to take into account newly emerging and increasingly popular courtship rituals. Chapter 3 focuses on less conventional courtship practices that were, nonetheless, widely used by people off all classes, including courtship advice columns and correspondence clubs, marriage bureaus, and matrimonial newspapers. Advertising for marriage partners or meeting them through networks outside the traditional circles of family and friendship had a long history, but these methods were becoming ubiquitous and were being justified as necessary in an increasingly urban society with a growing number of displaced people whose communal ties were weak or dissolving. This chapter will demonstrate both the benefits and pitfalls women faced as they sought to construct their own identities and gain a measure of self-determination by taking a more active role in finding husbands.

Chapter 4 examines the laws governing the wedding ceremony, including legal and illegal forms of marriage, types of marriage licenses, and the rules regarding the publication of the banns. This chapter also describes the emergence of the wedding planning industry with its emphasis on the purchase of appropriate clothing and other wedding accoutrements, the duties of the wedding party, the details of the celebration, and the importance of the honeymoon. Contrary to popular belief, most Victorian brides did not wear elaborate white dresses, though Queen Victoria set this example in her own wedding. Finally, this chapter outlines the conflicting views of fashionable weddings, whose expenses and extravagances came increasingly under fire. It further investigates the very different situation working-class couples faced in terms of settings and preparations for reciting their vows.

The concluding chapter examines what happened when the ideal of marriage failed to meet people's needs. The growth of the requirement of financial independence before marriage made England one of the oldest marrying populations in the Western world. The middle-class standard of living delayed marriage—sometimes indefinitely—for many, but many also chose not to marry for other reasons. In this final chapter I focus on those who lived without amorous relationships, at least for a time, including old maids and bachelors, widows and widowers, paying attention to the ways in which these folks struggled to carve out an acceptable niche for themselves in a world that privileged married couples. I also look at unmarried couples living in committed relationships, romantic friendships, and same-sex unions as I map out the terrain of partnerships that defied lawful or socially acceptable standards. Finally, I outline some of the outright challenges to the institution of marriage, illustrating that most of the criticisms of marriage at the end of the century continued to be based on the prevailing ideal of the companionate marriage.

2

Courtship Conduct

In courtship men are supposed to be in the active and women
in the passive voice.

—*London Journal*, March 1875

My belief is that if you have to be the aggressor, if you have to
pursue, if you have to do the asking out, nine times out of ten,
he's just not that into you.

—*He's Just Not That into You*, 2004

Just as they did in the Victorian era, many people today seek to improve
their inner lives as well as their social status by making successful connections with others, often through marriage. Most bookstores have an entire
section devoted to self-help literature, including books that offer expert
advice on dating, finding a spouse, and maintaining satisfying relationships. Greg Behrendt and Liz Tuccillo's *He's Just Not That into You* is one of
the most popular of the recent self-help books for single women. This book
is aimed at helping women secure fulfilling relationships that will lead to
the ultimate commitment: marriage. It is the brainchild of two writers for
the Emmy award-winning television series *Sex and the City* (HBO, 1998–
2004), which was itself based on a book by Candace Bushnell compiled
from her *New York Observer* dating advice column. Behrendt's conversations with Tuccillo about the difficulties many accomplished women have
finding suitable husbands inspired the story lines in the show as well as
the concept for the advice book, published the same year the television
series ended. In 2008 and 2009, respectively, the television series and the
advice book were adapted into major motion pictures. The aim of *He's Just*

Not That into You is to stop high-powered city women from treating their relationships like their careers. Instead of aggressively pursuing potential partners, Behrendt advocates a passive approach that he claims is more appealing to men. The advice offered to 21st-century women is, perhaps surprisingly, the same advice offered to Victorian women in the 1875 *London Journal:* "In courtship men are supposed to be in the active and women in the passive voice."[1]

He's Just Not That into You even looks like a Victorian advice manual: it is written in the form of letters exchanged between imaginary women readers and the authors, just as many Victorian conduct books were. Behrendt advises women advice seekers to sit back and let men take the lead in courtship, though he does so apologetically: "I know it's an infuriating concept—that men like to chase and you have to let us chase you. I know. It's insulting. It's frustrating. It's unfortunately the truth. My belief is that if you have to be the aggressor, if you have to pursue, if you have to do the asking out, nine times out of ten, he's just not that into you." Tuccillo responds with her own conversion narrative, providing a woman's perspective intended to convince skeptical readers of the wisdom of this seemingly antiquated advice:

> We're just supposed to put on our little dresses and do our hair and bat our eyes and hope *they* choose *us.* Why don't you just tie my corset too tight so I can faint in front of some man who'll scoop me out of the way just before the horse-drawn carriage runs over me? . . . But guess what? . . . Since I've been implementing Greg's handy-dandy "he's just not that into you" philosophy, I've been feeling surprisingly *more* powerful. Because if men are asking you out, if the men have to get your attention, then you, in fact, are the one in control.[2]

Sounding like a parody of a Victorian conduct book writer, complete with references to corsets and carriages, Tuccillo reluctantly embraces Victorian ideals of courtship conduct.

Conduct books, etiquette manuals, and self-help guides have enjoyed a mass market of consumers since the 19th century. In the Victorian era, these popular forms were aimed primarily at middle-class women, though there were many books geared toward men, children, and the working classes as well. Two of the best-remembered conduct book authors, Sarah Stickney Ellis and Isabella Beeton, focused on women's proper roles within the home. By providing advice related to establishing a happy household, living within one's means, maintaining a healthy marital relationship, and starting a family, their books offered both idealized images of middle-class life and practical guides for upward mobility. Conduct and etiquette books may also have been purely entertaining for some as they promoted stereotypes that many women realized were at best far from realistic and at worst ridiculous. Regardless of their presentation of largely unattainable goals, these books promoted the idea that readers could control their lives and their social status in some, albeit limited, ways. As Nancy Armstrong puts it, Victorian conduct books offered "the power of self-transformation" regardless of one's "material conditions."[3]

Conduct books motivated by the idea that manners were the outward expression of religious morals rather than determined by fashion or taste dominated the early part of the century. Such conduct literature was overtaken at mid-century by etiquette guides, which codified conventional rules of behavior. These guides were aimed at helping readers avoid the appearance of vulgarity and exhibited less regard for internal virtues or values. Ellis's series of books—including *The Women of England* (1843); *The Wives of England* (1843); *The Mothers of England* (1844); and *The Daughters of England* (1843)—promoted women's piety and domesticity with a religiously inflected nationalistic fervor. In *The Daughters of England*, Ellis declares that "the heart of woman, in all her tenderest and holiest feelings" is "beautifully exemplified in connection with the dignity of a British Queen" and "is the same beneath the shelter of a cottage, as under the canopy of a throne." She connects the average pious woman with the new Queen, thereby creating an image of a nation of superior, domestic women. On the other hand, *Mrs. Beeton's Book of Household Management* (1861) was aimed at training women to manage their houses, meals, and servants like "the commander of an army, or the leader of any enterprise."[4] Beeton gave women the status of authoritative professionals in charge of running the home rather than moral guides influencing their families. Ellis's books have the quality of sermons and are more properly classed within the genre of conduct literature, while Beeton's focus on providing concrete ways to maintain an efficient household leans more toward the etiquette and self-help genres.

In *Manners, Morals, and Class in England, 1774–1858*, Marjorie Morgan argues that "the eclipse of the conduct by the etiquette book in the nineteenth century suggests that the latter's fashionable behavioral code was, in some fundamental way, more compatible with England's highly competitive, commercial society than was the sincere behavioral code." Thus, etiquette permeated all ranks of society and all activities, even those beyond the woman's sphere of the drawing room, as it became *the* form of the "modern, urban industrial society." Deborah Gorham points out that two systems of assigning class status coexisted in the Victorian era: "one based on material wealth, and one based on the manifestation of certain personal and cultural attributes."[5] Etiquette books led the way to improving one's status within the second system, over which women had more control. Yet, the most potent power women had over their status in society was their choice of a spouse. Since most members of the middle class remained in the lower level of the class, employing only one or two servants and living rather modestly (as Beeton herself did), marrying into a more prosperous family was the best way to achieve genteel respectability. As a result, an entire category of advice books devoted to the rituals of court-ship emerged. While these books often reinforced the expectation that women should not actively pursue men, they also indicated that it was during courtship that women had the most control over the direction their lives would take.

In *Advice to Young Ladies on Their Duties and Conduct in Life* (1856), T. S. Arthur explains that ladies must carefully exercise their right to accept or reject gentlemen callers, making sure they do not associate with anyone exhibiting dishonorable behavior: "When the character of a young man is known to be bad . . . let him not, on any consideration, be admitted to a visiting acquaintance, nor, even in public assemblies, noticed, except with coldness and formality. His family connections, his education, manners, polish, intelligence, or ability to entertain, should be considered as nothing when put in the scale against his evil principles."[6] Though a woman was not supposed to visit a man or take the initiative to actively seek him out as a husband, she maintained the power of attraction, encouragement, and acceptance or repulsion and refusal just as Tuccillo points out to her 21st-century peers. So, while Arthur—and Behrendt and Tuccillo—require young ladies to remain outwardly passive, they are nevertheless expected to actively use their judgment and taste in selecting husbands.

The power to subtly woo and ultimately accept or decline a proposal allowed women a certain amount of socially acceptable power during courtship. Furthermore, as the century advanced, so too did views on women's initiative in courtship. An 1883 article in *Chambers's Journal* reflects this evolving view of women's roles:

> There is no definitive rule, even on such a fundamental point as whether the initiative and active negotiations shall devolve upon the lady or the gentleman. . . . According to popular tradition, it is the special prerogative of the fair sex to be wooed and won; but this is not by any means an invariable rule. It has many exceptions; and some who speak from personal experience as well as extensive observation, go so far as to declare that in the majority of instances it is really the ladies who do the courting, though the initiative and other formal steps may ostensibly lie with the enamoured swain.[7]

While certain rules prevailed and there was no shortage of advice about how to follow those rules, courtship standards were evolving and conduct literature evolved along with them. This chapter explores the intricacies of this complex courtship dance as portrayed in etiquette books, including how to choose a spouse, where and when to court, how to communicate with a lover in person and in writing, and how to respond to a proposal. It also examines the very different courtship practices of the working classes and delves into the more cynical realm of anticonduct literature, which drew attention to the absurdities of the prevailing standards of courtship.

COURTING LOVE

During the Victorian period, marriages were imagined as matches made for companionship and personal fulfillment as much as for status and power. Indeed, love was the driving force behind the concept of marriage, though finding a mate who was of at least equal status was a given in etiquette guides. Class, of course, played an important role in Victorian courtship practices. *The Etiquette of Love, Courtship, and Marriage* (1847) advises women that: "A lady of high rank does not raise her husband to the same position as she formerly occupied; but sinks down to his standard; but the gentleman raises the lady, however much below himself, to the same position in society." While class rules were easy to convey, many of these books struggled to address the subject that was, presumably, their central reason for existence: love. Interestingly, they often skirted around the definition of love, deeming it to be outside their scope and purpose. *The Etiquette of Courtship and Matrimony* (1865) claims that "it would be out of place in these pages to grapple with a subject so large as that of Love in its varied phases: a theme that must be left to poets, novelists, and moralists"; instead, etiquette books were typically written for the gentleman who had already wooed and won and to the lady who viewed "her admirer with preference" and deemed "him not unworthy of her favourable regard."[8]

Though love was assumed to be the basis of marriage, it was not explicitly defined. However, *The Etiquette of Love, Courtship, and Marriage* makes one lesson clear: "True love is sober, serious, and sedate" and not at all akin to flirtation, coquetry, or the "many false impressions" presented in "that unnatural system of philosophy found in novels and light reading." Reading fiction was frequently characterized as the antithesis of etiquette guides, which were assumed to be more realistic and practical. *The English Maiden* (1842) also eschewed the romanticized images found in novels and instead suggested a more straightforward approach to courtship. First and foremost, an honest self-presentation was required to enable a sound marital decision: "Suppose you have faults—and who has not?—why should they be cautiously concealed?" Instead, couples were urged to avoid misrepresentation, making it "a point of principle to disclose to each other their entire character" so that they could be certain that their love was true. Ladies were admonished not to fear being single and to make well-reasoned decisions about marriage that would be gratifying to themselves and not just to their friends and family. Maud Wheeler, in *Whom to Marry* (1894), set forth six tests of true love for her readers, including feeling long absences keenly, delighting in self-sacrifice for the loved one, and being unable to imagine loving another. For Wheeler, even love could be logically assessed. If love did not bloom prior to marriage, Wheeler warns, "the early months of married life" would inevitably bring "disenchantment and bitter regret."[9] In the world of etiquette literature, it was important to make marital choices informed by both the head and the heart.

Since arranged marriages were no longer fashionable, the preferences of young lovers were supremely important, though couples were cautioned against clandestine marriages or unions made in the face of continuing family opposition. As *The Etiquette of Love, Courtship, and Marriage* contends, parental objections, while often unjust, were the cause of two-thirds of unhappy marriages. Readers are advised that "Kings and Queens are not permitted to choose for themselves in matrimonial alliances, but their subjects are vested with this privilege, and it is their duty to exercise it, as their future happiness chiefly depends upon the choice they make." In contrast to Ellis's elevation of commoners to the status of royals, here the middle classes are reminded that they have the privilege of marital choice not afforded to royalty. However, to assist their judgment in matters of the heart, ladies were advised to consult the more objective opinions of their parents. Since a lady "has probably first met the gentleman at a ball, or other festive occasion, where the excitement of the scene has reflected on every object a roseate tint," she is most in need of "the very best advice accompanied with a considerate regard for her overwrought feelings" that only a mother can provide. Parents or paid chaperones were charged with assessing an admirer's rank and character, hopefully prior to the formation of an attachment. First and foremost, parents were expected to guide their children away from marrying too young. Indeed, the law required parental consent for those under the age of 21. Beyond considerations of the law, women's early engagement was frowned on since "in nine cases out of ten, this lover is not the one that would be accepted if the affections were free at twenty or twenty-one. . . . Nor is the love of a man, for a girl who is still too young to accept wisely an offer of marriage, a love that promises happiness as the fruit." Furthermore, marrying before 22 or 23 was considered detrimental to a woman's health due to the increased number of childbearing years she would experience. Wheeler goes so far as to provide a formula regarding the ideal age of marriage: "Perhaps the best standard as to the relative difference of ages most conducive to happiness between husband and wife is to halve the man's age, and then add seven to the remainder. . . . We estimate that a man of thirty is suited to a girl of two-and-twenty, by the same standard we reckon that a man of forty should choose a wife of twenty-seven."[10] This calculation was, indeed, on target with common practice. Middleclass men, on average, married in their early to mid-30s and women in their early to mid-20s.

Courtship was considered a trial period in which to examine one's potential partner to make sure they were suitable for a lifetime commitment. A woman was expected to scrutinize her suitor for signs of disrespectful behavior toward her or her family, a lack of religious feeling, or any inclination toward "expensive pleasures," "low and vulgar amusements," or "foppish, eccentric, or very slovenly" appearance. If any negative behaviors or traits came to light, she was urged to drop her beau immediately. Gentlemen were also on the lookout for ill-tempered or coquettish behavior, though to a lesser degree since they were expected to be certain of their choice before initiating contact with the family and seeking approval for courtship. A man was expected to determine if his potential bride was attentive to her household duties, affectionate to her parents, and pleasant to be around.[11] If she exhibited affectation, showy dress, or an eagerness for flattery or flirtation, a man was to consider himself forewarned. The biggest impediment to determining the character of one's future spouse was that young ladies and gentlemen were not allowed to spend time alone together. In fact, dating as we know it was nonexistent and all interactions between the sexes were expected to take place in public or under adult supervision. Social encounters were heavily monitored by chaperones until late in the century, when standards were loosened to allow more natural interactions between unmarried men and women. Chaperones were often either governesses or hired (and already married or widowed) society women whose job it was to protect their charges from male harassment in the streets and the pursuit of men of lower ranks at social events.[12]

Rhoda Broughton's 1867 novel *Cometh Up as a Flower* was considered scandalous in large part due to the depiction of the young heroine's unsupervised meetings with her lover. Nell LeStrange—who has no mother to guide her, a sister who eschews her company for visits to distant wealthy families, and a father preoccupied with his own financial difficulties—is left to wander about the countryside on her own. While on one of her graveyard rambles, she meets a mysterious man with whom she quickly falls in love. Captain M'Gregor, who is genuinely captivated by Nell, breaks all rules of propriety by showing up in her garden or at her doorstep unannounced and often alone. Before her father even knows M'Gregor's name, he witnesses the captain lying in the grass and holding hands with his daughter. Nell describes the scene:

> As he caught sight of the pretty *tableau vivant* we had kindly got up in his garden to surprise him, he looked extremely astonished and considerably displeased. Nor was the poor man much to blame, I think, finding his favourite daughter sitting in the dusk of the evening with a man, whom, to his certain knowledge, she had seen but twice before in her life, lying at her feet and clasping her hand, apparently unforbidden. . . . It was so infrequent that my father was angry with me that I was in a state of proportionable awe and wholesome fear when such a *contretemps* did arise. I snatched away my hand and jumped up.[13]

In response, M'Gregor lies about why he is there (he claims to have delivered a message from a neighbor with whom he is staying) and leaves abruptly. This unfortunate beginning for the couple guarantees that their love will be forbidden and Nell will be urged to marry the boring man preferred by her father.

Once a suitor was approved, the appropriate length of courtship for a middle- to upper-class couple was a serious issue to consider. While lengthy courtships were undesirable, they were expected to be long enough for couples to get to know each other as well as they could while still being monitored by chaperones or family members. The fear was that the longer the courtship lasted, the more likely it would disintegrate. Quarrels could occur, partners could change their minds, or new lovers could present themselves. Furthermore, there was an acute but unspoken anxiety about the possibility that extended courtships could lead to sexual intimacy before marriage, though the opportunities for sex were certainly hampered by the ever-present chaperone.

Members of the working class avoided strict courtship rules and were, some speculated, better off for it. Indeed, *The Etiquette of Marriage* (1902) proclaims the "respectable working classes" to be "as happy as those of any set of human beings." For them, "the process of natural selection has been usually followed. The 'keeping company' stage, though open to abuse, has an influence in leading even the callow and the uneducated to choose a nature they are likely to get on with." Interestingly, it is argued that the middle and upper classes could avoid more marriage disasters if they too were "able to indulge in a friendship" with their potential spouses before marriage just as the working classes did. However, the idea of adapting the practices of the lower classes defied the distinctions conveyed by courtship rituals in the first place. At the end of the century, Maud Wheeler confronts middle-class prudery and hypocrisy head on in an effort to loosen courtship strictures that dictated unmarried ladies and gentlemen should never be together without a chaperone:

> According to the ethics of society the lowest of low evening dresses is quite consistent with perfect modesty, whereas to regard a man as a friend, and to treat him as such—instead of viewing him in the light of some strange, unnatural, and dangerous creature—by walking out with him alone, or talking with him without a chaperone, is most improper, reprehensible behaviour. The world is always concerning itself frantically about appearances, and never about the reality of things.[14]

Wheeler points out that while gentlewomen could wear low-cut gowns to attract gentlemen, they could not talk privately with them once they had their attention. In her view, true love and companionship were impeded by these social niceties. The elaborate rituals of upper-class courtship are best illustrated by the London Season, during which the privileged few had the opportunity to court potential wives and husbands in a dizzying array of activities. Yet, the Season also offered young Victorians opportunities to work around courting restrictions by taking advantage of the freer interactions afforded by outdoor parties and sporting events.

THE LONDON SEASON

Despite the Victorian emphasis on love and companionship in middle- and upper-middle-class marriage, Gillis notes that "marriage played a central role in mobilizing wealth and power, and the control of courtship, particularly that of heirs and heiresses, remained essential. While young people were told that they must marry for love and were given certain latitude in the choice of mates, the courtship process was carefully constructed to prevent misalliances." The development of the London Season, with its network of approved courtship locations and opportunities, emerged in the 1820s in response to the influx of the newly rich—many of whom had recently amassed wealth from the profits of industry—into upper-class social circles. The highly structured rituals of the Season were an important way of ensuring the continuing power of the traditional landed elites. As other institutions took over much of this regulatory process—for example, political office became elective and civil service appointments became tied to examinations—the Season was more and more focused on courtship. The Season was the primary marriage market for dèbutantes who came out in society at about the age of 18. Girls expected to have at least two to four Seasons to find a husband before beginning to fade into spinsterhood. Society, strictly speaking, included fewer than 1,500 families whose daughters were formally introduced by presentation to Queen Victoria at court, which was a highlight of the Season. Daughters of the aristocracy were automatically eligible, though others could participate if they had the right contacts to recommend them. Girls coming out at court typically wore short-sleeved white dresses and decorated their hair with plumes of white feathers. They were expected to curtsy, kiss the Queen's hand, and then gracefully back out of the room. Women were also presented at court both before and after marriage to mark their change in status. Middle-class girls came out too, though typically at private balls or dances. The transition to womanhood was also indicated by a change in dress that included putting one's hair up and taking the hem of one's skirt down.[15]

The official Season ran from May to early August and coincided with Parliamentary sessions that brought influential families into the city. It opened with the May exhibition at the Royal Academy of Arts and ended with the start of grouse hunting season (August 12), which lured families back to their country estates in the north. The events of the Season included private balls and dances (the first distinguished by a guest list over 200, a full band, and elaborate floral arrangements), dinner parties, garden parties, concerts, theater and opera visits, riding or strolling in

Rotten Row, driving or picnicking in Hyde Park, attending the Derby at Ascott or Goodwood, and watching the Eton versus Harrow cricket match. For some, the Season was extended with pre-Season activities in April and post-Season hunting, yachting, and house parties. For most, the Season was filled with an exhausting array of events each day, including morning, afternoon, and evening activities each requiring appropriate dress.[16]

Samuel Beeton founded the *Queen* in 1861 to appeal to middle- and upper-middle-class ladies who participated in (or aspired to be a part of) the London Season. According to Margaret Beetham, the illustrated weekly paper eschewed domestic subjects for reports on Society gossip, etiquette, fashion, travel, and cultural events. In December 1861, the *Queen* provided an irreverent overview of the Season that highlights the sexual tension of its courtship rituals. This feature, which fills much of the magazine, reflects Michael Mason's claim that in many ways there was, in fact, a stricter code of behavior for wives than for unmarried girls. He cites foreign observations of English courtship rituals as evidence, concluding that "girls were flirtatious in effect if not in intention, and struck some—in fact many—commentators as frankly indecent in their conversation, or sexually shameless and predatory."[17] To mitigate the idea of the predatory female, "The Manoeuvering Mamma's Matrimonial Monitor, and Belgravian Belle's Bridal Beacon, Containing Twelve Hints for Bewitching Bachelors into Benedicts" attributes the manipulative courtship behavior to the mothers of the dèbutantes. The satirical tone also pokes fun at the hapless gentlemen who fall into the mammas' traps. For the most part, the young ladies remain unscathed by the sexually charged scenarios. The article is accompanied by 12 illustrations of "The Year in Society" that depict scenes from the endless courtship season.

Though January is a rather unpromising month for courtship, the *Queen* provides a tale that ends in marriage for Zenobia, whose proposal comes from a gentleman on ice skates proving "that love is never out of season." The moral of the story is that "when a young gentleman undertakes to teach a young lady the art of skating, the dangers she risks are small indeed compared with those which beset the tutor. True, she may tumble once or twice, and scramble on her hands and knees, and be laughed at, but his fall, poor man, will be a desperate one—he will fall in love." Zenobia naively hitches up her skirt to allow her legs to move more freely and in the process she unwittingly captivates her skating partner. The image of her legs combined with her cold fingers that have to be warmed by a gentleman's hands, her wobbly balance that must be stabilized on a gentleman's arm, and her tiny feet that need to be unbuckled from her skates bring the unsuspecting tutor literally to his knees. While kneeling on the ice, he spontaneously implores her "to bestow on him her foot in marriage, and she—sweet blushing thing—referred him to mamma."[18] While Zenobia could be seen as a dangerous temptress, the

Queen characterizes her as an innocent youth sent out on the ice by her knowing mother.

February brings the promising exchange of Valentines, but the *Queen* prefers March for courtship. This month brings winds that have the benefit of making a girl's "skirt leap madly into space, twisting and flapping as if it would burst from its gathers." This is "truly a heart-rending spectacle" likely to make "the fair creature . . . spiteful." The author reports that a friend "once endeavored to calm a frantic skirt, and had his face smacked, and we thanked the lady for the wholesome lesson she taught him." While flirting with exposed limbs and sexual innuendo, the *Queen* maintains the wholesomeness of its young ladies, who are either set up by their mothers or compromised by Mother Nature. Thus, the author advises avoiding the blustery weather by touring the flower show at the Crystal Palace in Sydenham: "For encouraging the affections of the sexes, the Crystal Palace is pre-eminently adapted. It is the shilling Garden of Paradise. Conversation cannot flag when so many objects suggest fresh subjects. And what opportunities are there for a girl of education to trot our her knowledge and assert herself!"[19] Whether tongue in cheek or not, ladies are encouraged to initiate conversations about nature and science while touring Prince Albert's Great Exhibition halls.

With the Season in full swing in May, June, and July, the *Queen* assures readers that they can look forward to attending masquerade balls, concerts, and the opera. August and September bring seaside and yachting excursions. Readers are playfully told that "morning on the sands must be very like waiting at the gates of Paradise, and in no hurry for the opening, through patient certainty of admittance. More love matches have been coaxed to declaration point through embroidery as the tide fell, than in any other condition of life." While lounging on the beaches is recommended to foster love, young ladies are warned to be wary of boating trips. The *Queen* explains, "Once a girl ventured on board a yacht and was so poorly she could not speak; and when the use of her tongue was restored to her, she inquired where she was, and they informed her she was off the coast of Spain, for a gale had suddenly taken hold of the little boat, and thrown it miles away from home."[20] Having thus disgraced herself by traveling all the way to Spain without a chaperone, the poor girl (who loves another) is forced to marry her wayward captain. This cautionary tale suggests the danger of unchaperoned activities, but yachting, hunting, and riding horses were attractive largely because they allowed mid-Victorian ladies to wander away from adults and escape the strict rules of chaperonage (Figure 2.1). A *Punch* cartoon from 1874 called "Kind and Considerate" explicitly illustrates this kind of deliberate wandering off (Figure 2.2). The young ladies and gentlemen in the cartoon set out on a boating excursion with the express purpose of evading the supervision of their chosen chaperone, who is not a good sailor and will likely leave them alone on the upper deck.

THE YEAR IN SOCIETY.

SEPTEMBER.—SOCIETY YACHTING.

OCTOBER.—SOCIETY IN "THE FIELD."

Charles does not think he ought to yield the whip to Charlotte without receiving a quid pro quo; and he only wants a rose. Her dear Cousin Isabella is not at all in love with Charles, of course; but . . . . .

Figure 2.1. "September.—Society Yachting" and "October.—Society in the Field." *The Queen* (December 21, 1861): 308. Harry Ransom Humanities Research Center, University of Texas at Austin.

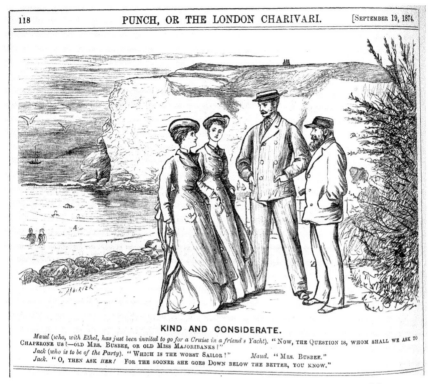

KIND AND CONSIDERATE.

Maud (who, with Ethel, has just been invited to go for a Cruise in a friend's Yacht). " Now, the Question is, whom shall we ask to Chaperone us ?—old Mrs. Busbee, or old Miss Majoribanks ?"

Jack (who is to be of the Party). " Which is the worst Sailor ?"   *Maud.* " Mrs. Busbee."

Jack. " O, then ask her ! For the sooner she goes down below the better, you know."

Figure 2.2. "Kind and Considerate." *Punch* (September 19, 1874): 118. Courtesy of the Division of Special Collections, Archives, and Rare Books, University of Missouri–Columbia.

The *Queen* concludes its parade of opportunities for courtship with the quieter events of November and December, including private dinner parties and country house visits. The illustration of "Society Passing a Dull Day at its Country House" depicts bored men looking longingly out windows and guests playing various household games, including billiards and a game called badminton battledore (Figure 2.3). Introduced by toymaker Isaac Spratt in 1860, this indoor or outdoor game involved partners hitting a shuttlecock back and forth with a solid racket, trying not to let it fall to the ground. With such humble home entertainments, the *Queen*'s "Year in Society" concludes, proving that courtship can happen any time of the year.

OTHER COURTSHIP LOCATIONS AND OPPORTUNITIES

Written by "The Lounger in Society," whose name evokes images of the privileged class to which he belonged, *The Glass of Fashion: A Universal Handbook of Social Etiquette and Home Culture for Ladies and Gentlemen* (1881) provided a more serious but still fun-loving catalog of possible courtship

THE YEAR IN SOCIETY.

NOVEMBER.—SOCIETY PASSING A DULL DAY AT ITS COUNTRY HOUSE.

Figure 2.3. "November.—Society Passing a Dull Day at the Country House." *The Queen* (December 21, 1861): 309. Harry Ransom Humanities Research Center, University of Texas at Austin.

scenarios for young people during the London Season, including calls, private theatricals, picnics, and balls. According to Sally Mitchell, the number of such guides to high society was "out of all proportion to the size of the population who actually observed these fine manners. Members of the upper class, for that matter, did not need books; they learned how to behave at home."[21] Those who aspired to a higher class status or wanted a glimpse of the high life probably bought most of these books.

With this in mind, *The Glass of Fashion* "is intended for both sexes and for all ages, as well as for all classes of society; for the quiet middle-class family whose ambition is restricted to an 'evening party' once a year not less than for the upper-class family whose members are 'presented at court.'" The Lounger reminds readers that "any one can learn to behave decorously at the dinner-table . . . but the difficulty is to learn how to control our temper . . . how to render our lives pleasant and gracious to ourselves and to others."[22] These final qualities are supposed to be those that define the gentleman and the lady, though these do not seem to be the qualities the books seeks to impart (presumably because they are natural and therefore unteachable traits). Instead, the book is a veritable encyclopedia of courtship practices to which many could aspire and about which all could dream.

While the advice offered by the Lounger tends toward stereotypical constructions of passive women and active men, it is clear that women rule courtship rituals. The Lounger's advice is, in fact, largely aimed at teaching *men* to successfully navigate women's realm of courtship. Beth L. Bailey, in her study of dating in contemporary America, points out that the shift from 19th-century courtship to 20th-century dating was marked by the displacement of these encounters from the private spaces and events controlled and orchestrated by women to public places and venues chosen by men and accessed by their money. Bailey argues that the result of this shift was, in fact, women's loss of control over premarital relationships by the mid-20th century.[23] The Victorian style of courtship, however restrictive and idealized, was in many ways a woman's game.

The *Glass of Fashion* sets forth behavioral standards intended to keep these gendered expectations intact and to prevent wagging tongues. For example, the book lays down rules for making social calls. A gentleman could not directly call on a young lady, but he could pay a visit to her mother, her aunt, or whatever other respectable married or widowed woman with whom the young lady was staying. The visit might include interaction with the young woman of interest, but would officially be paid to her guardian. The ritual of making calls was more commonly a part of women's social networking, but gentlemen did sometimes participate. Calls were to be made only during the particular days and times designated by the hostess to avoid disrupting housekeeping. Women generally held calling hours once a week between 3:00 and 6:00 P.M. Visits were expected to take no longer than 15 to 30 minutes. If a woman was busy or unwilling to receive guests it was acceptable for her to send servants to report that she was not at home. If this was the case, a visitor could leave a calling card imprinted with his or her name. As Leonore Davidoff explains, card leaving "was not synonymous with calling. It was, rather, a system of feeling the social climate before taking action." Calling cards, then, could be left simply to see if a return card or visit would be made. Returning a card or a visit signaled that a continuing acquaintance, and perhaps a developing friendship, was welcome. Calls were to be made on ceremonial occasions (weddings and births) and as acknowledgments of hospitality received (such as being invited to a dinner or a ball).[24]

Despite the rules of the ritual, the Lounger recommends "no more formality than is requisite to preserve order" during a call. It is certainly hard to imagine, but the Lounger expected an orderly encounter that was simultaneously unconstrained, open, and honest. As the Lounger humorously suggests, "Were it not for this excellent social institution, our English reserve and indifference would assume colossal proportions, and the hedge within which we enclose ourselves from contact with our fellows would become absolutely impassable." Though gentlemen could visit ladies under the conditions set forth above, "it need hardly be said that ladies never call upon gentlemen" unless married and calling on an old family friend.[25] Davidoff notes that while Sundays were traditionally reserved for close family and friends, "young and unmarried men paid their calls on Sundays, a practice sometimes called, a little maliciously, 'sowing seeds.' On the whole, however, they were rather pitied for having to do so as it was considered very much a part of a wife's or daughter's duty."[26] Still, making calls was considered the best way for a gentleman to get to know a lady because she could speak more freely and behave more naturally at home than in public. The Lounger maintains that "if you wish to know a young lady truly, you must see her at home, and by daylight. For myself, I do not think it a hardship to call upon an agreeable materfamilias and her charming daughters, and spend thirty or forty minutes in lively and intelligent talk. But you will say every materfamilias is not agreeable, and all daughters not charming. True: but my good sir, do you expect roses without thorns?" In addition to the call, there were several other kinds of household visits to which gentlemen might be invited by a young lady's female guardian. The invitation here was key—a young Victorian lady would be very unlikely to socialize with anyone not known to or approved of by her family. These invitational events included the afternoon party or at-home (a gathering often accompanied by music or other entertainment as well as coffee, tea, and dessert at which guests came and went freely between 4:00 and 7:00 P.M.); the conversazione or reception (typically more formal and held later in the evening with light refreshments or dinner, planned exhibits of a cultural sort, small groups engaging in artistic, scientific, or other kinds of conversation, or private theatricals); the tea party (an early evening event with 25 to 100 guests, including a buffet of tea, sherry, champagne, claret, sandwiches, biscuits, and cakes, and possibly featuring professional music); and the dinner party.[27]

As a part of these homely festivities, private theatricals or tableaux vivants might be presented or games like charades played. Such theatrical endeavors, as depicted in Jane Austen's *Mansfield Park*, Wilkie Collins's *No Name*, and Edith Wharton's *The House of Mirth*, presented opportunities for young ladies and gentlemen to take on alternate personas, to act out love scenes, and to wear daring costumes. As a result, they were often considered suspect. In *No Name*, Magdalen Vanstone discovers that she is "a born actress" while performing in a private theatrical production. Miss Garth, her governess, laments that though "her worst apprehension of results in connection with theatrical enterprise" was merely "levity of conduct with some of the gentlemen," she had not bargained for the more serious implications of the girl's behavior. "Magdalen, in the capacity of a thoughtless girl, was comparatively easy to deal with. Magdalen, in the character of a born actress threatened serious future difficulties." Miss Garth's worst fears are realized when Magdalen uses her acting abilities to disguise her true identity and dupe her miserly cousin into marrying her so that she can reclaim her lost family fortune, which he has unjustly inherited. While this ominous turn of events rooted in Magdalen's participation in private performance reflects a pervasive anxiety about theatricality, the Lounger dismisses such foreboding judgments. Instead, he is matter of fact in his recommendation that participants choose short scenes that require few performers and that ladies make their own costumes to display their sewing skills. He insists that "the chief amusement of amateur theatricals lies in the preliminary preparations and the rehearsals," which inevitably "achieves the most glorious conquests over the most extraordinary difficulties."[28] However, the Lounger was certainly aware that theatrical collaborations could present many opportunities to flirt and make conquests of another sort.

The Lounger recommended performing a tableau vivant if less time was available for preparation. Tableau vivant participants dressed up and arranged themselves into a scene, usually taken from a poem, novel, painting, or historical event. Among the scenes suggested by the Lounger are "Sleeping Beauty" and "Night and Morning," both of which involve creating sexually seductive images of women. "Night and Morning" involves:

Two ladies . . . one dark, the other fair. The dark one, with a black silk skirt and bodice, with arms bare, and tresses loose, lies in a graceful, half-reclining attitude, somewhat to the left, a yard or two of black tarlatan, covered with silver paper stars, being thrown loosely over her figure. Morning, in a simple white Greek dress, with hair down, and flowers in one hand, stands somewhat to the right, about a foot farther back than Night. Morning is exposed to the lime-light, while Night remains in shadow.

The Lounger adds slyly that the girl in the Greek dress "must not have any petticoats on," the dress must be "as limp as possible," and she must have bare shoulders and arms.[29] It is certainly clear why this would be an enticing scene.

Charades were likewise very popular. The Lounger explains that "whereas a tableau is generally intended as an artistic presentation of a poetic or fictitious subject, a charade is usually put forward in the light of a pictorial or pantomimic puzzle, the spectators being supposed to decipher a particular word signified by the movements and gestures of the actors." The greatest advantage to charades is that they require little planning: "Half-a-dozen persons—or more or fewer—with some notion of 'dressing-up,' and some taste for acting, fix upon a word (of two, or at most, three syllables)" that they then act out one syllable at a time, with the final act encapsulating the entire word. The Lounger's example is, fittingly, for the word *honeymoon*—perhaps the ultimate goal of the social encounters he describes in the book. The first scene involves eating honey, the second scene includes a poet on the sea reciting an ode to the moon, and the final scene depicts a bride and groom "seated at tea, in sweet companionship. The landlady enters with her bill. Pockets are turned out, but no money is forthcoming. Exit landlady in a rage, but the husband turns to his wife, and indicates that no vulgar cares . . . shall disturb their 'Honeymoon.' The audience are then requested to guess the word."[30] Such varying forms of private theatricals gave young people a chance to interact more freely with each other than they were able to do in other, more formal social settings and were, therefore, extremely popular.

Garden parties and picnics took courtship out of doors. The Lounger states that these romantic events are

> very popular among young people on account of the opportunities they afford for quiet flirtations. What sweet nothings may be whispered into willing ears while the band is playing. . . . What delicate attentions may be paid by courteous swain when Araminta exhibits her skill with bow and arrow! How lithe and graceful the figure of the fair Julia appears while she strives for victory at lawn-tennis! . . . A garden-party on a glowing summer noon seems like a page out of a poem, and reminds us of the romances of the old chivalry.[31]

In addition to music, archery, and tennis, croquet was a standard feature of garden parties. Due to the pairing off of guests as croquet partners, this outdoor amusement was often seen as particularly risqué. "The Romance of Croquet," an 1866 *Punch* parody of the game, declares that it offers "lots of opportunities" for "fluttering flirters" to say "sweet things."[32]

In Charlotte Yonge's *The Clever Woman of the Family*, "croquet fever" hits Bessie Keith, a coquettish character whose obsession with playing croquet even after marriage leads to the perception that she is involved in an extramarital affair that may account for her pregnancy. Though these rumors are ultimately disproven, her flirtations—and her life—come to an unfortunate end when Bessie trips over a croquet hoop in an effort to escape the unwanted advances of a man at a garden party. This ominous ending to Bessie's croquet fever may be far-fetched, but it illustrates how outdoor activities became opportunities to thwart strict courtship rules. By the 1870s roller skating and bicycling rivaled croquet in rebelliousness since they were also activities that facilitated the evasion of supervision.

Picnics were somewhat more sedate events, but they promised to nurture budding romances as well. At a picnic, the Lounger advises, "There should be a fair admixture of seniors to ensure order and decorum, but there should be a preponderance of young people—of young men, well-bred, well-mannered, and accomplished; of young girls, comely, intelligent, and agreeable. If among them there should be one or two couples with a marked preference for each other's society, all the better; they will set an example to the rest which in due time may bear fruit." However, it was frowned on for lovers to be too absorbed in each other to be good company for the rest of the group. The party would typically travel to a remote country spot without servants and with vast quantities of low-maintenance refreshments, including sandwiches, meatballs, salads, puddings, tarts, custards, and wine. One must be aware, though, that "the mustard *does* sometimes get into the raspberry tart, and picnic parties *do* sometimes forget the corkscrew." The Lounger asks what could be more conducive to young love than "the sunlit air; the blue arch above; the cool green foliage around; the songs of birds and the murmurs of the wind; the clear ringing laughter of happy voices; the flash and gleam of bright eyes; the grace of shapely forms—do not these combine in overpowering charm?"[33]

Balls were considered among the most important amorous events. It was one acceptable venue in which to meet members of the opposite sex to whom one had not yet been formally introduced. Attendees were expected to mingle and dance with many partners, which ensured lively engagement with new acquaintances as well as old ones. As the Lounger poetically intones:

The ball is the paradise of youth and love . . . the ball-room becomes an enchanted world of light and music and perfume . . . where sorrow is never seen, and past and future are forgotten in the innocent intoxications of the present. To the young ear, what is so delightful as merry music? To the youthful eye, what so attractive as the spectacle of fair forms gracefully revolving in the soft, sweet mazes of the mystic dance? And if we know that "at the ball" we shall meet that "other half" of one's self—Romeo or Juliet, as the case may be;

but Romeo without his melancholy, and Juliet without her tragedy—can it be wondered at that it draws us thither with an irresistible attraction?

He urges parents not to restrict their children's participation in such romantic events:

> Balls are not wholly free from alloy: they are not without the fell looks of jealousy, and the furtive glances of suspicion, and the hiss of wounded vanity; but what are these compared with the full flood of happiness which they pour into tender bosoms and manly hearts? . . . I confess I never could, nor can I now, detect their impropriety. Nor know I any pleasanter sight than that of a well-lighted room, echoing with merry music, in which a number of young men and maidens, the latter attired in bright and semi-diaphanous robes, their eyes shining with pleasure, and their rosy lips curved with happy smiles, are "threading the mazes" of the old-established quadrille, or circling round in the fascinating waltz. If you can dance no longer, my friend look on, and be happy in the happiness of others.[34]

Guest lists were supposed to be equally divided between ladies and gentlemen and made up primarily of eligibles who would dance and mingle freely. The music typically included a piano, a violin, and possibly a flute or harp, depending on the size of the room. Between 16 and 24 formal dances were planned with a break for refreshments and a light meal. This would include such repast as light wine, champagne, seltzer water, ices, fowls, birds, and fish, all served cold and carved so that the guests could eat and drink without a fuss. Guests were also issued programs with the dances listed on one side and a blank dance card on the other side so that they could keep track of their partners.

The ball presented many potential etiquette pitfalls. For example, the Lounger notes that "no lady will engage herself two-deep for any dance, nor will she, except in novels, throw over a partner she has once accepted for any new-comer, however 'desirable.'" Ladies were advised never to directly refuse a proposal to dance, but to decline with a polite excuse. Once she refused a partner, she was not supposed to dance with someone else. While *The Glass of Fashion* focuses on private balls where those invited are presumed respectable, many etiquette books warned women who attended larger public balls not to dance with men who had not been properly introduced to them by a trusted friend or family member. A gentleman, on the other hand, was obliged to dance with any partner suggested by the hostess as well as with the hostess herself. It was also considered polite for a gentleman to dance with any woman who was neglected. Balls presented a particularly challenging atmosphere for conversing well: "Under the hopeless conditions of heat, rapid exercise, excitement, and often fatigue as well" couples were thrown together with no idea about one another's "tone of mind" or interests, thus leading to clichéd talk on "stock subjects." The Lounger concludes that those with "congenial spirits" could transcend the trivialities of small talk even under these limiting circumstances.[35] Overall, the Lounger's advice defies the stereotype of etiquette books as a feminized and morally preachy genre. *The Glass of Fashion* appeals to men as well as women, asking them to embrace rules of courtship while still enjoying its rituals and behaving as naturally as possible.

EPISTOLARY COURTSHIP CONDUCT

Lucie Heaton Armstrong's *Letters to a Dèbutante* (1896) is essentially the female-oriented companion to *The Glass of Fashion*. Armstrong, author of the *Good Form* column in the *Lady's Pictorial* and another advice series in *Hearth and Home*, based her book on the letters she received from girls, many of whom were too embarrassed to ask friends or relatives for advice and whom, she claims, were often motherless. As a result, *Letters to a Dèbutante* is framed as a collection of letters written to Letty, an orphaned dèbutante making her way through society during the London Season, from her worldly aunt Priscilla. Priscilla, like the Lounger, offers a late-century perspective on the courtship rituals that had become commonplace but were unfamiliar to uninitiated aspirants to high society.

Priscilla begins by reassuring her insecure niece that "once you have mastered the laws of etiquette you will never be in doubt what to do, and the hesitation and embarrassment you speak of will pass away. Ease of manner is not attained by carelessness, but by knowledge—knowledge is power in society as elsewhere."[36] As their conversation unfolds, it indeed tells the story of Letty's increasing knowledge and power. Like the Lounger, Armstrong used humor to make her guidelines more interesting. She also engaged readers with a narrative of triumph for her main character. Interestingly, readers could infer Letty's progress only through her aunt's advice. Letty's articulation of her experiences are left to the imagination though it is clear what those experiences are from her aunt's replies. Thus, the book follows the conventions of the newspaper advice column by allowing Letty to become the perfect stand in for the average society girl.

Through the letters of the fictional aunt Priscilla, Armstrong traces the rules of etiquette in much the same way the Lounger does, running the gambit from at-homes to private walks and rides to country house visits, luncheons, dinners, and balls. The first lessons Letty learns are that she should never rise up from her seat when introduced to an unknown gentlemen during an at-home, she must never receive an unchaperoned call from a gentleman, she should never spend more than 20 minutes on a visit, she must not have calling cards of her own while still under the guardianship of others, and she should never take her gloves off at an afternoon tea—excepting the right glove and only to eat hot buttered cakes. As for walking alone, Pricilla notes, "Much more liberty falls to the lot of modern girls than was ever enjoyed in my young days. . . . You would not walk in the Park by yourself, especially on Sunday, nor would you be seen alone in a crowded thoroughfare very late in the afternoon; but otherwise you can go about very much as you please, and as long as you go quietly no one will ever remark you." Priscilla insists that maintaining a quiet demeanor in public is crucial and loud conversation in the street is "simply unpardonable" as are loitering before shop windows, turning one's head to look around in the street, and wearing bright colors. These prohibitions are striking for their clear aim of insuring that proper ladies are not confused with fancily dressed shop girls or prostitutes. Pricilla's commentary betrays an anxiety that with the increasing independence and mobility of women at the end of the century, society girls might actually be mistaken for independent working girls. Priscilla sets forth an entire "etiquette of walking" that distinguishes a lady from a common woman, just in case one's appearance was not enough to signal the difference. Ladies were supposed to keep to the right of the walkway in open streets, remain on the inside edge of park paths for protection from strangers, allow married women to precede them, and let gentlemen carry their parcels and steer them through a crowd.[37] These urban rituals conjure up images of young women moving freely through hustling and bustling centers of commerce and pleasure despite following very specific rules to do so.

When Letty is invited by an old family friend for a country house visit, she calls on her aunt for advice. Priscilla recommends that she pack lightly and not expect to be entertained every minute of the day and night. While such visits provided liberty to a girl, she advises Letty not to accept any outside invitation without consulting her hostess first and "not to be out so much that you appear to be turning your hostess' house into an hotel." Letty is urged to join in whatever household amusements are proposed by the hostess and to sing and play when invited. It is at this point that Mr. Edward Ironside, a childhood friend, appears in the narrative. On receiving Letty's report on her country visit, Priscilla writes:

> It was pleasant for you to have Mr Ironside sitting next to you at table, since you never feel shy with him, as you do with so many people, and you never feel as if he were laughing at you; and I am delighted that you enjoyed your day's hunting so much, and found the long ride home so agreeable. I don't quite see how it was that you both got lost, and were so late getting home, but these things will happen sometimes, and of course, neither of you know the country very well.[38]

Despite her concern for proper protocol, Letty manages to spend private time with her admirer. This budding romance certainly fits the ideals of Victorian courtship as it is based on a childhood friendship, forged by families of similar status, and involves two people who are clearly companionable.

When Letty is invited to a ball in London where Edward will also be a guest, she frets over whether or not he will ask her to dance. Priscilla tells her to show herself to advantage by wearing "a low dress" in white satin covered with tulle or chiffon and paired with a pearl necklace and a bouquet of white flowers or a white-feathered fan. On the pitfalls of dancing with bad partners, she advises "don't allow your partner to hold your hand out as if it were a pump-handle, or to whirl you round faster than you like. If he dances badly, simply stand still, say you are tired, or that you would like to watch the others a little—never permit him to make a sight of you, for people might think it was your fault." She notes that "everybody flirts more or less, nowadays, so I won't lay a veto on that; only don't make yourself noticeable with any one person—it would be very bad to get talked about in your first Season." Letty is told never to sit out two or three dances in a row and not to spend too much time "in cosy corners" as it would be "bad style." However, Priscilla concedes that "it is not a bit of good for me to tell you how many times you can dance with Edward Ironside. . . . I know perfectly well you won't keep to it if I tell you. Well, three times is supposed to be the discreet limit." Priscilla also insists that Letty allow the gentleman who takes her in to supper to escort her back to the ballroom as well. These seemingly contradictory rules strike a balance between interacting with a variety of gentlemen on the dance floor and demonstrating allegiance to one dinner escort. Letty, as her aunt predicts, is better at exclusivity than playing the field: "My little Letty! . . . to think your fate is settled, and you should have gone and got engaged at your very first ball! Well, I am truly surprised, my dear. I am so utterly astonished at Edward Ironside's proposal as you seem to have expected me to be."[39] Though Letty's courtship and proposal comes quickly and in person, others courted through correspondence.

LOVE LETTERS

In her study of American conduct literature, Karen Halttunan argues that the "demand for perfect self-restraint" in behavior "was in apparent conflict with the sentimental ideal of transparent emotional self-expression." The only way to reconcile these seemingly contradictory ideas was to insist that "all polite manners be completely natural" once ingrained by good breeding or etiquette lessons. This tension between the rules of courtship behavior and the expression of true love can be seen in *The Glass of Fashion* and *Letters to a Dèbutante*, but it is most obvious in letter-writing manuals since a letter is, as Halttunan suggests,

simultaneously "an act of emotional self-expression" and "a critical aspect
of genteel performance." "Although the avowed content of the polite letter was heart-felt sentiment, its form was rigorously self-restrained, styl-
ized, and most significant, standardized."[40] The love letter, then, embodies
the key contradiction in Victorian courtship practices: they are supposed
to be based on real feelings of affection and love, but they are bound by
social rules. Just as the ball at which a lady was expected to mingle with
many partners but avoid snubbing her dinner escort, the love letter and,
indeed, courtship itself were contradictory endeavors.

According to Catherine Golden, the introduction of the penny post in
1840 greatly increased the importance of love letters since they could now
be sent more cheaply and frequently. The tradition of making and sending
Valentines was also spurred on by Uniform Penny Postage. In 1841 Victorians sent over 400,000 Valentines and by 1871 that number had increased
threefold. But Valentines were only sent once a year; love letters were vi-
able year-round. *The Etiquette of Love, Courtship and Marriage* warns readers that "a far greater importance is attached to letter writing than most
people are aware of. A letter is the index of the mind. . . . What is spoken,
is in a great measure forgotten; but what is written remains, and can be
referred to at any time."[41] Writing love letters was considered very serious
business. As a result, many letter-writing manuals provided models that
beginners could follow to avoid making blunders.

The Letter Writer for Lovers (n.d.) explains that its model letters were chosen because they recommended an appropriate "tone rather than dictated
the terms of the letters" to be written. Yet, the author defends the possibility of using the models as they are, stating that they "may be fearlessly
used under any of the actual circumstances in view of which they have
been composed." *The Lover's Letter Writer for Ladies and Gentlemen* (1866), on
the other hand, uses footnotes to warn readers against the potential pitfalls
of copying its letters directly. One note warns that "this, and a few of the
following letters, are given as specimens of the *naïve* and lively style of correspondence, which *intimate acquaintance* alone can justify the use of. Our
readers must therefore be cautious in copying such examples." Another
note declares, "On grounds of plain *common sense*, we should not recommend this or the following letter for imitation; but people *will* send such
letters." Interestingly, most of these warnings occur in the "Gentlemen's
Letters" section of the book, indicating that it was the male of the species
who was presumed to write more effusive letters. The guide provides one
woman's harsh reprimand to "an absurdly Romantic Letter" from a suitor:

> I do not know whether your epistle was intended in jest, in which
> case its absurdity might have been excused. . . . But if you can really
> write *in earnest* . . . I must express my humble opinion that such is
> not the proper course by which to excite a reciprocal feeling. Regret-
> ting that you should have adopted a tone of writing which neither

modern usage, nor common sense at any time, could sanction, I remain, Sir, Your obedient servant.[42]

Thus, gender roles were reversed in love letter writing: women were presumed to be more restrained and reasonable in their responses to admirers and men more sentimental and romantic in their attempts to woo women. Indeed, courtship conduct books and letter-writing manuals provide a rare instance of the belief in women's ability to "keep their heads" rather than act impulsively "from the heart," demonstrating that while women were perhaps expected to need advice literature more than men, they were also expected to behave more rationally as a result of their training.

Letter-writing manuals encouraged writers to use simple and direct language that was not overly sentimental or bombastic and to be very discreet so as to avoid the possibility of embarrassment in case any letters reached unintended recipients. The fear that love letters would be shared by the recipients with family or friends or even exposed publicly in court by a breach of promise lawsuit (typically brought by a woman accusing a man of reneging on a marriage proposal) led many to advise against writing them at all. An exchange between Mrs. And Mr. Punch in "On Love Letters" makes the case against amorous epistles. After reading a report in the news about letters presented in a breach of promise suit that were covered in stars to represent kisses, Mrs. Punch declares that "a man ought to be punished for writing such idiotic love-letters." Mr. Punch replies, "Logical as ever, my adored . . . but it is in the fitness of things that a love letter should be idiotic. Love is a brief (very brief) madness." According to Francois Barret-Ducrocq, fallen women who applied for assistance at the London Foundling Hospital also used love letters as exculpatory evidence. "Snippets of sentimental conversation" were "attached carefully to their admission forms" to prove that they were not prostitutes, but rather mistreated victims. Despite the potential risks, *The Letter Writer for Lovers* maintains that "there is nothing derogatory in writing affectionately; on the contrary, if the engaged couple are really loving, and wish to express their feelings in loving phrases, let them by all means do so; but let this be done in a gentlemanlike and ladylike manner. A love letter never loses by being couched in grammatical terms, and with due regard to style and diction."[43]

Capitalizing on the popularity of the epistolary form for conduct books such as Armstrong's *Letters to a Dèbutante*, letter-writing guides not only offered model courtship epistles but also provided entertaining narratives developed in the letters themselves. *The Lover's Letter Writer* opens with a section on "Ladies' Letters" in which it traces one woman's responses to a gentleman who abruptly proposes and continues to persistently pursue her despite her initial refusal to marry him. The first response "From a Young Lady, in Answer to the Proposal of a Gentleman who had met her the previous evening" is dismissive but polite: "Without wishing to say anything harsh, I must confess that I do not feel any motive to entertain so hasty a proposal, and have felt bound to lay your letter before my parents, as I could not think of concealing from them any correspondence of such a description." "Another, More Favourable" response from the young lady while on a country house visit follows: "I cannot think of giving a sanction to further attentions on your part, without consulting Mrs.—. . . I have, therefore, placed your letter in her hands. I cannot deny feeling some pleasure in having elicited sentiments from you which appear to be founded in honourable good feeling, but must, for a time, beg of you to excuse me giving you any further sanction to your addresses." The next letter is titled "On receiving a Second Letter, after frequent meetings" and includes a cautious but encouraging message: "Let us not . . . be too hasty in our conclusions—let us not mistake momentary impulse for permanent impression; let us rather seek to know more of each other, to study each other's tempers, and to establish that sincere esteem which should, which must, be the foundation of every deeper feeling." The series concludes with a letter written "On more intimate Acquaintance" that implies an impending acceptance of the gentleman's proposal:

> We shall all be very happy to see you here. . . . When I say *we*, it of course includes some one in whose heart you now hold a place. . . . I believe we are to perform charades, or something of that sort and I have been occupied half the week cutting out old window-curtains and sofa-covers into absurd costumes, supposed to be Oriental. I know you are very clever at that sort of nonsense, so I hope you will come and have a good laugh. . . . P.S. Come early. I have something to say to you.[44]

Here we see a perfect example of the woman's control over courtship practices as well as her own feelings. She remains reasonable in the face of romantic pursuit and does not give in to effusive self-expression even when she is apparently conquered by her suitor.

The blossoming of courtship away from the watchful eyes of parents is a common theme in these guidebooks. *The Lover's Letter Writer* includes letters responding to requests for clandestine meetings as well as letters to parents about suitors met in their absence. Perhaps surprisingly, a great deal of support is offered for relationships forged beyond the bounds of family control. As the "more favourable" response to a proposed secret meeting states:

> Although my own conscience tells me that anything like clandestine conduct should be avoided, still I feel that we are most unhappily placed, and that the undue opposition on the part of my aunt, in seeking to force upon me a man whom I dislike, excuses to some extent what I cannot justify. . . . A few months more, however, will see me mistress of my own fortune and liberty, and then there will be no fur-

ther need of concealment. I shall be walking–at—o'clock, when we shall perhaps gain an opportunity of a few minutes' conversation.[45]

The ideals of romantic love and companionate marriage permeate the discourse of love letter writing manuals, often at the expense of following the rules of courtship set forth in other etiquette books.

Women were particularly encouraged to make marital decisions independently. A letter from *The Letter Writer for Lovers* entitled "From a Lady to her Father, Announcing a Proposal made to her" indicates a good deal of autonomy on the daughter's behalf. The lady reveals to her father that she has "something very important to tell . . . and I hope you will not scold me when you have read my news"; however, she does not seek permission for, but rather, approval of her wishes. Having already received and accepted a proposal at a picnic party, she tells her father, "You said I was always to follow the dictates of conscience, and my conscience is quite at ease." A similar letter from a daughter to her father explains,

> I yesterday had an offer of marriage . . . and I must confess that I gave him reason to believe that I entertained a sincere liking for him. I have known him, as you are aware, for a great many months, as he visits here a good deal. . . . I, of course, referred him to you for your consent to our engagement; but I did not hide from him (as he pressed me very much) that I hoped you would not withhold your sanction. . . . I am sure you will like him when you know him, and will receive him as my affianced husband.[46]

While the model responses from the father are a mixed bag, with two unfavorable and two favorable ones, it is clear that a woman's right to choose her partner for life is upheld.

The model letters reveal the challenges gentlemen faced not only in winning a bride but in pleasing her during the engagement. According to the letters, newly betrothed women commonly complained about their fiancé's prolonged absences, infrequent letters, frequent quarreling, and flirtations with other women. The gentlemen accused their fiancées of similar offenses. While an engaged couple was urged not to show off their status in public and to continue to pay polite attention to those of the opposite sex, this contradictory conception of courtship and marriage as both very private and very public affairs could easily result in misunderstandings. *The Letter Writer for Lovers* includes models "From a Lady to her Fiancé, complaining of his silence," "From a Lady, Upbraiding her Fiancé for not writing.—More Severe," "From a Gentleman to his Fiancée, complaining of her not writing to him," and "From a Gentleman, Remonstrating with a Lady on her Continued Silence.—Severely," as well as "A Lady to her Lover, who has Accused her of Flirting" and "From a Lady,

Remonstrating with her Fiancé for 'Flirting' at a Party." The lady's denial of flirting very pointedly puts her Fiancé in the wrong and once again reinforces the woman's upper hand in the land of courtship: "Your very absurd letter scarcely needs a reply. I am sorry to find that you are of such a jealous temperament, and think that I ever did or said any of the things you impute to me. It is too absurd for refutation. Of course, . . . I will be very glad to talk to you if you will come here to-day."[47] These letters expose the difficulty of striking the delicate balance between sociability and exclusivity during courtship and engagement.

Engagement was a period, as Sarah Grand notes in the *Woman at Home*, that allowed couples "a certain license" to become more "intimately acquainted than before, and of obtaining a better knowledge of each other's characters, tempers, tastes, and habits than they could have done in ordinary social intercourse." This was both beneficial and potentially detrimental given that it could lead to discord where harmony was assumed to exist. This is why short engagements, like short courtships, were recommended. However, engagements among the middle classes were typically longer—from six months to two years—than those in the upper echelons of society. The standards for the working classes were much less formal: "Two people with an affinity for each other strike up a friendship, and are practically said to be 'keeping company.' If their sentiments undergo no change, this stage is simply succeeded by the wedding itself." As *The Etiquette of Marriage* declares, "The wisest people sometimes make mistakes, and when a mistake *is* made in the choice of a husband or a wife, it is well if it is discovered before the nuptial knot is tied." Grand insists "it is justifiable to break off engagements, not only under special circumstances but under any circumstances which may threaten to bring unhappiness on a pair should they marry." *The Etiquette of Courtship and Matrimony* is even more explicit about what such circumstances might be. A woman who discovers "incompatible habits, ungentlemanly actions, anything tending to diminish that respect for the lover which should be felt for the husband; inconstancy, ill-governed temper" is determined to have "sufficient reasons for terminating an engagement." For a man, however, the standard was higher and more vague: "The reasons must be strong indeed that can sufficiently justify a man, placed in a position of an accepted suitor, in severing the ties by which he has bound himself to a lady with the avowed intention of making her his wife. His reasons for breaking off his engagement must be such as will not merely satisfy his own conscience, but will justify him in the eyes of the world." If faced with the necessity of breaking off an engagement, it is recommended that the communication "be made as tenderly as possible," especially if the bad news is delivered by the lady. In this case, it must be "so managed that not the slightest shadow of fickleness or want of faith may rest on the character of the lady. It must be remembered, however, that the termination of an engagement by a lady has the privilege of passing unchallenged: a lady not being bound to declare any other reason than her will. Nevertheless she owes it to her reputation that her decision should rest on a sufficient foundation." Clearly, the reputation of a woman could be more damaged than that of a man in the case of a broken engagement. However, as *The Etiquette of Marriage* points out, "It is less painful to suffer a sudden, sharp blow that is, after all, capable of healing, than to drag out a miserable existence with an unsympathetic partner." *The Etiquette of Marriage* even suggests keeping the engagement private for a time to provide "a little breathing space" that will enable "lovers to be pretty sure they have not mistaken their feelings."[48] As the model love letters indicate, while the period of engagement could be joyous, it was also potentially treacherous for partners who may not have spent any time alone before making a lifelong commitment to one another.

COURTSHIP AMONG THE WORKING CLASSES

The *Letter Writer for Lovers* devotes an entire section to letters from farmers, lady's maids, and men in service, while *The Lover's Letter Writer* includes a fair number of models for other working class suitors. *The Letter Writer for Lovers* explains in its preface that "it is manifestly impossible for any one individual to write a series of 'love letters' . . . which meet all cases and requirements: what would suit a person in one grade of society would be out of place in another."[49] Therefore, separate letters are provided for each class. What was courtship like among the working classes for whom no London Season was possible? Members of this class met at work, Sunday school, church, theaters, music halls, museums, weekly markets, and annual fairs. They socialized in taverns, coffee houses, gardens, and other public places. Workers organized their own dances and gatherings free from the supervision of elders. These relationships were more casual and free than those of the middle and upper classes and parents were less restrictive about their children's interactions with the opposite sex. Based on data collected from English parishes between 1800 and 1849, Penny Kane suggests that one-fifth to two-fifths of women were pregnant on marriage. Gillis adds that pregnancy was sometimes seen as a desirable way for a working class woman to secure a husband. Michael Mason argues that despite the "restricted evidence, pre-nuptial pregnancy and therefore pre-nuptial intercourse were indeed widespread phenomena" though it was more common in rural areas than in urban centers. Still, most couples probably aimed for a more respectable sexual restraint, especially by mid-century when middle-class ideals of marriage were spreading to the working classes. As Kane asserts, "If couples had been sexually active much before their marriages, we might expect that large numbers of 'shotgun' weddings would have moved the average age at marriage downward—and that did not happen." In fact, the rate of illegitimacy and prenuptial pregnancy actually declined compared to earlier periods, dropping 50 percent by the end of the century.[50]

According to Mason, Victorian observers "leapt too readily to adverse conclusions about the sexual morality of the working class on the strength of certain appearances. They applied inappropriate standards of decorum in speech and personal address, to conclude, for example, that certain kinds of swearing, or conventions of behaviour between young people, denoted sexual license." One ritual that many middle-class observers thought immoral was the habit of the working class Sunday. Many Londoners saw their only day off from work as an opportunity to mimic the upper classes in dress, drunkenness, and courtship on river trips to the Crystal Palace or on excursions to local parks and other attractions. Well-meaning observers may also have concluded that crowded living conditions among the poor led to sexual depravity or incest. The idea that unmarried members of both sexes might sleep together in the same room was, for many, indicative of loose morals. Barret-Ducrocq claims, "By contrast with the ideal image of the Victorian family—the essence of order and discipline, where everyone has a place to occupy, a role to fulfil, a room to live in—such proximity was seen as bruising to the sensibilities and disturbing to the mind." However, statistics do not reveal a correlation between housing density and rates of illegitimacy. Furthermore, Mason points out that many members of the working class applied strict rules for sleeping and dressing that enforced the separation of the sexes despite crowded conditions.[51]

By 1851 about one-third of women worked, most in shops, factories, or in domestic service. Urban dwellers and factory workers were often separated from their parents and extended families. They earned their own wages and worked and socialized in mixed company, which encouraged greater freedom in courtship. Even if living at home, young people had more independence than their middle-class counterparts and did not seek parental consent for marriage. Gillis contends that in both pastoral and industrial regions, "conditions conducive to female independence" prevailed as widows and unmarried women could rent or own small plots of land while supporting themselves "selling eggs and milk, brewing, laundering, or working in the handicrafts." Working women's earning power gave them even more influence in courtship. Yet, as Ginger Frost contends, the fact that "their courtship was informal and largely unsupervised" led to an explosion of "breach of promise" lawsuits among the working classes. The average length of time from courtship to proposal among the working classes was only nine months, while the median length of time between the engagement and marriage was three years. The longer engagement sometimes resulted in the disintegration of the relationship, usually to the woman's detriment. Breach of Promise suits were often won by women, allowing them compensation for the loss of their prime courting years if they could prove that they were misled and abandoned.[52]

The popularity of going into domestic service had declined by the end of the century in large part due to the greater independence factory and other workers had in comparison to those in service, whose lives were highly regulated by the families who employed them. Servants' clothes, leisure time, and courtship possibilities were restricted, making marriage and upward mobility more difficult. Overall, members of the working classes tended to marry earlier than those of the professional classes: in 1886 working-class men married at an average age of 24 while tradesmen married at 27 and their professional counterparts married at 31. These figures reflected the amount of money expected to set up an independent household for each respective class. However, servants tended to marry later or not at all. Gillis explains that servants

> normally came to the city without any inheritance beyond their labor power. It took years before they accumulated sufficient savings to marry . . . their courtships tended to be extended and even those with the most promising liaison often failed to consummate their marriages. Of all the groups in Victorian London's female population, it was servants who were most at risk of unwed motherhood, largely because there were so many obstacles to their nuptiality.

The tremendous cost of premarital pregnancy for domestic servants, who were typically dismissed for the offense, resulted in the high numbers of them among mothers abandoning children at the London Foundling Hospital and among women taken in by rescue organizations for fallen women.[53] Given this context, model letters from servant girls may have been included in love letter-writing manuals in part to convince their employers (who were more likely to purchase the manuals in the first place) to sympathize with the plight of their servants. More freedom in courtship could, perhaps, prevent clandestine relationships and their often disastrous results. However, these manuals turned a blind eye toward the very real possibility that servants could also become victims of members of the households for which they worked.

One letter from a servant to her suitor sounds more like a model for how to treat servants than a model for how servants should communicate with their lovers: "My mistress is so satisfied with me that she has increased my wages, besides making me a handsome present of clothes. I am in hopes that, with care and economy, we may both of us save something, and not start into married life, as many do, without a farthing to help us. As my mistress kindly permits me to go out on Sunday afternoon, I shall hope to meet you as usual." Model letters from servants frequently address financial concerns, suggesting the difficulty of preparing for marriage among the servant classes. As another female servant writes to her suitor: "Should you be so fortunate as to obtain the situation of which Mr.—has held out hopes, we shall be able to marry without fear. . . . Do not think that it is coldness that makes me object to our immediate happiness; it is only prudence that makes me wish to spare ourselves the risk of that poverty which too often leads to dissipation and misery on both sides." "A Manservant to the Object of his Affections" likewise writes:

> How often do I think of those innocent and happy days when much of our time was passed together. Servitude has since separated us; but if I may judge of your heart by my own, our feelings of affection towards each other have not undergone the slightest change. Our attachment is the same, and we must both long for that period when, freed from servitude, the useful toils of our past life may meet their reward.[54]

These model letters reveal that for the servant class it was often more difficult to obtain independence from employers than it was from parents.

Elizabeth Gaskell's *Cranford* dramatizes the problem of servant courtship. Though Cranford is a town filled with middle-class old maids and very few middle-class gentlemen, men "abounded in lower classes. The pretty neat servant-maids had their choice of desirable 'followers,' and their mistresses . . . might well feel a little anxious, lest the heads of their comely maids should be turned by the joiner, or the butcher, or the gardener; who were obliged, by their callings, to come to the house." Miss Matty forbids her maid Fanny to have followers. However, the narrator Mary notices that "a vision of a man seemed to haunt the kitchen. Fanny assured me that it was all fancy" but "I had seen a man's coat-tails whisk into the scullery once," and another time "there was a very odd appearance, singularly like a young man squeezed up between the clock and the back of the open kitchen door."[55] Miss Matty finally relaxes her restriction against followers, which was put in place by her father and carried on by her deceased sister, after reflecting on her own lost chance at love with a man disapproved of by her family.

In 1868, the *London Review* championed greater freedom for servants to openly court and marry without losing their positions. The article "The Courtship of Female Servants" goes so far as to call the restrictions on courtship inhumane: "Ladies who have to deal with nurserymaids, parlourmaids, and chambermaids, never think of these creatures as possessing a common nature with themselves. . . . The rules imposed on women in service exact a decorum and a morality which is regarded as a credential, like the physical recommendation of health or comeliness." The article declares this required credential unrealistic given that the typical servant was making her way with "no friends or relations" to guide her. As a result,

They go for a walk on their evening out, and are met by some plausible vagabond who manages to scrape an acquaintance with them somehow or other. Then an appointment for another meeting is made. The girl is induced on the next occasion to visit a low music-hall . . . or a cheap dancing saloon. The end might be predicted from the beginning. It may indeed happen that a servant in her solitary excursions becomes known to a respectable workman or mechanic. A courtship perfectly pure and honest may be exchanged by them.[56]

Then again, the liaisons these lonely girls made may not have been so admirable. From such beginnings, maids were often "ruined" and abandoned. The *London Review* argues that employer sanctions against female servants were the primary cause of infanticide as unfortunate women attempted to destroy the evidence of their secret relationships. The magazine advocates more open courtship practices and fewer restrictions by employers as a solution to numerous premarital pregnancies, breach of promise suits, and untimely dismissals.

While servants were presumably held to overly strict standards, some in the lower middle classes aspired to follow similarly restrictive middle- and upper-class courtship rituals. The *London Journal*, a magazine that catered to upwardly mobile working- and lower-middle-class readers, reflected the simultaneous resistance to and desire for higher standards of courtship conduct. The magazine sometimes overtly criticized the courtship rituals of the middle and upper classes and at other times lauded them as standards for readers to follow. One article pointed out the cruelties of courtship conduct, particularly for women. Given the propensity of men to mislead women with their courtship behavior, the magazine argues, middle-class women were often set up for disappointment: "our system of courtship seems especially designed for mischief. . . . For weeks, for months, for years, he worships at the feet of his fair one with compliment, flattery, and endless attentions. He seems the slave of her smallest wish. In all this there is much acting, often much conscious acting. Marriage is the dropping of the curtain."[57] Based on this critique of middle-class courtship, the working class system seemed more honest and wise (as even some middle-class conduct books acknowledged). However, the *London Journal* also ran its own courtship conduct series in 1849. Written by J. Parsons Hall, the series consists of brief weekly essays parroting standard courtship practices (against early marriages, against clandestine courtship, against flirting, and for modesty and self-control) but also freely acknowledging that following etiquette rules could lead to false behavior that was detrimental to relationships.

Just as courtship conduct could be misleading, so could overt displays of wealth. Not surprisingly for a magazine geared toward an audience unlikely to strike it rich, the *London Journal*'s etiquette column is especially cautious about the pursuit of wealth and status above love and companionship: "Marital happiness is not to be found in the depth of the bride's pocket, or the patronage or influence of her friends; it comes from a purer and more certain source; and young men, in making their election, should not allow themselves to be altogether blinded by the golden dust scattered before men's eyes by a rich man's daughter." Likewise, women are urged to seek a man whose behavior is more respectable than his status: "This is not a point which should be either sneered or laughed at; for, with the melancholy example of so many imprudent, and consequently unhappy, marriages before their eyes, the young girls of the present day are not quite so thoughtless as by many they are supposed to be." Greedy parents, particularly "mothers whose hearts are hardened, and their instincts deadened by the love of money" are remonstrated for participating in sanctioned prostitution by selling their daughters to the highest bidders, who often happen to be the oldest and most unsuitable partners. May–December marriages or marriages made solely based on financial arrangements were blamed for both infidelity and spousal murder.[58] That infidelity and murder are mentioned at all in a courtship etiquette guide is quite sensational and indicates the lingering suspicions about adopting the courtship rituals of the upper classes.

Continuing its sensational strain, the *Journal* warned women about being duped into marriage by dishonest men. Women were cautioned against rakes, fools, melancholy lovers, misers, and overly jealous men who could turn them into slaves. They are especially urged to acknowledge their own susceptibility to flattery: "The serpent often masks himself in the bloom of youth; and through an imperfect knowledge of the world, and an ignorance of wrong, many a maiden has allowed him to twine himself round her heart." Likewise, men are advised to avoid coquettes, who will only excite contempt and bring about "sorrow, doubt, and distrust" rather than "wedded happiness."[59] Etiquette advice in the *London Journal*, then, is offered with the understanding that proper courtship conduct does not ensure happiness. This version of courtship etiquette accepts that advice might help the working and lower middle classes rise to new positions of status through marriage, but maintains a healthy skepticism about the prospects for the success of such endeavors. While this skepticism is entirely suitable for a working class audience shut out of the pleasures and privileges of the London Season, it also pervades the genre of anticonduct literature.

ANTICONDUCT LITERATURE

Alongside all of the serious etiquette manuals crowding the shelves of booksellers, there were also a handful of anticonduct books, which capitalized on the humorous and absurdly embarrassing situations that could arise during courtship. Anticonduct books were sometimes outright fictional satires and other times masked as real advice manuals, but they were always sensationally cynical about courtship conduct. *Whom to Marry and How to Get Married! or, The Adventures of a Lady in Search of a Good Husband by One Who Has Refused "Twenty Excellent Offers at Least"* (1848) is a satirical novel that dramatically demonstrates the many pitfalls of courtship, whether it is pursued at home, in public, or through correspondence. Lotty, the narrator, receives at least 11 marriage proposals throughout the novel, each one more disastrous than the last. Whether she is motivated by love, money, or vanity, Lotty is repeatedly thwarted in her search for a husband. Lotty does not seem to learn from her mistakes unless, perhaps, she learns that there are so many kinds of courtship blunders to be made that learning about them is a lifelong endeavor.

Perhaps the most compelling episode in the novel involves a direct parody of the use of conduct literature. Following Lotty's romantic indiscretion with her tutor, for which her father blames her excessive novel reading, she is sent to boarding school to be reformed. The school is presided over by the two Misses Thimblebee, who base their curriculum on conduct book lessons despite the fact that being well versed in conduct book advice has obviously not worked for them. Miss Grace is a spinster and her sister, the ironically named Miss Prudence "had, in the flighty moments of her thirty-fifth year, been imprudent enough to rush blindly into matrimony with a certain gay commercial traveler . . . who had unfortunately been led astray . . . by an overfondness for the bottle." The sisters therefore live "in constant dread of seeing the hopeless prodigal husband" return to demand "all the ready cash" they have on the premises. The Misses Thimblebee, not surprisingly, fail to reform Lotty despite their constant quotation of maxims from *The Handbook of Toilet, Etiquette for the Ladies,* and *How to Live Upon Two Hundred a Year.* Their requirement of endless hours of ladylike pursuits such as "Berlin-wool work, or velvet painting, or embroidery, or japanning, or wax flowers, and other odd knick-knackeries" likewise fails to make an impression.[60] Instead of following the advice of the fair school marms, Lotty begins a clandestine correspondence with a classmate's brother. During one secret meeting between Lotty and this bumbling boy in the school's parlor, he is forced to hide in a large double-bass viol case that is subsequently delivered to the train station. Fearing for her suitor's life, Lotty confesses her transgressions to the Misses Thimblebee. Luckily, the boy is found and released before being stowed on the train as luggage. Unfortunately for Lotty, conduct book advice and instruction in ladylike accomplishments produce no better results than her novel reading.

Lotty's shenanigans do not end at boarding school. After returning home, her capers often include her silly mother, who ruins one marriage prospect from a dashing soldier when she interprets a general's proposal to bring a dozen "donkeys" to a picnic as an affectionate reference to his officers instead of to actual beasts of burden. She winds up insulting the entire regiment when she repeatedly uses the unflattering term to describe them. Lotty also faces a rivalry with her sister over a Lord, fights off both a vain clergyman and a swindler, and endures the death of her first husband, Captain Dawdle, in a horse race. After being left penniless by this tragedy she is forced to take a position as a governess, which she finds advertised in the newspaper. She ultimately marries Sir Luke, her employer, and triumphantly becomes a Lady. However, her marriage is immediately on the rocks as she spends her miserly husband's money recklessly and the neighbors look askance at Luke's unwise marriage to someone beneath him in both age and status. As a result, Lotty is forced to leave the high life and live on her own again, but the subtitle to the novel—*Twenty Excellent Offers at Least*—promises more proposals—and disasters—to come.

Similarly, the novel *Courtship as It Is, and as It Ought to Be* (1877) follows Jerome Bluster's unskillful attempt to court Amelia Somersdown as well as the rise of Jerome's ill-treated servant Nat, who unexpectedly inherits a fortune and proves to be more of a gentleman than his brutal master. Jerome blunders through several horribly inept attempts to win Amelia's heart: "Like all others who are the votaries of COURTSHIP AS IT IS, Jerome accepted everything as ominous of triumph, and made a virtue of his veriest vices" never recognizing that he is constantly embarrassing and offending Amelia rather than earning her affections. Instead of taking her silence as a sign of her disinterest, he takes it as "a tacit trophy of the secret working of affection." One highlight of his efforts occurs at a dinner party during which he:

> plunged the knife manfully into the smoking dish before him, and— Good Heavens! How fearful!—how luckless! The treacherous blade had slipped, sank into the rich essence of the veal, and Amelia, in conjunction with Jerome and a dozen more unfortunate sufferers, found herself blinded and besmeared by a copious shower of odorous sauce. What a catastrophe, to be sure! Jerome trembled, stammered, protested and implored: in vain he sought the encouraging smiles of Amelia, or the re-assuring forgiveness of others who had participated in the fall of fat: the ladies were too much pained and piqued to notice the remarks of poor Jerome, and their countenances completely overspread with gravity and gravy.

It is not Jerome's poor table manners or clumsiness that doom him, but rather his self-absorption and unnatural behavior. Jerome's courtship is "cold, methodical . . . without sympathy or sentiment, love or tenderness." Furthermore, his artificial advances are facilitated by Amelia's parents, whose involvement is decried by the narrator because "love is a voluntary plant: no family influence can summon it into being" or prevent it from growing.[61] After stalking and assaulting Amelia to no avail, Jerome seeks revenge for his scorned love by committing arson and attempting murder. Luckily, the perpetrator is the only one who perishes in his criminal scheme.

Readers are left with the following lesson: "It is the general character of those who practice courtship as it is, to set about their work with ostentatious shallowness, relying on such paltry subterfuges as all those which, even if they *could* lure the eye of women of good taste, must leave the heart untouched."[62] The hypocrisy of conduct book courtship is the primary target of this anticonduct tale. However, the novel ends with an example of "Courtship as it Ought to Be," illustrated by the return of the recently educated former servant Nate, who woos Amelia the right way, by forging a real relationship based on friendship, admiration, and affection rather than on empty conduct book rituals. Interestingly, it is once again a member of the working class who is able to behave naturally in love rather than being hampered by the rules of etiquette.

Strict courtship rules for the upper and middle echelons existed alongside more relaxed courtship practices for the working classes, revealing obvious lines of demarcation between them. Interestingly, it was members of the middle classes who expressed the most dissatisfaction with these behavioral differences though they also relied on them as signs of their own respectability. While the very highest and lowest classes of people could bend the rules, those who felt compelled to follow them imagined that they might be better off with the freedom afforded to those beneath and above them. However, they needed the rules and regulations to preserve their class status. The lower middle classes had more leeway to pick and choose from the established rituals of courtship, emulating certain elements while maintaining greater freedom. Likewise, women were more restricted by courtship etiquette than men, yet they held the power of decision making and the position of rationality in the dance of courtship. Men, on the other hand, were expected to take action and woo with an ardent passion that sometimes made them objects of ridicule. Thus, courtship took place on a woman's stage, but men were the primary actors. Resistance to courtship etiquette showed itself not only in the admiration of working class intimacy (excluding servants whose place in the upper-class home forced them to adhere to stricter rules), but also in the emergence of satirical anticonduct literature that boldly criticized the standards and expectations of courtship. Theses anticonduct messages likely played an important part in the growth of the alternative courtship practices that are the focus of the following chapter.

3

Victorian Match.com: Alternative Courtship Practices

MABEL MAYFLOWER, being in search of a husband, entreats some young gentleman to take compassion on her virgin loneliness. She is musical, fond of painting and poetry; can make herself very useful, also, in housekeeping affairs. She is a proficient in needlework, both ornamental and otherwise, and very clever in sewing on buttons! She is of a fair complexion, with auburn hair, and eyes of a blue-grey; rather tall, and will be twenty-five next June. A member of some profession (and not a tradesman) would be much preferred. Black wavy hair and dark eyes are Mabel's standard of perfection in a lover; so no "fair-haired laddie" need trouble her with his adoration.

—*London Journal*, May 1851

We will soon be able to do everything with electricity; who knows but some genius will invent something for the especial use of lovers? Something, for instance, to carry in their pockets, so when they are far away from each other, and pine for the sound of "that beloved voice," they will have only to take up this electrical apparatus, put their ears to it, and be happy. Ah! Blissful lovers of the future!

—*Wired Love*, 1880

"Finding Love: Why You Shouldn't Give Up." "Dating: When to Spend and When to Splurge." "5 Dating Rules You Should Never Break." These are just a few of the headlines recently featured on the computer dating website, eHarmony.com under the heading "Real People. Real Advice." As a religiously oriented dating service, eHarmony claims to have the highest marriage rate of all the dating websites. The site invites visitors to read articles to improve their chances of finding a spouse, to take the "patented Compatibility Matching System" inventory to generate a customized list of appropriate partners, and to write a personal profile that their matches will read before deciding whether or not they want to start an email correspondence or arrange a meeting. Similar dating forums such as Match.com (the most popular U.S. site, claiming 15 million members) and Chemistry.com (a spin-off of Match.com that uses a personality test designed by an anthropologist) are less focused on the immediate goal of marriage and more geared toward uniting romantic partners for short-term amusement or long-term relationships that may or may not include marriage. Regardless of the mission, online dating sites are surging in popularity among a generation of singles who have devoted their 20s and 30s to the establishment of their careers or who have been divorced and are seeking new partners. While the online dating phenomenon seems to be a wholly original invention of the computer age, its roots are firmly planted in the 19th-century periodical press. In fact, seeking "dating" advice, publishing personal advertisements, and exchanging letters and photographs with strangers were all common aspects of the Victorian world of alternative courtship practices recorded in the newspapers, magazines, and fiction of the period.

While courtship etiquette books were available in abundance, the conventional advice they offered failed to take into account newly emerging and increasingly popular courtship practices. Advertising for marriage partners or meeting them outside of the traditional networks of family and friends had a long history, but these methods became ubiquitous in an increasingly urban society with a growing number of displaced people whose communal ties were weak or dissolving. By about mid-century, personal marriage advertisements, professional matrimonial offices, and matchmaking correspondence clubs were recognized as possible—and perhaps necessary if not respectable—venues for seeking a spouse. No longer was it enough to rely on tight-knit social circles for introductions to acceptable mates; young people were taking the matter into their own hands. While clandestine communications with secret lovers had been common in the *Times*'s agony column for decades, now unmarried men and women were advertising to the unknown public, hoping to find the right partner for themselves rather than relying on family or friends to bring them together.

Though personal advertisements were considered distasteful and even dangerous, they were vehicles through which women, in particular, could begin to exert rhetorical power over the complex marriage market by articulating their needs and desires as well as convincing potential partners that they would be good wives. Although conduct books mapped out rules that reinforced the expectation that women would be politely passive during courtship, they also indicated that this was the time when women had the most control over the direction their lives would take. In this chapter, I will outline several examples of alternative courtship practices that illustrate both the benefits and pitfalls women faced as they constructed their own identities and gained greater self-determination by advertising for love. As the opening epigraph from Mabel Mayflower indicates, Victorian women were striking out on their own to seek partners that would meet their increasingly high expectations. Mabel and many other women like her were increasingly delineating very specific traits they sought in a husband and advertising the qualities they felt made them a desirable partner. However, they were also potentially putting themselves in a precarious social position in the process. Whether or not women like Mabel were actually seeking husbands or merely courting a good time, they were certainly taking a calculated risk by opening themselves up to the anonymous readers of mass-market periodicals.

COURTSHIP ADVICE COLUMNS

Advice columns, also known as agony columns, emerged in England in the late 17th century. In *Aunt Agony Advises*, Robin Kent traces their origins back to John Dutton's founding of the *Athenian Gazette* in 1691, which she calls "the first device for audience participation in the history of publishing." Dutton took the question and answer column out of the realm of politics and into the personal lives of magazine readers. Though the purpose of the published readers' questions varied widely—including many scientific, medical, and philosophical queries—a substantial portion of them were related to love, courtship, and marriage. This format was picked up and popularized by many editors including Richard Steele who made it the defining feature of his early 18th-century magazines, the *Tatler* and the *Spectator*. However, many of Steele's queries were fabricated to capture readers' attention. The popularity of the question and answer format among women encouraged its evolution into an advice or agony column often answered by a woman or a male editor using a feminine persona. The *Female Spectator*, under the editorship of novelist Eliza Haywood (1744–1746), and the *Old Maid*, edited by Frances Moore (1755–1756), established the "Agony Aunt" as a trusted female figure with whom readers could share their problems and seek advice.[1] Thereafter, many women's magazines were known for their agony columns.

By the 1840s and 1850s, agony columns had morphed into "Notices to Correspondents" sections, which appeared in penny family magazines aimed at men and women of the working and lower middle classes. These columns were a regular fixture alongside sensational and adventurous fiction serials, nonfiction articles on topics of broad interest, puzzles, recipes, household hints, poems, and practical information. According to Mitchell, as many as 78 penny magazines were issued in a single week in 1840. The

Family Herald (1842–1940) and the *London Journal* (1845–1928) dominated the mass-market readership, selling a combined total of three-quarters of a million copies each.[2] Periodicals such as *Reynolds's Miscellany* (1846–1869), the *Leisure Hour* (1852–1905), and *Cassell's Illustrated Family Paper* (1853–1867) soon joined the ranks of these best-selling periodicals. The repeal of the Stamp Act in 1855 (which eliminated a tax on newspapers) along with the introduction of faster printing presses and improved printing processes, falling paper prices, and an increasingly national distribution system that utilized the railroads contributed to the explosion of the mass-market press. As a result, for the first time working- and lower-middle-class families could afford their own magazines and newspapers.

This new audience was drawn primarily from the growing numbers of city dwellers, which as of the 1851 census made up more than half the population of England. These readers were interested in learning the manners and mores of those above them on the social scale. Their letters to correspondence columns reflected their anxieties about navigating the complex new social landscape of urban life. Mitchell observes that the predominance of letters "about matters of etiquette and general knowledge that would be obvious to anyone with a polite background and more than a rudimentary education" indicate the rapid and unsettling social mobility and sense of displacement among the writers.[3] Though this audience would not be able to afford expensive conduct books, they could take advantage of the free service provided by the correspondence columns of penny papers. As an added bonus, they could ask detailed and specific questions that pertained to their immediate circumstances.

While readers' letters were not printed alongside the editor's answers, the subject and tenor of the inquiry could usually be inferred from the response. When this was not the case, the often-amusing editorial response was entertaining enough on its own. A quick look at one issue of *Reynolds's Miscellany* provides some typical responses. In the December 1862 "Notices to Correspondents" section, *Reynolds's* editor harshly advised Bernard D. that "we cannot sympathize with your alleged grievance. On the contrary, we think that the young lady's father was perfectly right in objecting to you as a son in law on the ground of your being an idler, and living on your industrious relations. . . . The idler is apt, sooner or later, to become a fit candidate for the penitentiary." Directly following this admonition, the editor declares that George K. has "no business to keep [his] engagement with the daughter a secret from her parents. . . . The daughter herself ought to be ashamed of such a course of disrespect and deceit." Finally, John S. is informed that "it would be most rude and impertinent . . . to accost a lady whom you do not know. The fact that you have fallen in love with her would not be a sufficient justification." Judging by these entries, it is clear that advice columns were not just for women. The correspondence section was also an important forum for upwardly mobile men. In these examples, the men are uncertain about appropriate courtship practices and are reprimanded by the editor for their clumsily disrespectful efforts. Women, however, were not spared from the editor's chastisement. They often wrote to find out how far they could push the boundaries of ladylike behavior while maintaining their femininity and aspiring to a kind of middle-class gentility. For example, A.F. is advised that:

> A young lady should not make advances to a man whom she loves. If he has not told you he loves you, you must wait till he does. There are certain ways of bringing him to his senses, however, which are legitimate, and which every girl by instinct knows how to use. Should you bring him to a confession and declaration, you could then ask him for his miniature, and also correspond with him, without impropriety.[4]

Those who did not have the proper "instinct" (or training) were left in the dark or doomed to behave inappropriately. Much of the advice offered in these working-class magazines closely conforms to conduct book literature for the upper middle classes. Boundaries are drawn, rules enforced, and propriety preserved. But not all penny family magazines reiterated conduct book advice.

The *London Journal*, in keeping with its reputation as one of the more sensational penny family magazines, often published notices that hinted at far more controversial relationships and dilemmas such as the one in which Mary found herself. The editor advises her that "the man evidently does not seriously contemplate making you his wife. Accept the first eligible offer." Presumably, Mary was an unwed mother and the editor thought she should marry as quickly as possible to avoid a scandal. Similarly, Eliza Hargrave is warned away from a strange gentleman who spoke to her on her morning walk, inviting her to meet him in the evening: "in the event of her seeing him again," the editor warns, "it would be improper to speak to him . . . for the fellow is probably either some prowling, penniless adventurer or a rake on the look-out for a fresh victim." Likewise, Ann Agnes Morton is implored not to go to London with "the detestable wretch who calls himself your lover" unless he marries her as she "will be abandoned in a few weeks—perhaps days—to the stings of misery, and a biting, gnawing conscience."[5] These tidbits of advice imply a treacherous romantic environment in which much more is at stake than propriety. In these cases, the advice seekers are in danger of suffering severe consequences for their behavior. Yet, the editor implies that these are common scenarios. In this way advice columns diverged from conduct literature, providing a more realistic approach to the challenges of working-class courtship.

Correspondence columns proved so popular that middle-class magazines also got into the habit of providing advice for the love-lorn that

eschewed conduct book platitudes. "Cupid's Letter-Bag," a column focused on love problems in Samuel Beeton's *Englishwoman's Domestic
Magazine (EDM)*, often overtly rejected standard conduct book advice and
encouraged readers to be more actively involved in both its own pages
and the marriage market. The *EDM's* responses to readers were surprisingly bold, speaking frankly about the awkward and sometimes inappropriate situations in which the letter writers found themselves. This was
Beeton's first, and more cautious, foray into provocative conversation in
his magazine, which later featured a sexually charged correspondence
section discussing the pleasures and evils of tightly lacing one's corset.

The *EDM* filled a void in the market for women's periodicals in the
1850s. High-life fashion magazines begun in the early part of the century
were going out of style and the new penny press papers and mother's
magazines were on the rise. Launched in 1852, the *EDM* aimed to merge
the older and the newer forms. According to Megan Ward, the magazine

> targeted a middle- and lower-middle-class audience; at 2d. it was
> significantly less expensive than the one-shilling lady's magazines of
> the past. It was also less extravagant in appearance: about the size of
> a modern paperback book, with a plain cover and thirty-two pages
> of closely spaced type. Unlike the similarly priced *Family Friend* and
> *The Christian Lady's Magazine*, the *Englishwoman's Domestic Magazine*
> was not particularly concerned with religion; it celebrated instead
> the amalgam of domestic ideology with generic morality.[6]

The magazine was also more focused on practical advice and daily activities than other women's periodicals and invited its readers to contribute to
its conversations by submitting essays for its writing contests and sending
letters to its advice columns. Unlike many periodical correspondence sections, the *EDM* usually reprinted its letters rather than simply providing
mysterious answers to unknown questions. This gave readers a more visible role in shaping the focus and tenor of the magazine. While some of the
letters may have been written by Beeton or his paid contributors, it seems
likely that most were genuine given the small size of his staff, the repeated
invitations to readers to correspond, and the magazine's inclusion of the
letters, which bucked the wider trend. Even if the staff fabricated the letters, they hit on issues that certainly resonated with the magazine's readers. This new formula proved to be highly successful, bringing the *EDM* a
healthy audience of 60,000 by 1860.[7]

"Cupid's Letter-Bag" ran from June 1852 until April 1855 when it
merged with the more generalized "Englishwoman's Conversazione" advice column. The "Letter-Bag" created a space for women to share their
courtship experiences and ask very personal, even forbidden, questions
about their own romantic desires. Beetham argues that the magazine cast
"the correspondent . . . as the heroine of a romance, perplexed by the

difficulties of finding a way to marriage and full adult sexuality." Presumably many women could ask close female relatives or companions for advice or consult one of the many comprehensive conduct books. What was likely more difficult to find was a frank and objective male perspective on their specific problems. Beeton's "Cupid's Letter-Bag" offered this rare opportunity by providing more realistic and practical advice than most parents or etiquette books, delivered in a more "jocular and avuncular than magisterial and serious tone." While the editorial voice was masculine and superior, it was also supportive of women's education, property rights, and entry into the public realm. As Beetham puts it, the *EDM* encouraged women "to 'do,' not to 'be.'"[8]

"Cupid's Letter-Bag" encouraged women to act more boldly with men than was typical, as long as they did not behave in an overly flirtatious manner or deteriorate into coquetry. For example, when M.B. asks why she, "a pretty and engaging girl" according to her female friends, has "not as yet met with an admirer of the opposite sex," she is advised that "modesty, in some young ladies, amounts to reserve—this, we feel sure, must be the secret of M.B.'s want of success." Similarly, Kate laments her devotion to "a model of a young man, whom I am doomed to see every day. I feel I can never love another; but how to let him know it I cannot tell." The editor incredulously suggests that "surely . . . some method will suggest itself of making him acquainted with your love, which is all that can be possibly expected from you under the circumstances." Likewise, Eliza, who wonders why she has not been able to find a husband, is told that her retiring nature is perhaps misinterpreted as coldness. She is encouraged to "assume a less frigid manner" with potential suitors.[9] Each of these correspondents is urged to take action rather than waiting for a man to make the first move.

The *EDM* not only promoted more active women but also more intellectual ones. Coelebs (one of very few male correspondents and a likely candidate for a fraudulent one) professes to have been "most happy in the affections of a young lady, whom I have fondly pictured as my wife." That is, until he discovers that "she has taken to authorship, and has gained a prize" in the *EDM* writing competition. He laments that "if there is one thing I have a horror of more than another it is a *blue*. . . . Instead of darning stockings, I shall find her writing essays on 'the Rights of Woman.'" The editor gallantly defends "bluestockings," declaring that "Coelebs can never be so prejudiced or narrow minded as he would lead us to suppose. . . . For our own part, we consider the sympathy and affection of an intellectual woman one of the greatest boons heaven has bestowed on man."[10] Rather than posing a threat to marriage, Cupid proposes that educated women provide better companionship and sympathy for their husbands while also, conveniently, advertising the magazine's writing contests.

The *EDM* advocated revising the boundaries of male–female relationships to include friendship. While most conduct manuals advised against the development of close friendships with members of the opposite sex for fear that women might become the subject of gossip, Cupid promoted freer relationships between the sexes. Rose, a correspondent whose father was often away on business and who was frequently visited by a family friend, worries that she might be "acting wrongly by encouraging his visits." She claims that she and her gentleman visitor "mutually entertain for each other a feeling of friendship and nothing more, arising from our similarity of tastes." Instead of reprimanding Rose for her private visits with a single man in her father's absence, Cupid acknowledges that the situation would not be approved by many, but encourages it anyway:

> In the present state of society we dare hardly speak of *friendship* existing between persons of the opposite sexes. This arises from the artificial usages of civilized life—the simplest *civility* from a man being often construed by prudent parents and brothers into *particular attentions*. . . . As it is young persons, nay persons from twenty to seventy (so ridiculous have we become) cannot meet a few times without some love-affair being gossiped about. . . . Our own opinion is, that the more amalgamated the male and female characters the better; and such can only be effected through more frequent and more rational intercourse. There is no impropriety in Rose still continuing to receive the visits of her friend.

However, the editor does recommend having a chaperone to "stay the tongue of scandal." Similarly, Cupid tells Passion Flower, who worries about her escalating interactions with a gentleman in her social circle to whom she has not received a proper introduction, that "if desirous of cultivating your acquaintance, he should have sought an introduction through a lady friend. . . . So much, however, depends on the station of life, that what is considered etiquette by some would be looked upon as unnecessary formality by others."[11] Thus, the *EDM* acknowledges that class differences exist and gives license to some women to behave more freely than others based on their social context. This was a risky endeavor since it required the woman in question to exercise her own judgment rather than relying on the guidance of others.

"Cupid's Letter-Bag" also urged greater openness and honesty between men and women. When Bertha complains that she has "perceived a great coolness" lately in her fiancé and has heard rumors that he is attached to another and only wants to marry her for her money, Cupid insists that "openness and candor are indispensable. Tell your lover what you have heard, and offer to free him from the engagement if he wishes it. We prophesy if Bertha takes our advice, that when we hear next from her it will be to tell us she is happy with her beloved." In response to two sisters confused about which one is being courted by a visiting gentlemen, Cupid advises "that weak-minded young gentlemen often play off one sister against another . . . the boldest and most effectual way of exploding such a plot is for the sisters to take the young gentleman into a corner, and demand simultaneously and on the instant an explanation of his extraordinary and deceitful conduct." An even more sensational tale of a double-crossing suitor comes from Maria who found out from a friend that her fiancé had "presented me with the same locket and lock of hair which she had worn as his gift, and which she had returned when they quarreled! But that is not the worst. The note which accompanied it . . . is exactly the same word for word (with the exception of the difference of the name), as that which accompanied the same gift to my friend!" Cupid suggests that perhaps the gentleman was "of a business turn of mind; and liked to save as much trouble or time (in making love as in all things else) as he could." Yet, this generous view does not refute the fact that "he must be a decidedly bad bargain, either for love or friendship."[12] These sensational scenarios illustrate why the advice column was so adept at attracting correspondents as well as readers.

The *EDM* openly questioned parental authority. When Rosa raises the possibility of eloping with her lover because her family opposes him, Cupid acknowledges that "generally speaking" elopements "are unhappy matches." However, "it must not be concluded from this that *all* marriages so contracted must be unhappy." Defying one's family was sometimes justifiable. In the same issue, Blanche wonders if she "is acting wrong in continuing to hold a correspondence with a gentlemen" her family does not accept when "the only impediment to our happiness is a want of means." Cupid admits that "Prudence suggests that happiness can scarcely be expected from a marriage which is at its outset commenced in poverty" but cautions Blanche not to infer from this "that we are totally averse to marriages contracted on *small* means, so long as they are certain." Although the *EDM* advocated women's independence from parents as well as from restrictive social codes, Margaret Shaw contends, "It was a magazine written for young women who wanted to know how to manage the daily events of their lives, not the political and economic realities of women's general condition."[13] While not necessarily transforming gender roles or women's status in the public realm, the magazine made visible the challenges women faced as a result of societal expectations and restrictions. Exposing the inadequacy of ideals of feminine passivity, and advocating more active control of their romantic lives, the *EDM* did begin to change standards of courtship behavior.

By providing quick answers to women's romantic problems, "Cupid's Letter-Bag" participated in the transformation of periodicals into a highly interactive courtship forum that included full-fledged matchmaking publications such as the *Matrimonial News*. The growing familiarity with such public courtship practices in the periodical press induced more and more readers to seek potential spouses through advertisements, correspondence, the exchange of photographs, and even meetings hosted by "matrimonial agents." By the end of the century, the expectations of readers who used the periodical press for courtship were much like those of 21st-century users of Internet dating sites. Samuel Beeton's *Englishwoman's Domestic Magazine* was one key to this revolution in courtship.

PERSONAL ADVERTISEMENTS

If one did not want advice meted out by an unknown editor, but direct clandestine communication with a lover, a better venue would be the front page of the London *Times*. The second column of the most trusted newspaper in England inherited the moniker of the agony column for its "pathetic appeals for runaway husbands" and "plaintive cries for attention from 'lonely hearts.'" These notorious personal advertisements shifted the emphasis away from advice and toward the communication of coded messages, away from the mass audience and toward a more elite reader. The cost of the *Times* made it the province of upper-middle-class professionals, though servants may well have read their employers cast off copies. According to Matthew Rubery, "anecdotal evidence suggests that the personal advertisements may have been the most widely read section of the newspaper; Queen Victoria herself was said to have considered reading the personal advertisements a royal hobby." Reading these pages could be quite intriguing as respondents sought secret liaisons and sent desperate pleas to one another, once again disrupting the conventional ideals of conduct book courtship with equal doses of passion and angst. The *Times*'s agony column was such a popular pastime for leisure reading and code breaking that the *Leader*, an elite intellectual newspaper, devoted a regular column to reprinting portions of it. "The Romance of the *Times*" was aimed at reproducing

> the most remarkable of those mysterious advertisements which appear every day at the top of the second column of *Times*' front page. Some of the strangest glimpses into the romance of reality that any place presents—not excluding the police offices—are to be found in that dusky, hieroglyphical, yet most humanly-interesting, corner of the great diurnal. Tragedies, comedies, farces—love, wretchedness, despair—the outpourings of broken hearts, and the supplications of parents to their runaway children—the last struggles of desperate poverty, and the slow wiles of swindling—suggestions of strange plots, as yet in the bud—odd questions and answers asked too [sic] and fro between distant friends—the whole seen obscurely through a dim veil which it is out of our power to raise, and which gives to the fantastical details a sort of supernatural interest.

Rubery argues that the "ease with which women were able to access a newspaper made the personals a significant part of their emotional life" as both readers and writers of ads.[14] Who needed a novel when you had a real-life intrigue so readily at hand?

To capitalize on this thrilling genre, Alice Clay compiled a selection of the notices into a book in 1881. Clay introduces her *The Agony Column of the "Times," 1800–1870* with an explanation of how to crack the most common codes used by advertisers, providing examples of the coded messages for readers to decipher on their own. The use of secret codes indicates a desire among lovers to subvert traditional channels of communication, which would have been more strictly monitored by parents, family members, and servants. The remainder of Clay's book features deciphered or uncoded notices. Among the *Times* advertisements Clay assembles, many appear to be from individuals involved in clandestine affairs, such as this one posted on May 30, 1850: "A.W.—THE WOLF is NOT DEAD, but has been dangerously ill. Letters are intercepted. I trust no one. Break not your pledge. Communicate personally.—B." One can easily imagine the "Wolf" as a tyrannical husband and A.W. as the secret lover that B. hopes to contact. Likewise, M.H. desperately hopes to meet with S.P. in this August 28, 1850 message: "APPOINT the PLACE. Delay not; I trust to your word, but cannot live in this state of indecision. All will be well could I but see you. M.H." Along with scheduling secret meetings, miscommunications were frequent subjects of agony ads, such as this one from October 31, 1856: "S.M.J.—You little rogue, did you keep me waiting so long on Friday night and then not come, to punish me for the previous evening? I waited an hour. . . . Do write . . . and never doubt the continuance of affection and sweet remembrance of past happy days that still afford him happy reflection."[15] These daily reminders of the number of people breaking established rules of courtship printed in the nation's most respectable news venue help explain why conduct literature was so feverishly produced and purchased throughout the century. Conduct and etiquette books not only described acceptable courtship behaviors but also attempted to codify them.

If one wanted to find a new sweetheart instead of contacting a secret lover, the *Times* included some matrimonial advertisements. However, there were many other venues devoted to advertising for love. While the problem columns of penny magazines and papers increasingly included ads for marriage, some uniformly rejected the concept. *Bow Bells* (1862–1897), for example, carried on an active "Notice to Correspondents" section that frequently answered questions from readers interested in affairs of the heart and social propriety. However, the editor responded curtly to Annie's request to place a personal advertisement: "If you were a 'constant' reader of our publication, you would have seen that on many occasions we have declared that we will not insert matrimonial advertisements, and that we have determined them as immoral and indelicate to a degree. No respectable young man would take unto himself a wife through such a medium." *Reynolds's Miscellany* repeatedly made similar statements, one of which sarcastically noted that the magazine's editors did not "aspire to the honour of being considered matchmakers."[16] While marriage was frequently romanticized in conduct books, treated as melodrama in the *Times*'s agony column, and sensationalized in correspondence sections of magazines, the periodicals that included matrimonial advertisements reveal a much more businesslike approach to courtship.

The Victorian era's emphasis on love and companionship spawned an intense demand for marriage partners that traditional courtship methods failed to meet. Many thought advertising might be the answer to their courtship woes and were eager to participate in public matchmaking forums. Unlike some penny family magazines, the *London Journal* unabashedly printed matrimonial advertisements. The ads posted in the *London Journal* grew organically out of the "Notices to Correspondents" section and seem to have been driven primarily by reader demand as correspondents began to ask editors to print their personal ads or to connect them with other letter writers. The editors often obliged, but maintained control of the forum by summarizing—and editorializing on—what correspondents said rather than directly printing their profiles. In 1850, a handful of advertisements appeared in each issue, but by the middle of 1852 they had completely taken over the "Notices to Correspondents" section and soon began to spill over into the journal's companion publication, the *Weekly Times*, which started to reprint ads submitted by readers in their entirety. As Andrew King points out, for a brief period from September 1857 to July 1859 editor Mark Lemon removed the ads from the "Notices to Correspondents" section, causing the magazine's circulation to plummet and forcing him to resign.[17] The audience thus demanded and received the space to advertise for love.

The broad audience for matrimonial ads is evident from the range of eligible bachelors seeking wives in the *London Journal*. Advertisers identified themselves as farmers, mechanics, plumbers, engineers, engravers, sailors, merchants, clerks, tradesmen, government officials, military men, clergymen, and even gentlemen of property with declared incomes ranging from just shillings a week to £500 per year. Women seeking spouses were more likely to declare large inheritances to entice partners, such as Theresa who will have "a certain fortune of £5,000 on her wedding day." However, some advertisers were straightforward about the fact that they had little to offer in terms of money, including A Village Maid who claims to be "the daughter of a small farmer, and, never having enjoyed the opportunity of mixing in society, like a modest flower as she is, declares that she will not 'boast of herself,' having nothing to offer but a 'genuine heart.'"[18] Of course, without family connections to verify a potential partner's status, those who responded to ads had no way of knowing whether or not they were being duped. Regardless of this significant drawback, matrimonial advertising spread like wildfire. The fact that income and profession played such an important role in the ads indicates that financial considerations were crucial to the matches the advertisers sought, despite the insurmountable problem of not really knowing if the claims were true. While personal appearance and other qualities played a part in most profiles, they almost always began with the more practical matters of income and job for men or income and domestic abilities for women.

Why did such businesslike matrimonial ads become the norm at the same time marriage came to be seen as an individual choice based on mutual affection? One likely answer is that men and women new to the city were isolated, lonely, and in need of money. Mitchell explains, "Matrimonial advertisements can be seen as an attempt to fill a second role ordinarily taken by a social group instead of a magazine. . . . Changing social position isolated individuals. Ambitious men moved educationally and often physically away from their local roots. And if they became, in the process, too respectable to pick up girls in pubs and dance halls, their female counterparts had even fewer resources." Hermit is likely a typical case of a man seeking a companion in a new and alienating urban environment. The editor writes, "It is certainly a sad state of things to be alone, without friends to share your joys and soothe your sorrows; and this solitude is the more oppressive when in the heart of a great city. A loneliness creeps upon you even in the streets, and chills and damps strike to the very marrow. Poverty is a bitter curse, but there are many others quite as bitter. In our correspondent's case marriage will be an effectual remedy." Unfortunately, he goes on to suggest a course for finding a mate that sounds impossible for a man whose income was a mere £60 per year and whose moniker was Hermit: "He must endeavor to obtain introductions in respectable families. One friendship leads to the contraction of fifty others." Women had even fewer chances in their daily lives to actively seek partners. Therefore, they enthusiastically seized the opportunity to place personal ads. Kent states that "the problem pages of the 1850s and 1860s provide a picture of young women exceptionally ready to play an active part in courtship. Though these attempts were discouraged, the very fact that they appear so frequently suggests that, whatever the official view of flirting, Victorian girls pursued men with a single-mindedness rarely equaled before or since."[19] This active role, which went against much of the conduct book advice, was inherent in the form of the matrimonial advertisement.

Class issues were also a crucial component of the typical matrimonial ad. Hermit is advised that raising his status will be crucial to finding a suitable wife and Mabel (from the opening epigraph) expresses her disinclination to marry a tradesman, instead preferring someone of a higher profession. The *London Journal*'s editor frequently invoked class as a determining factor in matchmaking. The attention to class arises even when the advertisers themselves do not express concerns about it. Neglected Lily, for example, proclaims that she "has been setting her cap at the men for some years past, in the hopes of catching a husband, to no purpose. She now begs us to help her out of her dilemma." Her accomplishments include skills adaptable to both humble and gentlemanly homes. She claims to be able to "make pastry, wash, iron, knit" as well as sew "anything from a gentleman's shirt to a baby's cap," yet her "lively disposition" and "good temper" along with her ability to sing and play music would make her an asset in the parlor. The editor looks favorably enough on her profile to declare that "she will shortly have lots of proposals from the men, or the age of chivalry is past." Indeed, Neglected Lily does receive multiple responses between February and May of 1851. On March 1, 1851, an ironmonger offers himself to Lily; however, the editor does not approve of this match: "We will just hint to him that Lilies are not gathered without search and trouble." The editor also rejects Carolus, a widower with a child who earns £70 a year and "is no match for the 'Neglected Lily.' A hardy Daisy would suit him much better." Repeatedly, then, the editor tries to guide Lily away from partners he deems unsuitable based on their income or class status. Despite the editor's advice, she publicly accepts the offer of the widower and "promises to make him a good wife, and to be an affectionate mother to his child."[20] Though this seems like a happy ending, there was a serious problem with the logistical functioning of these early ads. Even if two advertisers expressed a mutual interest there seems to have been no direct way for them to contact each other. For their plans to work, the editor would have to intervene. Early on, then, the advertisements were nothing more than a titillating flirtation in print as there was no real mechanism for direct interaction between the participants.

The seeming futility of advertising for love is highlighted by the editor's notices about correspondent Edith Clavering. Edith tries to arrange a husband for her 19-year-old sister, who boasts a £100 per year income and an £80 life annuity. As the editor reports, "Edith thinks that 'M.S.' would be the man, and wishes him to appoint a place for an interview. The letter ends with a reference to a crescent in the vicinity of Belgrave Square; and says something about pink bonnets, black mantles, and deep-blue dresses. Might we venture to complete the insinuation and add . . . say noon" as a meeting time? Though the editor tries to help the couple set up a rendezvous, M.S. apparently never responds and no meeting occurs. By March 29, 1851, Edith's sister has received several published offers, the most promising of which was probably from Harry, 26, a "tall, dashing fellow" who offers to dote on her and provide £500 per annum.[21] Still, poor Edith's sister would not have had any way to directly contact her suitors. This problem, which made the matrimonial advertisements more entertaining than practical, was solved by the creation of new departments in the magazine.

By 1867 those placing personal ads are able to correspond directly through the *Weekly Times*. This newspaper, advertised in the *London Journal* and bundled with it by subscription, was one of the top three-penny Sunday papers.[22] Readers could place secondary advertisements in the paper to arrange private meetings. In January 1870, a new subsection of the "Notices to Correspondents" was introduced, called the *Weekly Times.* This column was followed by lists of people who sought to correspond privately with other advertisers or who wanted to announce that they would issue more thorough profiles in the weekend edition of the *Weekly Times.* To drum up business for the paper, the editor added enticing taglines speculating about which advertisers might publish their addresses in the *Times* for all to see.

In July 1868 the *Journal* also initiated sections that listed "Cartes de Visite Wanted" and "Cartes de Visite Received" to facilitate the exchange of photographs among personal advertisers. A carte de visite was an early photograph mounted on a two by four inch cardboard backing that was exchanged by friends and acquaintances (as calling cards would have been before 1854). The cards were so popular that by 1859 a new term, *cardomania,* was coined to describe the phenomenon of collecting them. Many Victorian parlors featured albums to display these photographic card collections. The *Journal* listed advertisers for whom they had cartes de visite and those who wanted to claim them were expected to submit the proper postage to the editorial office for delivery of the images. Certainly, there were some correspondents who participated in the personal ad bonanza primarily to collect cartes de visite, just as many today collect friends on social networking sites like Facebook.

By the 1870s, matrimonial ads dominated the "Notices to Correspondents" section of the *London Journal* and a "Women's Supplement" with fashion plates had also become a prominent feature. King argues that these elements indicate that the magazine had shifted from a masculine publication that included some women readers in the 1840s, to a feminine one that included some men in the 1870s. King goes so far as to speculate that many men bought the *London Journal* specifically for the matrimonial ads and that many women subscribed to the *Weekly Times* for the very same reason.[23] Matrimonial ads played a major role in transforming the contents and readership of the periodical and in sustaining its popularity.

Matrimonial advertisements were not just a hit among the lower and middling classes, however. Frances Power Cobbe laments the explosion of personal ads for the fashionable set on the front page of the June 8, 1869 newspaper the *Echo.* Cobbe complains that printing "such an advertisement" is at odds "with the character of a reputable journal."[24] Cobbe's objection is, in part, due to the coarseness of such ads. But she is also intensely concerned about the possibility of fraudulent self-representations that could lead women astray. The personal ad presented sensational dangers no matter what one's class status. Much like the popular genre of sensation fiction, matrimonial advertisements filtered up the social ladder rather than down it. While the middle and upper classes were not seriously reading the *London Journal*'s notices (or its cheap sensational literature), they embraced personal advertisements in other venues (and sensation novels in more expensive three-volume formats). By the 1870s, matrimonial newspapers had emerged as the primary site for middle- and upper-class matchmaking in the press.

MATRIMONIAL NEWSPAPERS

The *Matrimonial News* (1870–1895) was probably the most popular newspaper devoted solely to marriage. According to *Chambers's* it made as much as £20 a week for its proprietor during its first two years of publication. Its success spurred the development of many short-lived competitors, including: the *Matrimonial Chronicle* (1890–1893), the *Matrimonial Courier* (1891), the *Matrimonial Gazette*, renamed the *Matrimonial Herald* (1884–1895), the *Matrimonial Intelligencer* (1876), the *Matrimonial Journal* (1885), the *Matrimonial Post* (1898–1905), the *Matrimonial Record* (1882–1890), the *Matrimonial Register* (1896), the *Matrimonial Times* (1891), and *Matrimony* (1883). That the matrimonial newspaper business was becoming a pervasive part of late Victorian culture is undeniable. For example, the "Miscellaneous Advertisements" section of one issue of the *Penny Illustrated Paper and Illustrated Times* in 1910 featured 34 small ads, including three for matrimonial papers—*Matrimonial Times*, *Matrimonial Mail*, and *Matrimonial Magazine*—one each for the "Matrimonial Circle" correspondence club and a set of personal photo post cards, presumably to send to potential partners identified through matchmaking venues.[25]

Any given issue of a matrimonial paper would contain hundreds of personal advertisements. Spouse hunters could often place their profiles for free, but were expected to pay the subscription fee to receive the paper as well as a finder's fee on marriage. Advertisers were identified by number only, but the publisher would hold their names, addresses, and, cartes de visite to be released to admirers with their consent. If a match were a success, the couple would be required to pay a predetermined fee within a month of marriage. The editor of the *Matrimonial News* was also available for private consultations for an additional five shillings or to send private advice via post for the price of 12 postage stamps. While prices were amenable to some in the lower middle classes, the *Matrimonial News* was geared toward the middle and upper classes. Advertisers ranged in age from their 20s to their 70s and were divided fairly evenly by sex. Whether or not the ads were genuine or successful, of course, remains a mystery. *The Examiner*, at least, was skeptical: "Many of these advertisements are obviously of the kind known in American parlance as 'Bogus.' It is, for instance, inconceivable that no fewer than three Members of Parliament should at one and the same time be standing in need of the services of the Editor of the *Matrimonial News*."[26] Aside from their target audience, these ads were similar to the ones placed in the *London Journal*. However, the profiles were left to speak for themselves without editorial commentary.

An examination of a single issue of a similar paper, the *Marriage Post and Fashionable Marriage Adviser* for January 1907, reveals a diverse cross section of society seeking marriage partners. The tagline on the front cover proclaims it to be "the only Marriage Negotiator for the Nobility, Gentry, Commercial and all Classes," "the Largest and Most Successful Matrimonial Agency Throughout the Empire!," as well as "the Matrimonial Agency of the Civilized World" with a "World-Wide Reputation." Yet, the price of the paper was only three pence, or five pence if delivered in a "private envelope"; thus it was accessible to a wide range of readers. Those who wished to advertise were asked to include information about their "age, general appearance, position in life, nature of business or profession, and the amount of income" as well as "some description of the lady or gentlemen (as the case may be) with whom correspondence is desired." It is noted that all correspondence from the newspaper will be "enclosed in private envelopes, which can afford no indication of the nature of their contents," indicating the precarious reputation of matrimonial advertising despite its growing popularity.

The advertisements featured in the *Marriage Post* were divided into three categories in the following order: the first was for those willing to share their names and addresses with clients the editor determined were eligible; the second was for those who wanted to be notified before their personal information was shared with an admirer; and the third was for those whose information was freely available so that they could be contacted without the intervention of the editor. Those who wanted more personal consultations could pay additional fees to have a home visit from the editor or a neutral venue for meetings with other clients. This elaborately tiered system of matchmaking allowed participants to customize the services based on their own inclinations and income. The level of personal attention offered to the highest-paying clients must have made the system seem worthwhile for wealthy spouse hunters.

While most *Marriage Post* advertisers claimed to be members of the middle or upper echelons of society, some members of the working classes used its services—particularly domestic servants, who may have had easier access to the paper through their employers. The advertisements published in the *Marriage Post* are certainly more refined and genteel than those listed in the *London Journal*. Many advertisers claimed unusually high incomes and even royal titles. The following samples provide a taste of the profiles included:

Gentleman, bachelor, aged 36, tall, rather slight, dark brown hair and eyes, with about £1500 a year, principally derived from landed property in Australia. . . . Orphan ladies, or any willing to sojourn in Australia, are invited to correspond. Advertiser makes periodical visits to England.

A young Lady, 26, with a tobacconist's business and £14 weekly, desires correspondence with a bachelor about 30, with an income from
£200 a year.

A young lady in service, fair, height about 5 ft. 4 in., small cash in
bank, desires to correspond with a respectable working man, widower not objected to, but no children.

Widow lady, no family, aged 37, partner in restaurant business,
£100 per annum and share of profits yearly, desires marriage, bachelor or widow immaterial.

Spinster, possessing £1800, young, smart appearance, desires an
early introduction to a gentleman, aged from 25–30 preferred, and
connected with the theatrical profession.

Gentleman with £900 a year, aged 23, wishes to marry a lady not
influenced by monetary considerations; will not answer unless a
photo is enclosed.

Lady, 33, writing successful articles on literature and art, wishes to
correspond with literary man. Income at present derived from writings. On decease of relative (76), £200 a year, plate, jewellery, [sic]
family portraits and books.

A well known foreign Prince, European, aged 30, wishes to marry
a lady of large income or substantial amount at command.

Farmer (widower), aged 49, with £100 invested in farming, wishes
to correspond with lady 40 to 45 years of age with means. . . . This is
genuine.[27]

What really stands out here is the importance income plays for all of the
marriage advertisers. While those submitting profiles were told to include income, it often stands out as the crucial part of the ad in both the
London Journal and the *Marriage Post*. While conduct books were touting
love and companionship, those willing to advertise for love were perhaps
more desperate or more practical. Remarkably, even the gentleman who
claims to earn £900 a year and will not consider a woman without seeing
her photo (suggesting his own superficiality), seeks someone who is not
motivated by his income alone. The emphasis on beauty and money were
widely criticized despite the fact that it was assumed that couples should
be well matched in appearance, status, and income. Indeed, the prevailing
perception that matrimonial advertising was crass and uncouth as well as
dangerous inspired much of the writing about it in the press.

Matrimonial newspapers were criticized more vehemently than "Notices to Correspondents" columns, perhaps because personal ads had now
clearly infiltrated middle- and upper-class audiences. The most common
question critics sought to answer was why any respectable person would
engage in such abnormal courtship behavior in the first place. As *Chambers's* asks in November 1870: "With such evidence of recklessness with
which folks will rush into the state that has only two exits, divorce and

death, one can hardly wonder at some men being adventurous enough to seek a wife by advertisement—the most risky way imaginable of going about a business risky enough under the best of conditions." The author speculates that the risk is made acceptable by the promise that "desperate maidens, bashful bachelors, disconsolate widows, and consolable widowers, need despair no longer; they can now make known their connubial qualities for the small charge of sixpence." While the male marriage advertisers are often ridiculed, the women are typically pitied. Yet, as the *Illustrated Review* notes, if "any young gentleman remains too modest to announce his excellences" in an advertisement, "multitudes of charming young ladies here ask him to marry them; nay contend for the honour of comforting and aiding his desolate existence. 'Christine,' 'Clara,' 'Hilda,' and numbers more are 'ready to correspond' (such seems to be the established phrase) with him." It is interesting that the term *correspond* itself comes to stand in for something potentially more scandalous. The writer goes on to argue that while many of the ads are probably fake and could make a fool of any gentleman who answers them, "the egregious folly of the ladies who enter into correspondence with such advertisers can hardly be too strongly pointed out."[28] Women who corresponded with strangers were seen to be almost self-sacrificial, potentially on the way to falling from innocence into a tragic state of corruption.

Some critics turned their attention to matrimonial advertisements' display of distasteful immodesty or even fraudulent self-presentation. *All The Year Round* criticizes female advertisers who are "oblivious to the copy book maxim about self-praise." In its study of matrimonial ads, the magazine counts 5 women who claim themselves beautiful, 8 very handsome, 23 handsome, 16 very pretty, 16 pretty, 52 good-looking, 9 nice-looking, 29 of good appearance, and 8 attractive. Apparently only one poor woman failed in the art of self-promotion. She wrote, "Wanted a husband, by a spinster, aged thirty-eight, without money, and not good-looking. Should this meet the eye of any gentleman wanting a wife, and in a position, and generous enough to take one with these disadvantages, the editors can give address."[29] These exaggerated examples highlight the press's insistence on the untrustworthiness of matrimonial advertisements. Indeed, letters that were for a previous generation a proper expression of true feeling became for these journalists a false and potentially dangerous form of self-definition.

Fun magazine featured a series of parodies of matrimonial advertisements that focus on their misleading nature, which includes self-deception as much as lying to others. In "Matrimonial Advertisements. No. 1," Araminta Brown—who is "rich, beautiful, and accomplished" but "cannot find a gentleman quite suited to her mind"—receives a promising response from Mr. Bloaterbrain (Figure 3.1). However, when they meet for the first time, Bloaterbrain has filled his double-breasted coat with pocket handkerchiefs to make his figure more masculine and in line

MATRIMONIAL ADVERTISEMENTS.

No. 1.—ARAMINTA BROWN.

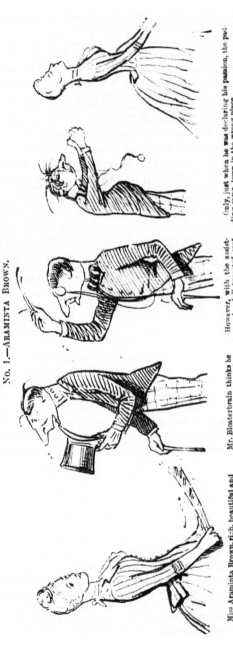

Miss Araminta Brown, rich, beautiful and accomplished, cannot find a gentleman quite suited to her mind, so advertises in a matrimonial paper.

Mr. Bloaterbrain thinks he will apply, but feels rather doubtful about his figure, which is NOT military.

However, with the assistance of a full breasted coat and a few pocket-handkerchiefs,

Only, just when he was declaring his passion, the padding came down in the wrong place.

REsULT.—*Decided refusal.*

Figure 3.1. "Matrimonial Advertisements. No. 1—Araminta Brown." *Fun* 51:1306 (May 21, 1890): 215. Image published with permission of ProQuest. Further reproduction is prohibited without permission.

with the military type he thinks will appeal to women. Just as he declares his passion for Araminta, his padding slips giving him a pudgy stomach instead of a full chest. Of course, Araminta immediately rejects him. In "Matrimonial Advertisements. No. 3," Miss Aurora Wailboan "writes in frantic desperation to a matrimonial paper." When she receives a visit from a rather "large-headed young man," she immediately falls in love, kisses him on the neck, and chases him through the house (Figure 3.2). Unfortunately for Aurora, the frightened man turns out to be the piano tuner and not a suitor answering her ad. These scenarios light-heartedly expose some pitfalls of courting through the press, but some observers imagined much more sinister results of the matrimonial advertising craze. These included the possibility that unwitting love seekers would be robbed, raped, or even murdered. The Red Barn murder case of 1827 was an early and notorious example. Not long after William Corder married a woman he met through a personal advertisement, he was convicted of killing his previous lover and burying her body in a barn. As Rubery notes, "Corder's last words allegedly cautioned his wife against remarrying by advertisement because 'it was a most dangerous way of getting a husband.'"[30] Critics feared that personal advertising was unwholesome at best and dangerous at worst, especially for women.

American psychologist Arthur MacDonald undertook what is perhaps the most in-depth study of personal advertisements among middle-class women in his 1897 book *Girls Who Answer Personals* (published as *Abnormal Woman* in its first edition two years earlier). MacDonald reprinted hundreds of letters received in response to fake personal ads he placed in newspapers in England, France, Germany, Canada, and the United States. He justifies his devious research methods by claiming that "considering the use to which the 'personal' column is generally put," he "did not think it wrong to make it serve as the means of sociological investigation." Furthermore, he reasons, "A woman who answers a public advertisement cannot expect her correspondence with a total stranger to be of a very confidential nature." MacDonald warns that his study of the new bachelor girl indicates a need for parents to provide proper home training and education to curb the tendencies of "women who have advanced ideas, but who are indiscreet in action." He argues that these women display "border-line abnormality" for their willingness to correspond with him.[31] Indeed, his conflicting claims that the women who answer personals are hypereducated and, therefore, unsuited to regular methods of finding a husband and that they simultaneously need to be better educated (presumably in modesty and submissiveness) highlight the ways in which women's growing power of self-definition within the alternative realm of courtship often produced a hysterical response. MacDonald's study also indicates that by the end of the century personal advertisements were seen as symbols of the breakdown of traditional gender roles.

Figure 3.2. "Matrimonial Advertisements. No. 3—Miss Aurora Wailboan." *Fun* 52:1315 (July 23, 1890): 38. Image published with permission of ProQuest. Further reproduction is prohibited without permission.

MacDonald characterizes personal ads as a sign of the collapse of modern social relations. For him this breakdown is something to be regretted; yet the women who write to him see it as a sign of hope for a future that they imagine will be less restrictive. For example, a correspondent from England, "Case 77," writes:

> I fear my opinions are not at all radical; they were once so, but time has modified them. I don't see, however, why women should not enjoy most, if not all, the privileges that man enjoys. As—in this country at least—we far outnumber the other sex, then it follows that a great number of us must remain unmarried, and a great proportion earn their own bread, it is only fair that we should have the same opportunity of acquiring a profession as our brothers have, and the chance of trying to compete with them in that profession. . . . Though a life of wedded bliss is what woman naturally desires, it is quite possible to be happy if one has work that keeps one's faculties fully employed and the mind interested.

MacDonald's correspondents repeatedly undercut his message by revealing their understanding of societal restrictions and openly rebelling against them. Several of the letter writers get to the heart of his claims by complaining about the state of women's education. One writer argues that a lack of formal education leaves women with a misguided sense of what to expect from life and no real skills to take care of themselves: "It is absolutely cruel," she writes, that "girls grow up with the idea that they are sure to marry" only to "realize too late they will have to fight their own battle of life without having received the slightest training." This writer refutes MacDonald's claim that women need more household education and less formal education by pointing out that traditional refinements are useless for women who cannot find husbands. As "Case 77" concludes, "some people have an idea that higher education unfits woman for the ordinary duties of everyday life, but that is all nonsense."[32]

Furthermore, many of these women had a healthy suspicion of MacDonald's motives and sometimes outsmarted him, calling into question his methods. For example, one woman inquired why he would write a personal ad if he were truly a respectable gentleman; another guessed that he was writing a study of national character since he accepted letters in a variety of languages; yet another refused to continue her correspondence unless he sent her handwritten (rather than typewritten) letters, correctly speculating that he was sending the same letters to a variety of women. Some correspondents demonstrated that they had their own ulterior motives. One hoped he would help publish her novel. Another asked him to send her money. It is clear that inasmuch as they may have wanted to find husbands, these women needed a way to support themselves with or without men.

As a whole, the "girls who answer personals" come across as savvy women who were looking for an exciting way to pass the time or to find a sympathetic soul with whom to share their troubles. Indeed, MacDonald admits in the conclusion to the first edition of his book that "a careful reading of the letters will show that the majority of correspondents do not seem to have anything special to do in life. Many are in abnormal conditions rather than abnormal themselves."[33] Perhaps this explains why he changed the title of his book when it came out in a second printing. The girls who answered his personals certainly do not sound abnormal, but rather painfully normal. They were lonely, bored, and seeking opportunities to demonstrate their worth. Pursuing romance and marriage were among their only options and they likely took the chance of answering MacDonald's personal ad because their choices were so limited.

MATRIMONIAL AGENCIES

In addition to the alternative methods of courtship that permeated the periodical press, matrimonial agencies that promised a more hands-on approach to matchmaking arose. Throughout the 19th century, the French were often singled out by the English for their decadence and suspect morality, so the abundance of criticism of French marriage bureaus in both fiction and journalism is not surprising. In January 1868 *Bentley's Miscellany* printed "Matrimonial Advertisements," a story that follows the intrigues of an eccentric French marriage broker who has very shady dealings but successfully unites couples. This "matrimonial ambassador" claims to have married "nearly one-third of all France." There were also reports of French marriage brokers who used secret observation rooms in which clients could view potential spouses through peep holes, accepting or rejecting them without the humiliation of a face-to-face meeting. Likewise, a German company is sarcastically praised in the *London Review* for brilliantly "reducing" marriage "to a system." The efficient "machinery" of the Schwartz company "offers to contract engagements between ladies and gentlemen, and to carry on the preliminaries of courtship for the small consideration which might repay the risk and trouble. We have as yet but insufficient means of estimating the success of this admirable corporation." The *Review* claims the company

> borrowed a leaf—the "Answers to Correspondents"—from our cheap pictorial journals. [Schwartz] has probably a huge album of *cartes*, or rather a whole library of albums. As operations are of a European and international character, it is likely that Schwartz has a French, a German, an American, and (why, after all, limit himself to Europe? Taste is cosmopolitan) possibly a Hottentot department. Think of the quantities of hair, the reams of letters, and the other

delicate embarrassments under which the postman labours, who discharges his daily freight at the office of this establishment?"

The *Review* satirically suggests taking this plan a step further by offering to send out traveling salesmen "with portfolios of sweet things in ladies and gentlemen, all over the country. These agents, of course, should be finished professors in the art of description and persuasion. Courtship by proxy ought, on every ground of reason and common sense, to become a popular practice."[34] By linking alternative courtship methods to foreign sources, these accounts attempt to preserve British superiority in such personal matters as courtship and marriage. While these examples discredit the French and German application of the entrepreneurial spirit to the sacred institution of marriage, it was often acknowledged that parallels to these systems were cropping up unexpectedly in England. Indeed, the *Review* accuses English magazines of providing the original spark for the idea of the matrimonial agency.

The popular press was likewise fascinated with French marriage clubs in which women agreed to bundle their money into several substantial portions that would be given away to a few members by lottery as a marriage settlement or dowry to entice a husband. If winners were not married within a year, the money would be returned to the pool to be redistributed.[35] Popular fiction was another logical place where fantastic tales of French brokers and lotteries could be easily melded with English settings and characters. One case in point is Charlotte O'Connor Eccles's novel *The Matrimonial Lottery* (1906), which not only brings a wild "Frenchified" marriage scheme to England but also illustrates how close to home the marriage contest really was. "Matrimonial lottery" was a common term used to describe the process of finding a mate in the more conventional way. Eccles's literalization of the phrase took the concept to a new level that was in tune with the bourgeoning of alternative courtship practices in England.

In the novel, the staff of the struggling periodical the *Comet* decides that it must immediately and dramatically increase its readership to survive. Following the course of the *London Journal*, the *Comet*'s editors determine that the best way to accomplish this is to cause a sensation among the ladies. For maximum impact, they create a matrimonial lottery tied to the purchase of the paper, with a coupon of entry in each issue. The contest will confer on one lucky lady the hand of an Irish count (who is, unbeknownst to the public, working as a contributor to the *Comet* to make back the fortune he has lost). According to their plan, capturing the interest of women readers also draws in a male audience: "Everyone bought *The Comet*. People wished to see what all the fuss was about, and became interested in the development of the scheme. Husbands brought each number home to their wives, who might have been expected to take no interest in the matter. Readers speculated whether the offer could possibly be genuine."

The paper sells out with each edition and over 100,000 women enter the contest, generating £40,000 to restore the count's fortune and ensure the success of *The Comet*. The staff is expanded to handle the onslaught of letters from "women of all ranks and ages; rich girls and poor, plain girls and pretty, old girls and young; anxious mothers on behalf of their daughters, guardians recommending their wards; ladies of fortune from the United States forwarded glowing accounts of their riches and charms."[36] The idea of the marriage lottery is merely an intensification of the crass competition for spouses that was already commonplace. New marriage schemes, then, were more than good plot devices, they were also a reality.

In 1851, *Chambers's Edinburgh Review* describes a London matrimonial agency run by a "Professor of Matrimony" who does not "furnish a love-powder, or a talisman, or a perfume, or a salve, or a potion. . . . All he gives you for your money is two superficial inches of a pamphlet" that include "nothing mysterious, nothing magical, nothing even poetical." Instead, "he offers to do all the courting himself for the entire bachelorhood and spinsterhood of the nation" based on the theory "that everyone wants to be married, and that nothing more is requisite than an introduction."[37] The writer concludes that obtaining a spouse through a broker is unsuitable for the romantic and self-conscious people of England (and, of course, better suited to the businesslike and morally suspect French). However, it was clear that such unconventional means of courtship were thriving at home as well as abroad. In the *Punch* cartoon "Pretty Innocent," a naïve young lady confuses the Register Office (where civil marriages were performed) with a matrimonial agent's office (Figure 3.3). She enters expecting to be matched up with a husband: "I thought yours was like every other registry office," she explains, "I put my name on your books, and you find somebody who wants me." The young woman's assumption that relying on a matrimonial agent was ordinary would likely have been framed by reading about such services in the newspapers. Her misunderstanding of the process of courtship is so shocking to the registrar that he flees his post, never to return.

Matrimonial agencies could not be dismissed as purely foreign institutions, though they often had cosmopolitan ties to Europe and connections to displaced Englishmen in the colonies or America. Despite resistance to women's newly aggressive attempts to find suitable husbands, the idea of a woman advertising herself as a product became more and more routine. For example, organizations like the Home and Colonial Matrimonial Agency, launched to assist adventurous Britons in finding marriage partners overseas, urged women to actively market themselves as wives. In its publication *How to Get a Husband and How to Get a Wife* (1888) the agency suggests that the inequality of the sexes on the British Isles (confirmed by the 1851 census, which recorded more women than men of marriageable age) "is aggravated in a large measure by the continual stream of emigration which draws off in such large numbers the young men from

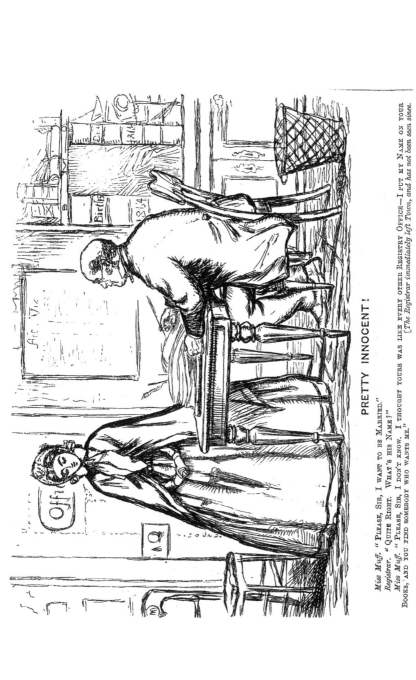

PRETTY INNOCENT!

Miss Muff. "PLEASE, SIR, I WANT TO BE MARRIED."
Registrar. "QUITE RIGHT. WHAT'S HIS NAME?"
Miss Muff. "PLEASE, SIR, I DON'T KNOW. I THOUGHT YOURS WAS LIKE EVERY OTHER REGISTRY OFFICE—I PUT MY NAME ON YOUR BOOKS, AND YOU FIND SOMEBODY WHO WANTS ME."
[*The Registrar immediately left Town, and has not been seen since.*]

Figure 3.3. "Pretty Innocent!" *Punch* (November 26, 1864): 224. Used by permission of the University of Missouri–Kansas City Libraries, Dr. Kenneth J. LaBudde Department of Special Collections.

our shores. The result is, to use a commercial phrase, the home market is overstocked or glutted." The agency argues that women must take matters into their own hands by rejecting the old idea that gives "the male sex the exclusive right of selecting partners for themselves, as if they either claimed or had any right to a monopoly of the privilege." As an alternative to the failing traditional modes of courtship, *How to Get a Husband* encourages women to approach marriage as a business:

> What does a merchant who has a certain class of goods to dispose of do in order to effect a clearance? Does he pretend that he is not willing to part with them—does he try to convey the impression that he is quite independent and indifferent as to whether they are disposed of or not—does he consign them to some secluded, out of the way corner of the premises and expect customers to be more eager to buy on that account? . . . Does he keep nothing but silks and finery where only the strongest and most homely fabrics are required, and that, too, in the face of a copious supply that is more than equal to the demand? Assuredly not; such conduct would not only prove the man to be unfit to be a merchant, but would bring him perilously near to, if not actually within the compass of, a straight-jacket and a lunatic asylum. Yet, thoughtlessly, because it is customary and reputed, dignified and respectable, our females in all positions of life mutilate and distort their matrimonial prospects in much the same way as their Chinese sisters do their feet.

Invoking asylums and Chinese foot binding to describe traditional courtship practices, the agency urges women to forge a new and "honourable path" that will "matrimonially revolutionize the nation."[38]

Readers were encouraged to send their names and addresses to Home and Colonial Matrimonial Agency's registrar, along with a personal profile, which would be identified by number and printed in advertisements and circulars "both at home and in the British Colonies." Once connections were made and correspondence begun, meetings could be arranged at the offices of the agency. If registrants were willing to meet gentlemen in the colonies, all arrangements, including travel, would be made by the agency. According to the brochure, "every woman will have a full knowledge of where and to whom she is going, and it lies with her personally to decide whether she accepts or declines after directly corresponding with her choice." A form was included to ensure that participants provided the relevant information in their profiles (including their age, profession, personal description, means, location preferred, and a photo if desired) and sample profiles were printed along with key words suggested for the personal description (such as amiable, refined, loving, gentle, domesticated, educated, sympathetic, cheerful, fair, dark, pretty, good-looking, widow, etc.).[39] These prefabricated profile suggestions clash with the spirit of innovation evoked by the agency's mission statement. Yet, those who were enticed to participate were made to feel that taking a radical step was necessary given a social and economic climate in which men were scarce and "good" men even harder to come by. The idea of women selling themselves as products is parodied in the *Punch* cartoon "A Caution" in which an unsuspecting woman waiting for an omnibus accidentally stands next to a sign that reads "Young Man Wanted" (Figure 3.4). The humor, of course, comes from the implication that the woman is advertising her need for a "young man," though the ad is presumably for the warehouse whose name appears on the threshold above. But the comic effect also comes from the equation of matrimonial advertising with prostitution since the woman (even if unwittingly) sells herself on the street.

The seriousness with which some were taking marriage agencies by the end of the century is evident in Swan's magazine the *Woman at Home*. A three-part series printed in February, March, and April of 1897 sought answers to the question "Should We Establish a Matrimonial Bureau?" The magazine printed responses from Walter Besant (a respected critic), W. T. Stead (a journalist and editor), "Madge" (an etiquette and advice columnist), Swan, and other regular contributors as well as readers. Besant suggests forming a series of social clubs rather than a full-fledged marriage bureau as "there is no need for a Matrimonial Bureau where there is social intercourse. Cannot some one establish a club, in every parish or every district . . . to which all young people of good character would be admitted? . . . At the club would be held concerts, dances, theatrical performances, quiet evenings of talk and rest." Besant sees this as far superior to and more natural than "the shameless Register which proclaims that a girl wishes to meet a man who will marry her, that she is five feet six inches in height, that she is considered good-looking, that she has a good temper and is 'domesticated.'" Other contributors build on Besant's proposal. Stead, for example, discusses his investigation into existing matrimonial bureaus. After assigning a female employee to write personal advertisements for agencies under the personas of both a man and a woman and carrying on correspondence related to both ads, Stead reports that this experiment "convinced me absolutely of two things. First, that there is a great need for an honest matrimonial agency; and secondly, that all the then existing agencies were worse than worthless. In nine cases out of ten the advertisements were answered by people who either wanted a mistress or wanted cash." Like Stead, one reader recommends the establishment of a reputable matrimonial bureau, which would be no worse than the existing social machinery for courtship: "Is it not more sincere, more honourable, and even more romantic than many of the methods approvingly resorted to by correct society for the same end?"[40]

In her conclusion to the series, Swan claims that 90 percent of those writing in on the subject favored some sort of matrimonial agency. She sees this as

A CAUTION

TO YOUNG LADIES WAITING FOR AN OMNIBUS.

Figure 3.4. "A Caution." *Punch* (December 3, 1864): 225. Used by permission of the University of Missouri–Kansas City Libraries, Dr. Kenneth J. LaBudde Department of Special Collections.

proof at least that I was right in my contention that many unmarried persons evidently suffer greatly from loneliness and isolation. At the same time, the majority of those who have written appear to shrink from the idea of the Matrimonial Bureau pure and simple, and the suggestion which was admirably offered by Sir W. Besant that a club for social intercourse should be established in every country parish, and in every district in large cities, seems to meet with general approval. I am myself of the opinion that if it were possible to carry this suggestion into practice, the whole problem would in some manner be solved. As Sir Walter truly says, in the social life of such clubs would be found the real or natural bureau, the bureau without a book.[41]

Following the conclusion of the matrimonial bureau series, interest remained high as letters continued to pour in, some asking to join the bureau, others to receive the addresses of single women or men whose responses had been printed in the magazine. Swan included some of these in her regular "Love, Courtship and Marriage Column" before finally announcing that conversation on the subject was concluded and informing readers that there was no actual bureau created by the magazine. However, there was at least one concrete result of the conversation in Swan's magazine: W. T. Stead's "Wedding Ring Circle."

MATCHMAKING CORRESPONDENCE CLUBS

The Wedding Ring Circle, a matchmaking correspondence group launched by Stead and advertised in his magazine the *Review of Reviews* between 1897 and 1900, was a direct result of the forum on the efficacy of establishing matrimonial bureaus in the *Woman at Home*. In the forum, "Madge" recommended the creation of a correspondence club to which Stead replied in the February 1897 *Review of Reviews* that "nothing would be easier than to work a series of matrimonial circles." By April he announced the founding of a club that would allow the opportunity for open, intellectual communication between the sexes. Stead invited interested readers to send their names and addresses "for the purpose of making acquaintances which possibly might ripen in a matrimonial direction." He suggests that the first contributor to the Circle

write a letter setting forth what he or she would like to find in the shape of a partner for life. I would then send this to one of the opposite sex, who would add his or her contribution, and then return it to me, by whom both contributions would be sent on to number three, and so on. This differs from the original proposal . . . in that it secures privacy, for as originally proposed, the names of all the members of the circle were to be written on the inside cover, so that every one could know his fellow contributors. . . . But in the more delicate Platonic Friendship or Matrimonial Bureau Circle, it is quite certain that many would only contribute to it at first under a seal of secrecy. . . . I will, as soon as I receive twelve names, put the circular in circulation and see what results follow.

Membership requests started pouring in and within a few months the Wedding Ring Circle was up and running. After getting the club off the ground, subscribers were asked to pay a yearly rate of 10 shillings for the benefit of having their letters passed along to their assigned correspondence group. Stead assembled the groups based on members' initial profiles. If two correspondents notified Stead of their desire to communicate privately, he would release their full names and addresses so that they could pursue a more intimate connection.[42]

In 1898, the popular correspondence club expanded its mission to include the *Round-About*, a monthly supplement to which members of the Circle could contribute essays, travelogues, and photographs. The *Round-About* also printed subscriber's profiles and allowed them to break out of their assigned circles to communicate directly with others, thereby encouraging greater participant control. Nonmembers could subscribe too, so the *Round-About* had a broader audience of potential pen pals. As Stead described it, the "circles rendered it possible to facilitate introductions within small groups" that "correspond to so many drawing-rooms" whereas the *Round-About* was more of a "common hall, or ball-room." H. G. Cocks explains that in addition to the printed profiles, "each member had access to the photograph album containing members' pictures, and the autograph album containing their thoughts on 'the subject that interests them most.'" The albums were held at the *Round-About* office in London where the letters and requests for direct communication were vetted.[43]

Following a prominent two-page spread advertising the Wedding Ring Circle and its member profiles in the July 1897 *Review*, Stead included a brief column discussing the progress of his matchmaking service in every subsequent issue of the magazine. At first, these were simple explanations of the Circle's operating procedures, but later they provided a more philosophical rationale for the group. Stead's justifications were apparently intended to counteract personal attacks on the Wedding Ring Circle such as the one appearing in the sporting magazine *County Gentleman* in 1898. This periodical sarcastically reports that the notorious journalist and editor's "wild career has now reached another stage" as "the president of a matrimonial agency." The brief notice paints a strange picture of this "queer" man and his "crowd of unattached or semi-detached people." They are imagined assembled around a meeting table with Mr. Stead "in the chair" as a kind of ringmaster, a P. T. Barnum of matrimony.[44] Stead had previously written a scandalous exposé on child prostitution, *The Maiden Tribute of Modern Babylon* (1885), for which he was brought to trial and imprisoned for three months. The journalistic investigation on which the book was based had included the "abduction" of a 13-year-old girl he helped purchase from her mother to demonstrate the dangers and realities of "white slavery" (or prostitution) rings. Given this sordid chapter from Stead's recent past, it is not surprising that his supposedly virtuous efforts as a matrimonial agent aroused considerable suspicion. Stead no doubt took the criticism as a cue to step up the rhetorical packaging of his correspondence club, setting a socially progressive rationale for the endeavor.

In February 1899, Stead argues that the Wedding Ring Circle will "enable scattered human units to free themselves from something of the doom of solitude which hangs like a pall over so many existences." In providing such a service, Stead claims, he "marks a step onward in the evolution of human society" replacing "the masked ball of former times" without promoting the abuses they entailed ("of which the less said the better") by affording the rare and valuable "opportunity for the free interchange of ideas and sentiments which would otherwise be impossible." Here Stead displaces the notion that correspondence is somehow a licentious activity by brushing that charge off onto an older venue for courtship: the masked ball. Next to this equally anonymous and potentially more subversive example, courtship correspondence clubs appear safe and even wholesome. Stead goes on to argue that while the Wedding Ring Circle "fulfills its highest end when it succeeds in bringing about that complete union of man and woman that takes place in an ideal marriage" it can also forge "pleasant acquaintances, which are often far more intimate because of their anonymity" since "the best and most lasting friendships are those which are based upon the discovery of a real sympathy and fellow-feeling in the depths of the heart, which in ordinary society are carefully concealed."[45] Stead directly attacks the superficial social system of the London Season with its exclusivity and triviality and proposes a more free and open—though initially anonymous—scheme to replace it.

Likewise, Stead argues that a particular kind of modern alienation from one's community lent significance and heft to his group, which ironically formed more genuine bonds out of anonymous relationships than more socially acceptable matchmaking practices. He even goes so far as to claim that his club could help erase social and gender inequalities. Stead envisions not only successfully making love matches but also changing the world. He clarifies this newfound mission in January 1900: "Some half-a-dozen marriages have been arranged, to say nothing of many intellectual friendships between men and women; but if this scheme is to succeed as it should, and prove useful to the crowds of isolated individuals who have no link or connection to bring them within knowledge of each other, much more has to be achieved in 1900." In October of the same year, Stead announces that "it may be considered a matter for much congratulation" that the circular has reached nearly 700 members "from all parts of the civilized world" who have contributed to its efforts to promote intellectual exchange between men and women that "will take years, if not centuries, to remove." He argues that the club resists the "tide of prejudice against its formation and continued existence" to transform the nature of men's and women's relationships.[46] Stead's overarching argument, then, is that the Wedding Ring Circle allowed its participants to forge more meaningful relationships, whether friendships or marriages, through its unconventional courtship practices.

HIGH-TECH COURTSHIP

At the turn of the century, the idea of alternative courtship began to take on new, technological dimensions. The advent of the typewriter, the telephone, and—especially—the telegraph created even more complex scenarios for anonymous and long-distance courtship. In 1877 Alexander Graham Bell demonstrated the telephone to Queen Victoria by making calls from her home on the Isle of Wight to London. Commercial long-distance calling using existing telegraph wires began a year later. Telephone exchanges that connected calls from place to place employed operators who were later replaced by electronic systems as the use of the telephone rapidly expanded across the country.[47] The possibility of connecting with someone at a long distance was promising for romantic liaisons, yet there were many drawbacks. Early phone connections were notoriously unreliable and unclear. "The Telephonic Love-Song," a satirical poem printed in *Punch* in 1893, illustrates the pitfalls of communicating by the still unreliable telephone:

Love, are you there? Most patiently I've waited
    To hear the answering tinkle on my bell;
Have then the central offices belated
    Not switched me on as yet to thy hotel?
Or is—oh bitter thought—a rival hated
    Addressing thee by phone as well?
Love, are you there? Distracted, I repine; . . .
The suitor in happier days of old,
    When he would woo his lady-love divine,
Beneath her window his affection told
    In skillful verse and neatly balanced line;
And even if he sometimes caught a cold,
    His was a less prosaic way than mine;
Then they'd embrace—no doubt it was not proper,
But I can only kiss a plate of copper!
Oh come, my love, and speak to me again,
    Say that you live for my unworthy sake,
And kindly make each syllable quite plain,
    To guard against all subsequent mistake;
And soon may fortune reunite us twain,
    Communication never more to break!
Take up your tube in answer to my prayer;
Once more I speak my greeting—*Are you there?*[48]

Despite the drawbacks, telephones—if working properly—provided an intimate sense of connection with the person on the other end whose voice and emotion one could actually hear.

The typewriter and the telegraph, on the other hand, provided the possibility of more anonymous communication and, therefore, left room for the same kinds of intrigue and imposture possible in matrimonial ads. Anonymously written love letters could be typed and mailed or telegraphed to an unsuspecting recipient. It is no accident that several of Arthur MacDonald's subjects in *Girls Who Answer Personals* doubted his veracity because he had typed his letters to them. Telegrams were similarly manufactured messages that lacked the signature or voice of the sender. In 1897, London had over 300 telegraph offices open from 8:00 A.M. to 8:00 P.M. and employed 2,214 female operators (about a third of the total number of operators) to send close to 30 million telegrams.[49] Telegraph lines connected the entire British Empire, spreading from England to India, Australia, New Zealand, Canada, and the eastern coast of Africa. Telegrams were exchanged between England and the United States, the first of which was between Queen Victoria and President Buchanan in 1858. This instant global communication system literally changed the world. The telegraph has been called the "Victorian Internet" for good reason. As Tom Standage explains, "the journey of an email message, as it hops from mail server to mail server toward its destination, mirrors the passage of a telegram from one telegraph office to the next."[50] But it was the telegraph operators themselves, rather than the messages they sent for their customers, that captured the imagination of the public and spurred an entirely new genre of fiction: the telegraphic romance.

Katherine Stubbs describes the telegraph as a sort of party line over which any operator on a given circuit could listen in to the frequent conversations that arose in the lulls between the rapid transmission of paid messages by Morse code. Though operators were supposed to identify themselves by code name, there was no way of confirming the sex or true identity of the person on the other end of the wire. The result was a form of anonymity similar to that experienced on the Internet.[51] The parallels between telegraphic romances and today's online dating forums are quite striking, though the telegraph was limited to a small group of skilled operators. The romanticization of the telegraph office is especially interesting considering that women operators were often of a higher class than their male counterparts, though they were paid a lower wage. It seems that the anxiety this class and pay imbalance spurred on both sides was eased by telegraphers' own depictions of women operators as easily tamed—or even expelled from the profession—by love. The genre of the telegraphic romance was typically written by telegraph operators for industry magazines. These tales and poems often explore the clashing worlds of femininity and professionalism, expressing anxieties about the advancement of women and using courtship over the wires as a way to put women back into the home, thus providing a satisfying romantic conclusion as well as a socially conservative one. Yet, telegraph operators were considered bohemian and were often equated with unconventional types such as artists or actors. This image was reinforced by their self-depiction as a youthful and progressive bunch, even if their stories happened to be reassuring to the status quo.[52]

"Kate: An Electromagnetic Romance" was published in *Lightning Flashes and Electric Dashes* (1877), a collection of stories written by telegraph operators for other operators. It follows a love affair between Kate, a train station telegraph operator, and John, her train engineer beau. Because John frequently travels he alerts Kate of his arrival at the station by spelling her name out in Morse code on his train whistle. When another station operator deciphers this public call, Kate devises a new system of communicating with John by private telegraph. The couple assemble their own wire powered by a home made pickle jar battery that rings a bell in Kate's office each time John's train is about to enter the station. This clever strategy allows them to meet every time John passes through without calling attention to their clandestine affair: "So the lovers met each day, and none knew how she was made aware of his approach with such absolute certainty. Science applied to love, or rather love applied to science, can move the world." After Kate's private knowledge of John's approaching train alerts her to an impending crash with another train, she prevents the catastrophe by signaling John to stop before it is too late. Upon solving the mystery of how the wreck was avoided, the president of the train company fires Kate and promotes John to chief engineer, thereby clearing their way to marriage. The fact that Kate is fired for her heroism is not an issue within the story because her real reward is marriage. When the president announces Kate's dismissal and John's promotion, a "tremendous cheer" breaks out from the crowd and after "many handshakings for John, and hearty kisses for Kate" the couple is expected to live happily ever after.[53] Despite their high-tech courtship in which Kate takes a leading role, the couple will presumably live a very conventional married life.

Ella Cheever Thayer's *Wired Love: A Romance of Dots and Dashes* (1880) is probably the best example of the telegraphic romance and one of the first written for a general audience. Whether or not Thayer was a telegraph operator is unclear, but she was certainly inspired by the tales in *Lightning Flashes and Electric Dashes*. Thayer takes the genre to a new level, developing the plot and characters into a full-length novel. As the book's title page indicates, the novel tells "'The old, old story,'—in a new, new way." In *Wired Love*, it is the mystery of not knowing if one is communicating with a man or a woman that sparks excitement in the relationship between the telegraph operators who, of course, turn out to be of the opposite sex. It is in the process of trying to decipher each other's identity—in between sending paid telegraphic transactions—that they fall in love. The freedom of their interactions and their witty verbal sparring create a kind of intimacy that the main character, Nattie Rogers, has never experienced. When Nattie finally meets her mystery friend Clem—after a case of mistaken identity with another (red-headed, short, and fat) telegraph operator who mischievously tries to sabotage their affair—she finds that she cannot continue her lighthearted affair in person. The intensity of their connection is due in large part to the novelty of communicating without the filter of social status or conventional gender roles. However, their face-to-face meetings thwart this freedom as social mores begin to encroach on their unconventional openness.

Clem first reveals his identity to Nattie by tapping out a message in Morse code with a pencil as they sit in the parlor of her boarding house. No one else is aware of this private conversation, though it takes place in front of other tenants. Nattie responds in code with a pair of scissors. At first, the two are delighted to have found each other. When Clem moves into the same boarding house, they continue their intimate though public communication by stringing up a telegraph wire between their bedrooms. This allows them to communicate freely late at night and for Nattie to wake Clem up with a telegraphic message in the morning. However, when they are not communicating over the wires, Nattie finds herself constrained by more traditional feminine reserve as she "sometimes felt that a certain something that had been on the wire was lacking now. . . . One reason of this she knew was her own inability to conquer a sort of timidity she felt in his presence." After a series of misunderstandings fueled by Nattie's anxiety about communicating openly with Clem in person, Nattie concludes, "romances, whether 'wired' or taken in the ordinary way, were certainly very unwieldy things to manage." Yet, Nattie finds the solution to her worries in Clem's final, desperate message "in dots and dashes" declaring his love for her. This direct (though still mediated) expression of love "more potent than electricity, required no interpreter."[54] Nattie and Clem are drawn together by codes and electricity that allow them to enact a very potent if rare version of alternative courtship.

In imagining the romantic possibilities of the future, one character in *Wired Love* conjures up a technology that would be even more democratic than the telegraph:

> We will soon be able to do everything with electricity; who knows but some genius will invent something for the especial use of lovers? Something, for instance, to carry in their pockets, so when they are far away from each other, and pine for the sound of "that beloved voice," they will have only to take up this electrical apparatus, put their ears to it, and be happy. Ah! Blissful lovers of the future![55]

This hand held device that everyone can carry with them sounds strikingly similar to a cell phone. While these ubiquitous devices certainly do make lovers easily accessible and constantly connected, it is questionable whether or not they make love more blissful. For the Victorians as for us, technology was both a potential boon and a possible burden.

The examples of unconventional practices I've outlined in this chapter reveal a remarkably modern system of courtship that takes advantage of technological advances in printing, publishing, advertising, and communication systems. This vision of chaotic technological connection in an increasingly alienated society is at odds with the traditional, orderly, and hierarchical image of courtship presented in many conduct books. These alternatives are, perhaps, most striking for their depiction of the increasingly dynamic roles women played in seeking satisfying personal lives. Exercising their rhetorical power in courtship advertisements and correspondence, or even over the telegraph wires, allowed women to abandon their passive voices for more active, engaged, and public ones. However, as with new technologies, unconventional courtship practices could be stigmatized as well as romanticized. Furthermore, participating in alternative courtship methods did not necessarily translate into living an alternative lifestyle. Despite the controversial ways some Victorians met, they were probably just as likely as their more conventional counterparts to have standard weddings and adhere to traditional notions of marriage. The next chapter outlines the legal and social parameters of the wedding and the increasing significance of the ceremony, the celebration, and the honeymoon.

The Wedding

Of all the events which characterize the history of human life, none are looked forward to with such pleasing anticipation,— none associated with such happy reminiscences as the day of marriage.

—*The Etiquette of Love, Courtship, and Marriage*, 1847

Marriage is a breaking up of old associations—an estrangement from old friends and acquaintances—a separation from accustomed habits and feelings.

—*The Etiquette of Love, Courtship, and Marriage*, 1847

The Victorian wedding was a highly anticipated event, even the primary goal of a woman's life. For better or for worse it was also a transfer of control from family to husband and an uncertain leap of faith. The opening proclamations about the transformative nature of marriage from *The Etiquette of Love, Courtship, and Marriage*—the first anticipating a promising new existence and the second lamenting the loss of everything one has known—suitably embody the contradictions of marriage for women. Despite being encouraged to look forward to one's wedding day as a sign of personal success, women were also warned that marriage was not "a season for unmitigated rejoicing" but rather an "important step" with serious ramifications. This admonishment to respect marriage as a duty to be performed only with a worthy man is, rather discordantly, followed by a blithe description of the honeymoon trip and the pleasures of setting up a household that would have left women readers blissfully ignorant of and unprepared for the dramatic transition from maiden-hood to wifehood.[1]

Of course, there were many conduct books, like those written by Ellis and Beeton, that offered a roadmap for wifehood, but the fact remained that there was a large chasm between courtship and marriage that could not be bridged except by going through the wedding ceremony, celebration, and honeymoon and coming out on the other side a wife. The transition was crucial but the only thing marking it was the ceremonial event. Thus, wedding and honeymoon planning became a cottage industry, a nascent version of the massive commercial enterprise it is today. Instead of wedding planning Web sites like the Knot, which provides a wedding checklist, budget calculator, shopping guide, and personalized event homepage, Victorians had access to etiquette books and newspaper accounts of elite weddings to use as models. The *Illustrated London News* readers were apparently fascinated by "fashionable" weddings, described in an ongoing series of articles throughout the century, as well as by royal marriages, featured in special supplements that included lavish illustrations and photographs. In contrast to the attention devoted to elite weddings in the press, there are comparatively few accounts of the details of middle-class wedding ceremonies in novels of the period. Despite the fact that marriage was a central plot point of Victorian fiction, the wedding itself remained woefully neglected by authors. Judith Flanders suggests that "diaries and letters are, even more unexpectedly, not much more informative" than novels because wedding ceremonies had not yet achieved the iconic status that they have today.[2] Or, perhaps, this neglect was the result of such ceremonial details being so obvious that it was not thought necessary to dwell on them.

As the advice books suggest, middle- and upper-class Victorians put a great deal of effort into planning their weddings. The 1855 *Illustrated London News* cartoon "A Panorama of a Fashionable Wedding" provides a humorous behind-the-scenes view of such an event as it parodies the stereotypical roles of various wedding participants (Figure 4.1). The key players include the hysterical bride, her weepy mother and emotional father, the maid with smelling salts to revive the aforementioned members of the bridal party, the gaggle of bridesmaids, the sleepy bridegroom, the critical socialites inside the church, and the rowdy mob of gawkers waiting outside. Though planning a proper wedding would not solve the problem of how to mentally transform oneself from maiden to wife, it could channel a bride's nervous energy and give her a sense of authority and control that would prefigure her role as mistress of her own household. This chapter explores the significance of wedding rituals for Victorian couples for whom the public ceremony of marriage and the forced isolation of the honeymoon marked the end of their old lives and the establishment of a new kind of companionate coupledom.

Figure 4.1. "A Panorama of a Fashionable Wedding." *Illustrated London News* (October 20, 1855): 484. Used by permission of the University of Missouri–Kansas City Libraries, Dr. Kenneth J. LaBudde Department of Special Collections.

LAWS GOVERNING THE WEDDING

The forms a wedding took in the 19th century were reliant on changes made in the laws governing marriage in the 18th century, on a shift in population from rural areas to urban centers, and on the increasing influence of the middle classes. For much of the 17th and 18th centuries, weddings, especially in rural areas, were rowdy, multiday, communal events, what Gillis refers to as "big weddings." The big wedding emphasized the relationship between the marrying couple and their community with wedding processions that moved through village streets engaging cheering and jeering crowds of onlookers. These weddings culminated in large and raucous parties complete with music and dancing. Lawrence Stone points out that,

> far more people and institutions had a vested interest in the process of marriage than merely the man and woman involved, their rivals and their competitors. There were also . . . influential kin, masters, or patrons—who often assumed the right of control or veto and were in a position to enforce their will by the granting or withholding of favours, be it money, house, property, or good will. . . . Lower down the social scale, there were neighbors, who had to be persuaded to accept the couple into their midst as a morally bonded domestic unit.

Marriage vied with inheritance as the most important way to transmit power and wealth. As a result, it was a significant legal affair that affected the entire community. However, the laws surrounding wedding ceremonies lacked uniformity and often left couples in the precarious position of not knowing if they were legally married despite having followed customary local marriage practices. Before 1753 ceremonies did not have to be held in churches and, following the Book of Common Prayer, only required the verbal consent of both partners confirmed by two witnesses. However, such verbal contracts had no legal standing.[3] Rebecca Probert argues that "an exchange of consent was not a full alternative to regular marriage—in that it did not carry the same legal rights" and most couples chose to be married by a clergyman even if they had an existing verbal contract. Stone explains that a verbal contract could have advantages for women as it "gave the husband no rights over his wife's property; it imposed on the wife none of the disabilities of 'coverture.'" However, its primary disadvantage was a big one: "it gave children no claim on their parents' property as legitimate heirs."[4] In part to remedy these inconsistencies, Parliament began to tighten laws related to marriage, culminating in the most significant and comprehensive reforms in 1753.

By the late 18th century, the number of working-class people engaged in urban wage labor (rather than in agricultural work) had dramatically increased. Workers left their families and moved to towns and cities, becoming more self-sufficient and less reliant on their local communities. As a result, the elaborate public ritual of the big wedding controlled by parents and the community dwindled. Weddings became more personal, simple, and sedate. Rural couples, as Gillis states, "simply walked to church on their wedding morning accompanied by a handful of friends, and then returned to work in the afternoon." Helena Michie argues that "privacy became part of the wedding ceremony and its attendant rituals. While ritual is by nature social, and while marriage itself is a social and legal act, at this historical moment privacy became increasingly the idiom in which these important public acts were carried out."[5] While late 18th- and 19th-century couples may have come to prefer more privacy, marriage ceremonies were shaped by government regulations that required public acknowledgment.

With the passage of Lord Hardwicke's 1753 Marriage Act, valid weddings could only be conducted by ordained Anglican clergymen in official churches after the intent of a couple to marry was announced publicly for three consecutive weeks, referred to as the reading of the banns. The couple was required to visit their parish clergyman to announce their plans to marry at least seven days before the clergyman would read the banns at the Sunday service. If the parties lived in different parishes, the banns were required to be published in both of them. A marriage could not be performed for parties under the age of 21 without the consent of a parent. If a parent objected to the marriage on the reading of the banns, the officiating clergyman could not proceed with the service. Other legal objections to a marriage were bigamous intent or consanguinity (a closeness of relation that would bar marriage). Charlotte Brontë's *Jane Eyre* provides a heart-wrenching scene of an objection to the marriage of Jane and Edward Rochester lodged, in most dramatic fashion, on the day of the wedding. Jane narrates her experience this way: after the "explanation of the intent of matrimony was gone through" and the clergyman asked "if either of you know any impediment why ye may not lawfully be joined together in matrimony," a stranger advances to the altar. Jane asks,

> When is the pause after that sentence ever broken by reply? Not, perhaps, once in a hundred years. And the clergyman who had not lifted his eyes from his book, and had held his breath but for a moment, was proceeding: his hand was already stretched toward Mr. Rochester, as his lips unclosed to ask, "Wilt thou have this woman for thy wedded wife?"—when a distinct and near voice said:—"The Marriage cannot go on: I declare the existence of an impediment."

Rochester moves "as if an earthquake had rolled under his feet" but "taking firmer footing" implores the clergyman to proceed. The clergyman, however, is compelled to hear the charge, which Mr. Briggs, a London solicitor, announces as "the existence of a previous marriage. Mr Rochester has a wife now living."[6] Briggs presents a copy of the marriage register to prove that Rochester is already married to Bertha Mason and Bertha's brother corroborates this. The marriage is called off and Jane escapes the fate of becoming the second wife of a bigamist.

The reading of the banns was considered a crucial way to prevent such illegal unions. However, even couples marrying in accordance with the law might want to avoid the publicity of the banns, particularly if they were remarrying soon after a spouse's death, if there was a great age difference between them, if they were of different religions, or if there was a premarital pregnancy. As an alternative to marriage by the banns, couples could apply for a license, though this was more expensive and had a waiting period equivalent to the process of publishing the banns. Furthermore, to obtain a license, the bride or groom was required to reside in the area of the church for a month. The Archbishop of Canterbury could award a special license that dispensed with the waiting period, but this was very expensive and intended primarily for those of high rank such as peers, peeresses, baronets, knights, and members of Parliament.[7] In an age when divorce was rare, these measures were deemed important protections against forcible marriages or elopements. Any clergyman who knowingly officiated a wedding in any place other than a church or public chapel without the required banns or license was to be transported to America for 14 years and any person falsifying a marriage registry was considered a felon and subject to the death penalty. Under Hardwicke's Act, members of other faiths could marry in their own churches, but their marriages were not legal. Exceptions were made for the marriages of Quakers and Jews, which were considered valid.

Prior to the 1753 Act, a wide variety of secretive, hasty, and frugal folks flocked to Fleet Street to marry. As John Cordy Jeaffreson describes it in *Brides and Bridals*, "Long before the Fleet became the chief prison in London for debtors, its chapel was used . . . for the solemnization of matrimony, when any of its inmates cared to add the fetters of wedlock to the manacles placed upon them by their gaolers." Soon, Fleet marriages spread to the area surrounding the prison and a clandestine marriage industry was born. Jeaffreson confirms the wide appeal of Fleet Street marriage, stating that in London, "clandestine wedlock was almost universal amongst the very poor, very general in the lower of the middle classes, frequent in the higher middle grades, and not uncommon amongst the rich and aristocratic." "Our Marriage-Laws," published in 1875 in *Chambers's*, describes the pre-Hardwicke Fleet Street marriage scene as one in which matrimony was hawked by street vendors who invited passersby in for cheap matrimonial services in private residences or pubs. The writer recalls his youth when such invitations often "came from a dirty profligate-looking fellow, wearing a slovenly parson's costume, generally attached to one of the numerous taverns in the locality, over the door of which was inscribed: 'Marriages performed within.'" Fleet parsons even began traveling distances of up to 30 miles to "execute clandestine weddings by midnight in rural taverns or churches, or in the parlours of manor-houses." Jeaffreson rather hysterically claims that at the height of the Fleet's popularity:

> Foolish men were entrapped by artful conspirators, induced to drink drugged liquor, and in the stupefaction of drunkenness married to abandoned creatures. Girls were seized in the suburbs, or even in the chief thoroughfares of towns, and carried off to dens near Fleet Ditch, where they were constrained to go through the forms of matrimony with their captors. School-boys, on their way through London to their homes in the country, were kidnapped and married to syrens unfit to become members of any decent family. At the most popular seasons for marriage, the Fleet quarter was kept in continual uproar by companies of sailors and other working-men, who came to the Fleet to be married in the tens and twenties, and kept their nuptial feasts in the taverns of the district with scandalous riot, to the inexpressible disgust of the decent residents of the district. . . . Every duchess knew some young lady who had escaped from her chaperone at a ball, or at the door of a theatre, driven to the Fleet quarter in a hackney-coach, and been changed into a wife almost before her proper guardian had missed her.[8]

As Jeaffreson's account reveals, concerns about clandestine marriage reached the level of a moral panic among the propertied classes who were threatened by the chaotic influence of romantic love, passing lust, or purely mercenary intentions that enticed couples to Fleet Street. Clandestine marriages threatened orderly, family-sanctioned matches that preserved property, wealth, and power.[9] Furthermore, while they could be challenged in court, they were valid if proven to have actually taken place.

The 1753 Marriage Act was aimed at preventing clandestine marriages, yet it was likely more successful at making marriage more difficult for all except the rich, who could afford to circumvent the laws if they chose, and members of the royal family, who were not bound by the laws to begin with. Probert argues that clandestine unions were not all of the Fleet Street variety. In fact, they "varied considerably," including "marriages actually celebrated in church that were clandestine only in that they did not comply with all of the requirements of canon law." Probert claims that the 1753 "Marriage Act should be seen as a part of a gradual progression towards regularity and formality rather than an abrupt shift in the regulation of marriage. It was consistent with the move from custom to law within Georgian society, and with the move from spiritual to secular forms of regulation."[10] While the changes brought about by Hardwicke may well have coincided with larger trends already underway, the act had many opponents, some of whom were members of Parliament.

It was not lost on members of Parliament that the new marriage laws might pose a hardship for the working classes. MP Henry Fox (who clandestinely married a woman above him in class status—Lady Caroline Lennox, the eldest daughter of the Duke of Richmond) objected to the 1753 Act on the grounds that it would make marriage more public and expensive and therefore discourage legal unions among workers who were opposed to the public calling of the banns and would not be able to afford a license. Likewise, Robert Nugent argued in Parliament that clandestine marriage was essentially the poor man's marriage license and that the immediate result of the new law would be to impede the marriage of sailors, soldiers, and itinerant laborers, who moved frequently and would have difficulty following the requirement of publishing the banns. He also saw the act as disastrous for working-class women who would, presumably, have a more difficult time convincing men to marry them if they were already pregnant due to the publicity associated with marriage by banns.[11]

Members of the merchant and trade classes who benefited from intermarriage with the landed classes also opposed the Hardwicke Act. In fact, Stephen Parker argues that strategic cross-class unions were increasingly beneficial to both classes since the combination of land and commercial wealth "formed a balanced portfolio with the latter helping to finance improvements in the former." Furthermore, primogeniture (the practice of bequeathing land to the first born son) was becoming less important as the rising bourgeoisie "were more likely to treat their children equally and distribute wealth amongst them." For groups aspiring to improve their social and economic status, romantic love and companionate marriage were on the rise while strict parental control over marriage was in decline. Regardless of objections to the law that crossed class boundaries, Lord Hardwicke's Act passed with a large majority in Parliament.[12]

As a result, Fleet Marriages came to an end. Two veterans of the Fleet clergy stayed on to challenge the law, but were immediately arrested, prosecuted, and transported just as the law promised. Regardless of Hardwicke's regulations, people continued to seek quick, cheap, and easy forms of marriage. One way to evade the Act was to falsify one's residence in a large town where the clergyman could not know all of his parishioners and have the banns read or the license obtained there. Another way around the law was to obtain a Scots marriage. To be legally married in Scotland, couples merely had to acknowledge one another as husband and wife in front of witnesses (in accordance with Book of Common Prayer guidelines). The minimum age to marry was also much lower—14 for boys and 12 for girls—and parental consent was not required. Scots marriages were also recognized as valid in England. These factors made Scotland the new Mecca for eloping couples—rich and poor—who would cross the border to marry. At first, elopers headed straight to Edinburgh to be wed. Jeaffreson describes the "matrimonial 'couplers' of Edinburgh" as far seedier than even those surrounding the Fleet as they were typically not ordained members of the clergy, but discredited lawyers' clerks or "lacqueys discarded from domestic service on account of their dishonesty" who "loitered around the yards of Canongate inns, ready, for any sum from a guinea to a shilling, to do any work that was not hard work." Gretna Green became even more popular than Edinburgh for those who "did not care to undergo the additional expense and fatigue" of travel to the northern capital for "an unedifying ceremony that could be more quickly and conventionally accomplished at the little village of Gretna, to fugitives from England the most accessible point of Scotland." This closer location was also more convenient for those who were pursued by family or friends trying to prevent the match.[13] Soon, couplers were everywhere in Gretna Green, offering special packages that included food and lodging for couples celebrating their weddings. With the spread of the railroad, Gretna Green marriages increased in popularity until the law was changed in 1856 to require at least one member of the marrying pair to live in Scotland for three weeks prior to the wedding. This change, coupled with the legalization of civil and nonconformist religious marriages in England, eliminated both the benefit and the demand for Scots marriage.

The Civil Marriage Act of 1836 extended the movement toward secular marriage by granting civil services conducted by a government registrar and officially recognizing weddings in churches other than the Church of England (and those ceremonies performed by Quakers and Jews) if conducted in a licensed place of worship with a civil registrar present.[14] The costs associated with the traditional banns included voluntary fees paid to the clergyman, which could range from £5 to £25 "according to the liberality of the bridegroom," as well as to the clerk, who could collect between £1 and £5. Marriage at the office of the registrar was considerably less expensive at 10–15 shillings.[15] Both nonconformist marriage and marriage by registrar were subject to the same rules as Church of England weddings, including the three-week waiting period and the publication of intent to marry. However, civil marriage differed in its requirement that a public declaration of intent to marry be posted in a Notice Book, which allowed more privacy than the banns. In some areas, mostly those with nonchurch wedding traditions from the pre-Hardwicke days, marriages by civil registry were as high as 65 percent.[16]

Despite the widening options for legal marriage, the vast majority of weddings still took place in the Church of England. In 1844, for example, there were 3,446 civil marriages, 2,280 Roman Catholic weddings, and 6,515 other denominational ceremonies. In contrast, 120,000 weddings were held in the official state church abiding by the reading of the banns. As *The Etiquette of Modern Society* proclaims, marriage by registrar was "perfectly legal, but by no means popular." The 1856 Act that required residency for Scottish marriages also made civil weddings easier and cheaper to obtain in England by lowering fees to about seven shillings and eliminating the requirement for publicity altogether. Regardless of the convenience, lower cost, and lack of publicity, in 1864 the national rate of register office marriages was still only 8 percent.[17]

Parker claims that civil unions, while not as popular as traditional ceremonies, were remarkable for catering to the growing public demand for more flexibility and privacy in legal marriage after the dissatisfaction with many of Hardwicke's restrictions. He cites increasing urbanization, growing religious dissent, and the 1832 Reform Act—which brought greater class diversity into the political process—as key factors driving civil marriage law. The new marriage code was less concerned with "the disruption of property through improvident marriages" than Hardwicke's Act since there was less reliance on landed property for the consolidation of wealth and power. Furthermore, it reflected the pervasiveness of the companionate ideal and the decreasing emphasis on parental control over marriage. Michie argues that the greater regulation of marriage in the late 18th and early 19th century shifted "the meaning of marriage in two opposite directions: while, on the one hand, the legal power to define marriage moved toward the more impersonal realm of government, on the other hand, the power to define it in day-to-day terms became the provenance of the married couple, that community of two that replaced larger and more mobile communities of friends, neighbors, and relatives."[18] A detailed exploration of the wedding, celebration, and honeymoon will illustrate the increasing importance of these private marriage rituals.

FAMILY WEDDING PREPARATIONS

The opening chapter of Elizabeth Gaskell's *North and South*, "Haste to the Wedding," provides Margaret Hale's view of her cousin Edith Shaw's prewedding activities. When Edith falls asleep on the sofa after a farewell dinner with family friends during which she chats herself to exhaustion about "wedding dresses, and wedding ceremonies; and Captain Lennox," her groom to be, Mrs. Shaw asks Margaret to assume her cousin's place by trying on the Indian shawls from her wedding trousseau, for which "no expense" had been "spared." Margaret obligingly fetches the shawls "which had already been exhibited four or five times that day" for admiring guests, some of whom could not afford such luxuries for their own daughters' weddings. Margaret wonders, "if a marriage must always be proceeded by what you call a whirlwind, or whether in some cases there might not rather be a calm and peaceful time just before it." She asks if "ordering the trousseau, the wedding breakfast, writing the notes of invitation" are "quite necessary troubles" as "an indescribable weariness of all the arrangements for a pretty effect, in which Edith had been busied as supreme authority for the last six weeks, oppressed her." The groom's brother tells her that "there are forms and ceremonies to be gone through, not so much to satisfy oneself, as to stop the world's mouth." But Margaret persists in imagining a simple wedding: "I should like to walk to church through the shade of the trees; and not to have so many bridesmaids and to have no wedding-breakfast."[19] Margaret thus resists what by mid-century had become the fashionable wedding, with its elaborate preparations and expected formalities.

As *The Etiquette of Modern Society* testifies, the "minutiae of etiquette" in wedding planning were "liable to continual fluctuation" according to the changing fashions.[20] However, we can glean a basic, if idealized, understanding of the details of preparing for a Victorian wedding from the guidebooks devoted to marriage. These books delineate the wedding preparations that were the responsibility of the bride, the groom, family members, and friends. Though the wedding was now a personal event, those close to the couple played significant roles in carrying out the wedding rituals.

The father of the bride typically bore the main costs of the wedding ceremony and festivities, including any presents for the groom, the decorations for the church, the music, the wedding carriages, and the reception. If his means allowed it, the father would also sign a marriage settlement drawn up by representatives acting for him and the groom, which would provide his daughter with her own money. The father likewise sent his daughter off to her new home with a trousseau. The bride's trousseau included a wardrobe of underclothes, nightgowns, dresses, and other personal items that could also include silver, linen, and household equipment. *The Etiquette of Marriage* advises against spending too much on an overly abundant or elaborate suit of clothes, but to have "a serviceable outfit of good, well-made clothes" including a "proper travelling dress, morning, afternoon, and visiting gowns" as well as dinner or evening wear, and a "reasonable number" of hats and capes to match. In 1856 the *Illustrated London News* described one fashionable woman's trousseau that would have been well beyond what most middle-class women could afford. It included five autumn dresses: one of green silk trimmed with black velvet, one of blue silk with "handsome bordered flounces," a "drab silk trimmed with bands of a darker shade on the flounces," "a very charming *chiné* silk," and a skirt of burgundy with a matching velvet jacket. This wardrobe also featured lighter dresses including a white tarlatan with ivy and violet embroidered sleeves, a dress of pink organdy and black lace, a white moiré gown for evening gatherings, and a white tulle ball gown trimmed with scarlet geraniums. According to the *ILN*, "the quantity and beauty of linen and lingerie provided for this trousseau, were in harmony with the profusion of more showy articles."[21] This was certainly a wardrobe that readers, like the admirers of Edith Shaw's shawls, would envy or emulate rather than use as a realistic model.

The bride was expected to set the wedding date, which could be any time of the year, though summer was often preferred. Popular days for weddings were weekdays rather than weekends, in keeping with the popular verse:

Monday for health,
Tuesday for wealth,

Wednesday best day of all;
Thursday for crosses,
Friday for losses,
And Saturday no luck at all.

The Etiquette of Marriage notes that "the last doleful prophesy does not seem to affect society brides at all, as Saturday is the favoured day for royal and society weddings." Sunday weddings, neglected entirely by the rhyme, were, according to Jeaffreson, considered by some to be an "outrageous exhibition of impiety." Among the working classes, the best day for marriage was most often payday, which happened to be Saturday for many industrial workers. Workers also favored holiday weddings, such as Christmas or Easter, because they were more likely to have time off.[22]

Once the date was set, the mother of the bride was expected to announce the wedding to close relatives, while the bride to be could write to her close friends to report the news. Society weddings were announced in the newspapers, though the date would only be provided to those who were invited to the ceremony. Invitations were sent two or three weeks prior to the wedding and guests were expected to respond immediately. The style of invitations, like all other wedding trends, changed with each generation. *The Etiquette of Marriage* suggests that they should be printed in silver lettering on white cards of whatever shape or size the bride preferred or on a regular sheet of paper folded into an oblong shape with a gummed flap for mailing and printed with silver lettering. The editor advises against overelaborate displays such as "crests, large and many-coloured monograms, or large lettering in addresses" and steers readers toward "note-paper which is good and thick, but otherwise plain, white, cream-laid." Furthermore, it is recommended that the "wording of the wedding invitation" be "severe in its simplicity" but suitable for the type of event, whether humble or elaborate, small or large. *The Etiquette of Marriage* provides a model invitation with "correct wording":

MR. AND MRS. SMITH
Request the pleasure
of
MR. and MRS. JONES'
Company at the
Marriage
of their daughter EDITH and
MR. HERBERT WARD
at
St. George's, Hanover Square,

On Wednesday, 24th April 1901, at 2 P.M.,
and afterwards
at
100 Grosvenor Square

The invitations would be preprinted except for the guests' names, which would be filled out by hand. If the wedding included only close family and friends, the invitations could be completely hand-written, usually by the mother of the bride. RSVPs were to be provided in the same style: "Mr. and Mrs. Jones have much pleasure in accepting Mr. and Mrs. Smith's kind invitation to the marriage of their daughter at St. George's, Hanover Square, on Wednesday, 24th April, and afterward at 100 Grosvenor Square."[23] It was appropriate to accept the wedding ceremony invitation but not the reception or vice versa. Guests who accepted invitations were expected to send gifts ahead of time and, as a result, the guest list was supposed to include only people well known to the bride or groom.

Presents were often sent a few weeks before the wedding, though the timing of the gifts varied. It was recommended that friends "avoid giving presents of an absurd character" and instead "bestow things of real service" to the couple according to their station in society. For example, giving "an elaborate jewel-case to a couple of the lower middle-class, or a valuable punch-bowl to a teetotal pair" would "appear almost as impertinences." It was better to determine what was really needed and to make inquiries to avoid duplicate gifts. Appropriate gifts included "china, crystal, ornaments, embroideries . . . tea services, canteens of plate, . . . and similar household or table appointments."[24]

Jeaffreson claims that gifts for middle-class weddings could range from £50 to £1,500, though it is difficult to imagine any truly middle-class person spending as much as that on a wedding gift. Gifts were often displayed at an afternoon tea the day before the wedding or during the wedding breakfast, labeled with the names of the gift givers. *The Etiquette of Marriage* warned that "in arranging these it is well to remember that cheques, no matter for what amount, should not be shown. A card with the donor's name, with 'Cheque' written on it is sufficient, but frequently the giver of a sum of money adds a trifle in the way of plate or ornament, which can be placed among the other gifts." Brides were to acknowledge gifts on receipt and notify guests of duplicate gifts immediately, if necessary. Interestingly, *The Etiquette of Marriage* allows that money is only an appropriate gift when given by "parents, wealthy uncles, or thoughtful relatives and friends." Much was made of the Scottish tradition of the penny wedding, at which each guest contributed cash (ranging from one shilling to half a crown), which was used to cover the cost of the wedding feast and to buy furniture and staples. This was variously thought to be vulgar or practical, depending on the point of view. As the *London Journal* remarks, it is really no worse than the predominant "system of inviting people to the bridal reception and expecting them to make a valuable present" that amounts to "a serious tax" on wedding guests.[25]

Before the wedding, the parents of the bride often held a dinner to introduce the groom to family and friends. As one writer joked, at such prewedding dinner parties, "when the house should be getting quietest things are getting into a commotion. The bridesmaids are clustering around the bride elect, as a queen bee. . . . [However], there is one person who is probably overlooked and despised, and considered an interloper and a nuisance if he takes any active part in the proceedings. This is the bridegroom elect."[26] Indeed, in the wedding dinner scene in *North and South*, the groom is absent altogether. The groom was, however, central to many of the most important wedding plans.

The bridegroom was expected, in consultation with his bride, to set up his household prior to the wedding, furnishing an entire home from scratch if possible (presumably he would not marry if he could not afford to set up a household). In addition to securing the banns or license, the groom also chose the wedding ring, which was typically a simple gold band. Furthermore, *The Etiquette of Modern Society* explains, "when the proposal of a suitor is accepted, it is usual for him to present his betrothed with some keepsake. This generally takes the form of an 'engagement' ring, which, during the period of betrothal is worn by itself on the third finger of the left hand by the lady, until at marriage the wedding ring takes its place." The engagement ring was a visible symbol of the state of betrothal that *The Etiquette of Courtship and Matrimony* calls an "approximation to marriage" often "considered in a very sacred light" as "the lady's honour is now in her lover's hands." *The Etiquette of Marriage* outlines another reason for the engagement ring, which is "not by any means compulsory" but rather, "from the more utilitarian standpoint," a way "to keep others from imagining that the lady is free to be wooed and won." This advice book also recommends that women have a say in choosing their rings, especially in regard to the stone. However, feminine readers are warned that "it is very bad form to exact from a man a ring more expensive than his means will afford. No doubt diamonds are preferred by many, but the sentiment will be no less sincere, and the affection may be more durable and grateful, if there is no feeling of taxation" placed on the gentleman. The book suggests that a gentleman make a private appointment with a jeweler to select rings in his price range before bringing his fiancée along to choose from the narrowed selection. While gemstones could vary depending on taste and income, opals were believed to be omens of bad luck and pearls too fragile, so both were discouraged. Moonstones (which were supposed to be lucky), sapphires (symbols of undying affection), and rubies (representing intense devotion) were recommended as alternatives to diamonds.[27]

There were many explanations about why the tradition of the wedding ring persisted despite the fact that it was not technically required. The January 1858 *London Journal* states that "the ring is no longer essential to the marriage ceremony, the Act of Parliament passed in 1857 having instituted marriage to be a civil contract; though it does not forbid the use of the ring, which holds its accustomed place to distinguish the maiden from the wife. . . . Its continual use furnishes another of the many proofs that customs and habits . . . are stronger and more permanent than written laws." The *Journal* goes on to tell the story of a man who went to the altar without a ring for his bride and after being chastised by the registrar because "the absence of the ring would expose the wife to insult after marriage," the man immediately "fetched one" bringing tears to his bride's eyes. The persistence of the ring as a symbol was often discussed in relation to the modern science of anatomy rather than in reference to religious laws or local customs. Jeaffreson explains that the wedding ring was worn on the fourth finger of the left hand next to the little finger because of the belief that this finger had a vein leading directly to the heart. In the *London Reader*, we find a similar claim couched in more up-to-date medical terms: "There are facts which belong to the ring finger which render it in a peculiar manner an appropriate emblem of the matrimonial union. It is the only finger where two principle nerves belong to two distinct trunks; the thumb is supplied with its principal nerves from the radial nerve, as are also the fore finger, the middle finger . . . the side of the ring finger next the little finger is supplied by the ulnar nerve."[28] The ring, then, was central to the expression of love and devotion if not required by law.

The groom was also expected to provide "a handsome locket, necklet or other article of jewellery [sic]" for the bride to wear on the wedding day.[29] He might present the bridesmaids with lockets or other small gifts such as bracelets, necklaces, rings, pendants, or brooches, often chosen by the bride. Prince Albert, for example, designed a gold and porcelain orange blossom broach for Queen Victoria on their engagement, as well as a turquoise beaded eagle broach for their bridesmaids. In addition, the groom purchased the bouquets for the bride and bridesmaids, to be sent to each lady on the morning of the wedding ceremony. The bride's bouquet was typically made of orange blossoms and other white flowers such as camellias, azaleas, or gardenias. The bridesmaids' bouquets often reflected the colors chosen for their dresses and might be replaced by baskets of flowers if the maids were children. Finally, the groom would present the groomsmen or best man with a ring or scarf pin.[30]

DUTIES OF THE BRIDAL PARTY

The number of bridesmaids and groomsmen were often equal at mid-century, but by the end of the century using only a best man was in fashion. The bride could have as many maids as she wished, varying in number from one to ten. *The Etiquette of Marriage* notes that "it is in better taste in ordinary social circles to limit bridesmaids to two, three, or four, as more are not only useless but involve the bridegroom in serious and unnecessary expenditure." Bridesmaids were typically unmarried sisters, close friends of the bride, or sisters of the groom. A bride's elder sisters, even if unmarried, would not typically serve as bridesmaids. *The Etiquette of Courtship and Matrimony* recommends that one lady be appointed principal bridesmaid. The chief bridesmaid, or maid of honor, was advised to provide support to the bride in the days leading up to the wedding by offering assistance with shopping, sewing, clothing preparation, dressing, and so on, particularly in middle-class households that did not employ a lady's maid to attend to such matters. The maid of honor also held the bride's bouquet and gloves during the ceremony and the signing of the wedding register and helped the bride prepare for her wedding journey, attending to her small luggage and helping her change from her wedding dress into her traveling clothes.[31]

The other bridesmaids had fewer duties, mostly involving the cards and cake: "On the second bridesmaid devolves, with her principal, the duty of sending out the cards; and on the third bridesmaid, in conjunction with the remaining beauties of her choir, the onerous office of attending to certain ministrations and mysteries connected with the wedding cake." The tradition of the cake started with throwing grain over the bride's head and later evolved into baking wedding biscuits or oatmeal cakes to feed the guests (in Scotland these were accompanied by shots of whiskey for all attendees). Sometimes a small cake was made to crumble over the bride's head and a large cake to adorn the banquet table and to serve to guests. In the 18th century methods were borrowed from French pastry chefs who transformed the cake into an icon of the wedding ceremony adorned with a hard white sugary crust, flowers, and other "toys figurative of the delights of matrimony." The cake could cost anywhere from £5 to £25 and became increasingly elaborate.[32]

Messrs. Bollard of Chester, makers of wedding cakes for the Royal family, explained that the process of baking a cake lasted from five to seven hours but "no cake is sent out until it has matured for at least six months." This process indicates that while Victorian cakes looked much like wedding cakes today, with a sugar and egg white frosting and elaborate decoration, they were akin to what we would call a fruit cake, a densely packed confection not at all like our light sponge cakes. The *Illustrated London News* included a magnificent illustration of a Royal wedding cake designed by M. Jules Le Blond for the wedding of Queen Victoria's eldest daughter (also Victoria) to the Prussian Crown Prince on January 25, 1858. The cake is described as "between six and seven feet in height . . . divided from the base to the top into three compartments all in white" and featuring eight columns, a dome, and an altar with two Cupids holding a medallion with Princess Royal Victoria on one side and Prince Frederick William of Prussia on the other. It was covered with jasmine and orange blossoms as well as rows of pearls dividing each portion of cake.[33]

While most brides had much more modest wedding cakes than the royal family, they followed the same traditions. Prior to the wedding, "one portion of the wedding cake is cut into small oblong pieces, and passed by the bridesmaids through the wedding ring, which is delivered to their charge for this purpose. The pieces of cake are afterward put up in ornamental paper, generally pink or white, enameled, and tied with bows of silvered paper." Early in the century, the bridesmaids would send pieces of the cake out to those who did not attend the reception, but this ritual was later taken over by the bakery that made the cake, or it was skipped altogether. After the wedding cake was eaten at the reception and sent home with wedding guests, it was served at the bride's at-home on her return from her honeymoon. A slice might also be preserved as a wedding keepsake.[34] Queen Victoria kept hers in an engraved silver box, where it can still be seen today at Windsor Castle.

In addition to their cake-related duties, bridesmaids also prepared the wedding favors, which they took to the church on the morning of the wedding. Favors might include flower petals to be strewn along the bride's path on leaving the church and small floral arrangements to be pinned to men's coats and servants' hats. All of the maids were expected to attend to the guests at the reception, making sure no one was neglected. They might also call on the bride's mother while the bride was away on her honeymoon "not staying long enough to make the visit an infliction, but to . . . endeavor if possible to fulfill something of the daughter's duties to her."[35]

The best man was in charge of the wedding ring and was supposed to ensure that "when the bridegroom puts on his wedding waistcoat, he does not omit to put the wedding ring into the corner of the left-hand pocket." *The Etiquette of Marriage* goes on to say that the "duties of the groomsman are more onerous in many ways than those of the bridesmaid, or perhaps it would be more correct to say they are more responsible." His primary role was to take care of business transactions for the bridegroom: arranging legal matters, seeing that all necessary papers were in order, paying fees to the clergyman, driving the bridegroom to the church well in advance of the arrival of the bride, escorting the maid of honor to the vestry for the signing of the register, and assisting with the wedding breakfast arrangements.[36] He also took care of the heavy luggage for the wedding journey and made sure a wedding announcement appeared in the newspaper.

WEDDING ATTIRE

Throughout the century, brides wore dresses of various colors and styles for their weddings. Often, the wedding dress was a woman's best dress.

Sometimes it was purchased for the wedding but was worn on other occasions as well. These versatile wedding dresses could be light brown, blue, lavender, gray, or silver. JoAnne Olian explains that between 1860 and 1912, wedding dress styles changed swiftly, matching the general fashion trends:

> At first, the crinoline held out the enormously full skirts of wedding dresses measuring five yards around at the hem, which gradually flattened in front and bunched up in back until they formed a bustle in the 1870s. By 1880 the bride was encased in an unyielding hourglass-shaped bodice and pencil-slim skirt that gave way to a revival of the bustle in the mid eighties. In 1890, the back fullness deflated and the yardage was transformed into a skirt that flared at the hem. The emphasis shifted to the sleeve, which looked increasingly like the . . . leg-of-mutton it was often called. By the turn of the century, fullness shifted to the derriere, a result of the S-shaped corset that thrust the top half of the body forward in a matronly monobosom effect while the lower half stuck out prominently behind.[37]

Dresses could be made of silk, satin, brocade, or muslin, depending on a bride's taste and budget. The bride would also wear a wreath of orange blossoms on her head, along with a veil of lace, net, or tulle. In 1851, the *Home Circle* suggested that morning wedding dresses be made out of plain white muslin or net, or white damask silk with plain sleeves, while an afternoon or evening wedding dress (fairly rare until later in the century) be made with white satin with lace flounces and orange blossoms and small white roses for the trim and headdress (Figure 4.2).[38]

Although some since the mid-18th century had worn white wedding dresses, Queen Victoria established the trend when she wore a white gown to marry Prince Albert. William Spooner's souvenir panorama of the Royal wedding depicts the Queen's wedding procession, including 12 bridesmaids also clad in white, making its way through St. James's Palace toward the altar of the Chapel Royal for the ceremony (Figure 4.3). However, white was not a color that would wear well. If one did purchase a white gown, it would likely be retrimmed (removing the obligatory orange blossoms and replacing them with some other ribbon, flower, or ornament) or dyed a darker hue for subsequent use. Since most dresses were made with separate bodices and skirts, they could also be pieced out and made into ball or visiting dresses, with new but matching top or bottom pieces, but these options posed additional expenses that many could not afford. A surviving wedding dress bill from 1850 indicates a total expenditure of £20 for materials, not including a seamstress to make the dress. "Wedding Extravagances" sums up the challenge of the white wedding dress this way: "of what use is the costly white silk bridal dress, which in all human probability will never in its original state be worn again? It will, of course,

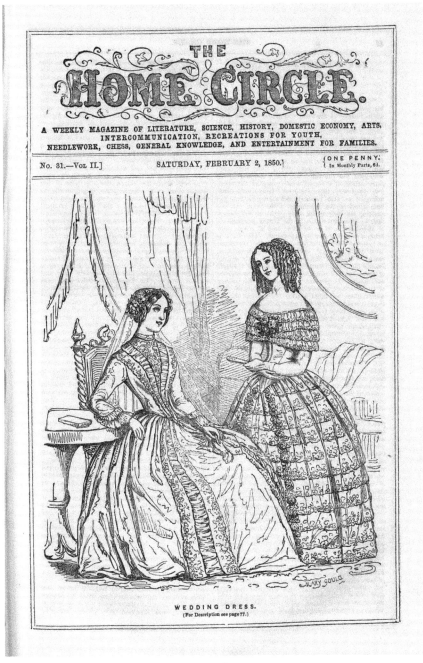

Figure 4.2. "Wedding Dress." *The Home Circle* (February 2, 1850): 65. Harry Ransom Humanities Research Center, University of Texas at Austin.

Figure 4.3. William Spooner's panoramic view of the Queen's wedding procession. The Royal Collection, © 2011 Her Majesty Queen Elizabeth II.

be laid up carefully, and looked at occasionally with tender sentimental interest; but by-and-by, in a year or two, it will seem old-fashioned, and most probably be picked to pieces and dyed some serviceable colour."[39]

By 1865 the tradition of the white wedding dress was well enough established that *The Etiquette of Courtship and Matrimony* suggested, "A bride's costume should be white, or some hue as close as possible to it. Fawn colour, grey, and lavender are entirely out of fashion." In 1873 Jeaffreson claimed that "in our polite and richer classes, the girl who arranges to be married in any colour but white, takes a sure means of making her bridal doings talked about as savouring of eccentricity."[40] A stunning white Honiton lace wedding dress worn in 1865 illustrates the wide, flat-fronted, rear-protruding skirt in fashion at the time—as opposed to the bell-shaped crinoline skirts of the 1850s (Figure 4.4). By the end of the century, white

Figure 4.4. Honiton lace wedding dress and veil. © Victoria and Albert Museum, London.

wedding dresses were considered orthodox; however, *The Etiquette of Marriage* declares that if a woman's "taste in evening and dinner dress runs to some colour or style other than white or bridal attire, she may add one or more extra" dresses to her trousseau and "dispense with the bride's robe." The predominance of afternoon rather than morning weddings in the 1880s brought about significant change as the traditional wedding dress was sometimes replaced by a going-away or travel dress in a bolder shade.[41] An eggplant-hued dress worn for a wedding in 1879 illustrates the change in both color and style, with an emphasis on a fitted bodice suggesting a jacket, and slender skirt featuring a rear bustle and train (Figure 4.5). A remarrying widow was another exception to the general trend.

Figure 4.5. Satin dress, trimmed with applied beading, chenille tassels, and needle lace. © Victoria and Albert Museum, London.

Widows were expected to wear bonnets instead of wreaths and veils, along with colored silk dresses. A widow would not wear white or orange blossoms, which "are only worn by maiden brides." Her bouquet would have colored flowers and she would likely have only one bridesmaid.[42]

The bride chose the bridesmaids dresses, consulting the ladies about color, material, and style. Although Queen Victoria chose white for her bridesmaids, "pale shades, selected to suit the complexions and styles of the various girls" were preferred. By about mid-century bridesmaids' dresses were expected to frame and contrast with the bride rather than echo her. Bridesmaids might dress "in pairs, each two alike, but sometimes all wear a similar costume. Pink and light blue . . . are admissible colours. . . . The whole costume of a bridesmaid should have a very light but brilliant effect, and . . . so constituted in style and colour as to look well by the side of and about the bride . . . helping to throw into the foreground the dress of the bride, and make her prominent, as the principal person in the tableau."[43] In contrast to this ideal, Edwin Grey's *Cottage Life in a Hertfordshire Village* describes rural weddings of the 1870s this way:

> The dresses of the bride to be and her attendant maiden (for only one girl friend accompanied her) were very generally made of some serviceable material of a pretty shade, with a bonnet or hat to correspond, the young women no doubt having in mind that these dresses would, as a matter of course, come in afterwards as best, that is for Sunday wear, holidays, and so on. . . . Carriages, retinue of bridesmaids, veils, wreaths of orange blossoms, etc were not then in vogue at the weddings of farm workers' daughters.

Most working-class city dwellers wed in their regular clothes and returned to work after the ceremony. According to Gillis, "the patrician white wedding, with its giving away of the virgin bride in white, was an expression of the kind of patriarchy that had very little resonance among the urban plebians."[44]

From the 1830s through the 1850s, men wore dark blue or black waistcoats in silk or velvet that were often emblazoned with brightly colored embroidery. The somber tones of the coats contrasted with the colorful designs and the lighter hued trousers. The waistcoat depicted in Figure 4.6 is made of silk damask patterned with a foliate design and embroidered with green floral sprigs (which cannot be seen in the photograph). This flashy style of dress was falling out of favor by the 1860s. In 1865 *The Etiquette of Courtship and Matrimony* recommends that the dress of the groomsmen "should be light and elegant; a dress coat, formerly considered indispensable, is no longer adopted." By 1881 *The Etiquette of Modern Society* expected the groom to wear a "blue frock-coat, or morning coat, trousers of a very light tint, light-colored neck-tie, thin kid or patent-leather boots, and white kid gloves" as well as a "glossy silk hat"

Figure 4.6. Silk damask waistcoat. © Victoria and Albert Museum, London.

and "a small white button-hole bouquet."[45] Figure 4.7 depicts a double-breasted frock coat worn for a wedding in 1871. Contrasting trousers in a dark grey were paired with the black wool jacket, though more and more men were donning trousers of the same color as their jackets (referred to as "dittos"). As *The Etiquette of Marriage* points out, by the end of the century, there was "little variety in male attire, so that the bridegroom is not confronted with much choice or difficulty in that direction. The groomsman and the bridegroom are practically dressed alike." However, the guidebook goes on to describe some remaining fluctuation in color and style: "A correct suit for such an occasion would include grey trousers, not however, startlingly light, black or dark grey frock coat, white tie, grey, tan, or straw-coloured gloves. . . . If the wedding takes

Figure 4.7. Double-breasted wool frock coat. © Victoria and Albert Museum, London.

place in summer, a white waist-coat is permissible. . . . the white tie may be exchanged for one of palest French grey, or the gloves be of a delicate tint of lavender." By the end of the century, black had become the typical color for the men's attire and three piece suits (often called leisure suits) were worn rather than the longer frock coats or fancy waistcoats with tails.[46]

THE CEREMONY

Church wedding ceremonies were scheduled between 8 A.M. and noon, unless exempted by a special license. The bridegroom and best man arrived first at the church to pay the fees and await the wedding

guests and the wedding party. The guests usually arrived by 11:00, followed by the bridesmaids and the bride's sister(s) or mother who waited
to greet the bride at the church door where she was to be escorted into
the church by her father. If she had no sisters, her father could instead
receive her at the door and her mother could escort her. Taking her father's right arm (or the right arm of a brother or whoever was to give her
away), the bride proceeded through a double line of bridesmaids into
the church to meet her fiancé at the altar. The bridesmaids followed her
down the aisle where she stood to the left of the groom, with her father
to her left, her married sisters and mother to his left, and the bridesmaids
behind them with the head bridesmaid first in line. Alternatively, the
bridegroom could escort the bride up the aisle to the center front where
the bride's family, the bridesmaids, and the groomsmen awaited. According to *The Etiquette of Courtship and Marriage*, "the words 'I will' are
to be pronounced distinctly and audibly by both parties, such being the
all-important part of the ceremony . . . the declaration of the bride and
bridegroom that they are voluntary parties to their holy union in marriage." Likewise,

> the words "honour and obey" must also be distinctly spoken by the
> bride. They constitute an essential part of the obligation and contract
> of matrimony on her part. It may not be amiss here to inform our
> fair readers that on the marriage of our gracious Sovereign Queen
> Victoria . . . her majesty carefully and most judiciously emphasized
> these words, thereby manifesting that though a Queen in station, yet
> in her wedded and private life she sought no exemption from this
> obligation, and in this respect placed herself on the same level with
> the humblest village matron in her dominions.

Following the service, the bride took the groom's left arm and followed
the clergyman to the vestry to sign the marriage register and be congratu-
lated by the wedding party. Probert explains that the 1753 Marriage Act
stipulated "that the registration of the marriage should take place 'immediately after the Celebration of every Marriage,' and should be signed by
the minister, the parties themselves, and two attesting witnesses."[47] The
bride and groom then returned down the aisle together, the veil lifted, followed by the groomsmen and bridesmaids. The bride and groom drove
away first, followed by the bridesmaids and groomsmen and then by the
bride's mother and father and the groom's mother and father so that they
would all arrive at the wedding celebration prior to the guests.

Rural weddings among the working classes were much different affairs.
As Grey recalls, cottage weddings in the 1870s "were simple, homely affairs, though often pretty and picturesque in their rural surroundings."
The best man often gave the bride away since her father "would have
to be at his work on the farm, for he could ill afford any reduction of his

small wage owing to loss of time; however, he would be in at the evening's merriment." Gillis argues that compared to middle-class women, "working women were neither so subject to their fathers nor so subservient to their husbands, a condition reflected in their preference for ceremonies that were restricted to the exchange of consents, with vows of obedience mumbled or left out entirely." Among urban workers in northern factory towns, "the closest thing to a 'public bridal' was breakfast at a local beer shop, where it was customary to take up a collection to help the couple furnish their rented room." The drastic transition from daughter to wife, son to husband was not so great among the working classes who were often already separated from their families and communities and might also be parents themselves when they came to the bridal altar.[48]

THE CELEBRATION

Wedding celebrations among the working classes included only immediate family and were typically held in the evening, after work hours. There was a wedding cake and gifts, but these were only from close family and friends and would consist of food or small useful household items. However, the celebration was an increasingly lavish production among the middle and upper classes. The bride's mother made most of the arrangements for the wedding reception, determining the number of guests, amount of food, and style of the event. Until the end of the century, when a wedding reception or ball was introduced that could be held at a hotel or other public venue, the celebration was typically a breakfast held at the bride's home immediately following the ceremony. At this celebration, which could be a sit-down or stand-up affair, the bride would usually make an appearance. Sometimes, though, she retired to her room to avoid "the fatigue and embarrassment of appearing at the breakfast table. When this occurs, her place beside the bridegroom must be occupied by a near relation or friend." *The Etiquette of Courtship and Matrimony* points out that "the rationale or original intention of this wedding assemblage" was to "give publicity to the fact that the bride is leaving her paternal home with the consent and approbation of her parents." All present were to wear their most festive clothing and no black dress was permitted, even for widows who were instead expected to wear silver gray.[49]

The Etiquette of Modern Society recommends that a horseshoe-shaped table be used at a sit-down celebration so that the "wedded pair are seated at the outside of the curve, the bride on the husband's right hand, with her father and his mother next, while her mother and father-in-law sit on the bridegroom's left, and the bridesmaids are disposed on either side." Though the celebration was called a breakfast, the food was luncheon fare, including soups, game, and champagne (instead of coffee or tea). The wedding cake was the centerpiece of the table and "often tastefully surrounded with flowers, among which those of the fragrant orange ought to be conspicuous." At the end of the meal, "the bride takes a knife and makes a cut into the bride-cake, which is placed before her and then removed, cut into little slices, some of which is handed round, and every one is expected to taste it." Next, the groom proposed a toast to the health of his wife's parents, with other toasts to follow.[50]

In *The Glass of Fashion*, "The Lounger in Society" declares that speeches should "give the assurance that there is no reserve in the heartiness and *totality* of satisfaction and welcome on both sides with which the alliance is regarded" without displaying a "gush and effusion" of sentiment. Another keen observer described the winding down of the ideal wedding breakfast this way:

> All the healths have been drunk. The father has honestly said that his girl has been a good girl all her days, and will prove herself a good wife. The bridegroom has made an honest, sincere, manly speech, which has under hopeful skies confirmed every golden opinion. The young gentleman who has proposed the bridesmaids has done it so brilliantly, he might propose to any one of them on the spot with every probability of being accepted. The old friend of the family has not been forgotten. The doctor, who took the bride through her juvenile measles, has been feelingly remembered. An excuse has been found for every one proposing the health of every one on public or private grounds—so we can hardly be blamed if we think ourselves the most meritorious set of beings in the kingdom.

After basking in the glory of such a scene (usually until about 3:00 P.M.), the bride changed into her traveling outfit. The bride would be showered with rice as she reemerged and the maid of honor and the best man would each throw a satin slipper at the couple as they departed for the honeymoon. These traditions symbolized that the bride was, as the Lounger notes, "thus passing out of the world of her maiden youth into the new vague world of married life."[51]

By the end of the century, when ecclesiastical rules permitted weddings to be performed between 9 A.M. and 3 P.M. (rather than 9 A.M. and noon), afternoon tea parties became a popular form for the reception because they were potentially less expensive and could accommodate more guests. Likewise, balls or soirees were given in the evening. The Lounger took a more cynical view of the wedding breakfast in *The Glass of Fashion*. He claimed that the wedding breakfast fell out of fashion because it had

> little to recommend and justify it as the custom of celebrating the marriage ceremony in the morning. There is something unnatural and unreal in such a repast under such conditions; it is not less a burden to the guests, condemned to drink wine and listen to bad speeches in the middle of the day, than to the bride and bridegroom,

who after the excitement of so solemn and important a ceremony, should surely be allowed a little time for quiet reflection and repose. Nor does it seem fitting the parting of the bride with her parents and sisters should be witnessed by a host of guests assembled for the purpose of amusement. All those things, moreover, tend to disguise the grave character of the act by which a young girl is taken from her home and its loving shelter, and plunged into a new world of duties and responsibilities; the act by which she sets a seal upon her past, and opens the book of a mysterious future.

Likewise, Jeaffreson calls the wedding breakfast "a cumbrous and distressing anachronism" destined to be replaced by a bridal dinner and dance.[52] And, indeed it was.

While the couple was away on their honeymoon, the bridesmaids sent wedding cards to friends of the couple who may not have been invited to the ceremony or the breakfast to indicate the change in status of the newlyweds. In 1865, *The Etiquette of Courtship and Matrimony* noted that the distribution of wedding cards has "long been regarded as an important social duty" carried out by the bridesmaids the day following the wedding. Cards were sent "to all whom [the bride] has been in the habit of receiving or visiting while at her father's house," but who had not been invited to the wedding celebration. This was sometimes a final farewell to past friends given that the bride could use the card as a means of "dropping such acquaintances as she may not be desirous of retaining in her wedded life." Card recipients would know they were unwelcome if the new address of the bride and groom was omitted from the card, whereas if it was included, sometimes along with the words "At Home," it was known that they were welcome to pay a visit. However, instead of sending cards, it was becoming standard practice to invite these people to the church for the ceremony instead. By the end of the century, the newspaper marriage announcement would sometimes advertise the at-home days of the bride along with her address, thereby eliminating the need for cards.[53]

As *The Etiquette of Courtship and Matrimony* declares: "On the return of the wedded pair from their honeymoon trip, about a month or six weeks after the wedding, they were, until recently, expected to be 'At home'; but the formality of reception days is now generally exploded." Still, close friends were expected to pay the couple a visit, whether formal reception days were set or not. During these visits, the bride would wear her wedding dress and serve leftover wedding cake and wine. She would be accompanied by her husband, or, if he was at work, by her mother or sister(s). Wedding visits were to be repaid within a few days, either by the couple or the bridesmaids on their behalf. *The Etiquette of Love, Courtship, and Marriage* points out that "if parties wait upon you and you do not return the call, it is a well known rule in Etiquette that you do not wish to form acquaintance with them. Your conduct in so doing may give umbrage to the parties, but that is not your consideration. Your future intercourse in society will be materially influenced by the decision you now establish, and what is the good of forming acquaintance where there is no similarity of rank; no congeniality of taste, or sentiment, or disposition, or pursuits?"[54] The onerous nature of the ritual of sending cards and exchanging visits perhaps ultimately contributed to its demise.

THE HONEYMOON

By the 1830s and 1840s, honeymoons were a crucial part of the marriage ritual. Jeaffreson argues that the introduction of the wedding trip in the 18th century had, by the 19th century, become "so agreeable to lovers of both sexes that the new fashion became yearly more general." The custom was now "indispensable" among "modest gentlefolk in the middle rank of life" and "even in the grades of country-town 'respectability.'" The honeymoon could last anywhere from a weekend to several months, depending on the distance traveled and the couple's income. Popular honeymoon destinations ranged from English seaside resort towns such as Devon and Brighton, or the Lake District—for those working with tight budgets or under time constraints—to farther flung places including Venice, Rome, or Paris. The very wealthy could take extensive European tours lasting months. Jeaffreson names the Isle of Wight as "a favorite haunt of newly-married couples, as soon as the honeymoon trip had become a universal incident of wedlock" due, in part, to its close proximately to London. He remarks on the "charming scenery" and "attractive honeymoon hotels," lamenting that "in later years the increasing facilities for travel have caused the majority of our spouses to regard the trip to the nearest of our Channel Islands as too tame and unadventurous for the happy pair who have the time and money for a run to the Pyrenees, Switzerland, or the Italian lakes."[55] According to Michie's study of 61 newlywed couples, 56 percent of them opted to stay close to home, taking domestic honeymoons, while 26 percent went on continental tours, and 13 percent made some combination of domestic trips and continental tours. The majority of her honeymooning husbands were of the professional/intellectual classes, though there were also merchants and businessmen, military men, clergymen, and a small number of clerks.[56] Honeymooning was, for practical reasons, the purview of the middle and upper classes, but by the end of the century the habit had infiltrated the upper working classes as well. For working-class couples, however, honeymoons were less likely. A simple walk in the countryside or a day off work to celebrate a marriage would be considered a luxury among the poor.

Though some honeymooners were accompanied by or met up with friends or family members, the idea was that the couple could begin their intimate relationship alone, away from the prying eyes of their families and friends. As early as 1847, *The Etiquette of Love, Courtship, and Matrimony* notes that couples "now . . . generally go alone" on their wedding tours. Michie argues that the honeymoon thus functioned as a "journey toward the conjugal" in which the couple took primacy over the family or the community.[57] However, as many observers noted, the couple still faced the prying eyes of strangers, as is illustrated in the *Punch* cartoon "The Happy Pair Then Left Town" (Figure 4.8). Here, the newlywed bride tries to be the consummate wife by serving her husband's tea, but she betrays her inexperience when she asks what kind of brew he prefers. The couple's lack of knowledge about each other becomes the object of amusement for the servants.

For some, however, the honeymoon was not at all amusing. It was at best a boring responsibility and at worst a burden on one's mental and physical health. *How to Be Happy Though Married* offers this cynical view of the ritual:

> You take . . . a man and a woman, who in nine cases out of ten know very little about each other (though they generally fancy they do), you cut off the woman from all her female friends, you deprive the man of his ordinary business and ordinary pleasures, and you

Figure 4.8. "The Happy Pair Then Left Town." *Punch* (November 16, 1867): 198. Courtesy of the Division of Special Collections, Archives, and Rare Books, University of Missouri–Columbia.

condemn this unhappy pair to spend a month of enforced seclusion in each other's society. If they marry in the summer and start on tour, the man is oppressed with the plethora of sight-seeing while the lady, as often as not, becomes seriously ill from fatigue and excitement.

How to Be Happy imagines that the working classes are at an advantage in avoiding the detrimental effects of honeymoon trips: "When Hodge [a condescending term for a rural worker] and his sweetheart crown their pastoral loves in the quiet old country church, they take a pleasant drive or a walk in their finery, and settle down at once to connubial comfort in the cot beside the wood. Why do their richer neighbors deny themselves this happiness and invent troubles?" The poem "Honeymoon Reflections" printed in London Society also articulates the potential disenchantment that could result on the honeymoon:

> And so you're on your honeymoon,
> And wear a golden fetter;
> You speculate—'tis rather soon—
> "Is it for worse or better?"
> You're thinking of a year ago—
> Twas just such sunny weather—
> But somehow time went not so slow
> When we two were together.[58]

More serious than mere boredom or poor health was the potential for a disastrous trip that could serve as a bad beginning for the marriage.

In "A Quiet Honeymoon," a short story published in All the Year Round in 1878, a young bride is determined to take a quaint wedding trip to a small northern English village "entirely out of the Lake district" to accommodate her struggling artist husband's meager finances. The idealistic Rose imagines that it will be a "nice, quiet honeymoon" even though her husband Jack asks her plaintively if she thinks her love for him "is strong enough to bear a fortnight of complete seclusion." As Jack fears, this trip fails to meet his beloved's expectations: on a chilly, rainy September day, the two are dropped off with all their luggage at the nearest station to Kissington, but they are eight miles away from the village and there is no regular transportation to their destination. After waiting hours to put their luggage on a pig cart, they walk behind it all the way to the village. Jack narrates their calamitous affair:

> Just when we were believing that we had walked sixteen miles at the very least, and were seriously thinking about giving up the struggle, we came upon . . . a long, straggling, dead-alive sort of village, with . . . about a hundred and fifty small tumble-down houses

and cottages scattered around, without any pretence at order or arrangement. This was the death-blow to all our hopes, and so utterly forlorn and wretched was the appearance of the place, that two big tears began to course slowly down my darling's cheeks.

While bickering over their predicament, they discover that their trunks have been thrown into the road: "The pigs were mixed up heterogeneously with our luggage, my wife's bonnet was smashed, and one of the juvenile pigs, evidently seized with a desire to closely study the latest Paris fashions, was poking his nose into the broken box and its delicate contents. Rose did not cry now—hers was a grief too deep for tears." Next, they realize that there is no proper hotel in town but only two beer shops with makeshift rooms for rent. After finding more suitable lodging in a private home, the couple cobbles together meals from "gory slabs of meat," potatoes, and tins of oxtail soup available at a local shop. To top it off, they are scolded by their landlady who does not want them chatting by candlelight so late at night. When Rose begs Jack to take her home, he reminds her that she "said [her] love was so strong that it would stand anything." She replies that she "didn't bargain for this" and besides, "we weren't married then." Still, they return with the knowledge that they can "make a dinner out of the most unpromising materials" and are consoled by the fact that there will be "no more 'quiet honeymoons.'"[59] Despite their miserable trip, enabled by Rose's idealization of the honeymoon, this couple still has hope for a happy future. However, the ritual of the honeymoon is seriously discredited by their experience.

Michie argues that the honeymoon became "a geographical and psychological site for the transformation from single to married subject." This transformation included a newly formed sexual bond as well as an intensified emotional one. The experience proved to be overwhelming for some. Among the middle classes, many men gained their sexual experience with prostitutes and most women had little to no sexual experience, both of which could lead to distorted expectations. The famous honeymoon of Victorian art critic John Ruskin and his beautiful young wife Effie Gray is a case in point. The marriage was never consummated and was eventually annulled. According to many scholars, Ruskin's refusal or inability to consummate his marriage was probably related to his unrealistic expectations about what a woman's body should look like. Indeed, Effie claimed in a letter to her father that Ruskin "imagined women were quite different to what he saw I was."[60] While we can never know what Ruskin thought or what he saw, it is clear that the experience of the wedding night was not what he'd imagined it would be. As Phyllis Rose puts it, "The ignorance in the case was not so clear and simple. It was ignorance mixed with self-deception, an unfamiliarity with women combined with a vivid and yet wholly unrealistic imaginative vision of what they should be— both physically and morally—added to motives and aversions so deeply buried in the subconscious that I hardly dare to speculate upon them." She argues that the honeymoon, "a supercharged transition from innocence to experience . . . may well have been a barbaric trial for at least one, and sometimes for both, of the newly married pair." To counteract such a terrifying plunge into sexuality, clergyman and novelist Charles Kingsley and his wife Fanny—who wrote famously passionate and sexually charged letters to one another throughout their lives—devoted the first month of their honeymoon to getting comfortable with each other before they consummated their marriage. Perhaps this approach would have helped Marian Evans (aka novelist George Eliot) and John Cross, whom she married after the death of her longtime partner George Henry Lewes. Two weeks into their honeymoon in Venice, Cross leapt from a hotel window into the Grand Canal, presumably in a suicide attempt. His brother had to be called in to assist and the honeymoon was abruptly ended. While doctors blamed a fever, speculation about their age difference—he was 40 and she was 60—was rampant, but Evans did not, according to Rose, "seem to have thought that her husband jumped out of the window to escape her."[61] While Ruskin and Cross were both distraught honeymoon husbands, the experience of extreme honeymoon anxiety was likely more common among women.

Michie argues that for women, especially, the break with their families and awakening to sexuality and devotion to conjugality could be traumatic, evoking a loss of connection rather than a sense of newfound identity. Since women were understandably reluctant to put their honeymoon trauma into writing, the intense anxieties surrounding the honeymoon were most often expressed in fiction. Michie identifies the genre of the "honeymoon gothic" as containing three main elements: the revelation of one's true character, the emergence of secrets and perhaps violence, and the use of gothic elements from ghosts to murders.[62] Wilkie Collins's novel *The Law and the Lady*, serialized in the *Graphic* from September 1874 to March 1875, provides a prime example of this form as it begins with a horrible honeymoon discovery that frames the entire plot of the novel. The first four chapters ("The Bride's Mistake," "The Bride's Thoughts," "Ramsgate Sands," and "On the Way Home") explore the ill-fated marriage and honeymoon of Eustace and Valeria Woodville. The marriage is marred from the start by a lack of wedding guests and Valeria's mistake of signing her married rather than her maiden name in the wedding register, an error that she calls an "ominous" harbinger of "evil to come." On the ride to their seaside honeymoon destination, Valeria wonders at the startling silence between them: "Had we already exhausted the narrow yet eloquent vocabulary of love? . . . I can hardly determine; I only know that a time came when under some strange influence our lips were closed toward each other."[63] Valeria soon discovers that this lack of communication is the least of her worries. While walking on the beach she accidentally meets Eustace's mother (who vigorously opposed the marriage and whom Valeria can only identify based on

a photograph hidden in her husband's dressing case). Through this encounter, Valeria realizes that Eustace has married her under an assumed
name because he was previously married. After further investigation, she
discovers that her husband was accused of murdering his first wife and
that a Scottish court arrived at the verdict of "Not Proven" due to lack of
evidence. This verdict leaves Eustace in a precarious position because it
does not clear him of the charge. Though Eustace refuses to tell Valeria
anything about his case, she sets out to prove his innocence and clear his
name, which becomes her occupation for the rest of the novel. All of the
elements of the honeymoon gothic are present in Collins's book, though
the honeymoon comprises only a few pages of the long work.

Gothic short stories that focus on the honeymoon were plentiful in popular periodical publications as well. In Chambers's "A Terrible Wedding-
Trip," a two-part story that coincided with the serial run of The Law and
the Lady, the narrator Ada falls in love at first sight with a wealthy young
man on a visit to the seaside resort of Torquay. Herbert St. Julien, the handsome, raven-haired 28-year-old proposes to her after only six weeks and
within another month marries her. Herbert leaves her for two weeks to
prepare for their wedding and trip and returns "pale and worn" with an
alarming "change in his expression—an indefinable peculiarity about his
whole aspect." Dr. Adair—whose previous marriage proposal Ada had
rejected on the grounds that she "had learned to regard the good doctor
in the light of a father"—and Ada's mother take her to the train station for
her honeymoon trip, despite their concerns about her husband's health.[64]
Once seated on the train, Herbert becomes agitated and begins talking
incoherently, asking Ada if she is his first wife or his second. Ada fears he
has lost his mind, noting that her "horrible suspicion passed into a still
more horrible certainty." As her husband's rant intensifies, she examines
the railway guide to determine how long it will be before the next stop,
discovering that she must wait at least an hour: "I could only resolve to
remain perfectly quiet and self-possessed, and to pray that Herbert might
not in the meantime become violent." However, after releasing "a strange,
unearthly laugh, ending in a wild shriek," Herbert whips out a penknife
and announces that he will cut his wife's eye out to prepare her to visit
the Cyclops![65] After humoring her husband while trying to escape from
his grasp, Ada realizes that she is on the wrong side of the train to pull
the cord that signals the train to stop. Under great distress, she faints only
to awaken and find the good doctor, who had stowed away on the train,
keeping watch over her. Herbert turns out to be a recovering lunatic who
is sent to an asylum where he dies two years later, allowing Ada to marry
her more worthy suitor, Dr. Adair. This gothic honeymoon tale sensationally dramatizes the threat of the unknown that punctuates the first experience of conjugal isolation.

George Gissing's "The Honeymoon" is much less gothic, but much
more chilling in its message about the dangers of unexpected marital

incompatibility. Published in the *English Illustrated Magazine* in 1894, the story begins with the marriage of Phyllis, a wealthy manufacturing heiress, to Charles Waldron, a financially strapped journalist whose "views appeared to harmonize with hers" in every way during their courtship. When the compliant Charles allows her to choose their honeymoon location, she settles on a small cottage in the seaside town of Sark, imagining a romantic scene of "green seas roaring upon cliffs of granite—ideal music for the commencement of a wedded life which she determined should at all hazards avoid the humdrum." Phyllis arrives at her destination with great optimism for her future with Charles, feeling that "she knew him; oh, she knew him perfectly!"[66]

Meanwhile, Phyllis has written a novel that has been accepted by a respectable firm and in a few weeks she is expecting the final proofs. Though she knows Charles is not fond of fiction, she assumes he is supportive or her writing career. Unfortunately, he takes the honeymoon as an opportunity to inform her that he will not allow her to publish her book because it just "won't do." He claims that "an escapade of this sort would shame us. I have a serious career before me, and can't afford to be made ridiculous." Horrified by this change in her husband, Phyllis angrily demands to know if he deliberately deceived her. Charles responds that he had merely "foresaw how much easier such little discussions would be after we had become man and wife." Though she "felt as though she had dreamt a voyage on the summer seas and had awoke to find herself shipwrecked," she concludes that this "cold, deceitful, tyrannous man . . . is doubtless the very man to succeed brilliantly." Phyllis bitterly but silently accedes to his wishes, giving up her budding writing career.[67] While this is an extreme case of waking up to find you do not know your spouse, it echoes the situation of many women who must have been startled to find themselves suddenly beholden to the whims of the man they married.

ADMONISHING THE FASHIONABLE WEDDING

In the Victorian period, just as today, people complained that wedding expenditures were getting out of hand. It was recommended, "so long as things are nice and sufficient, and the welcome of guests sincere, there is no occasion for extravagance. Better far is it for a young couple, who are to live on a limited income, to begin modestly and in accordance with their future condition, than, for the mere sake of display, to spend what would represent to them nearly a year's income." In a leader for the newspaper *The Echo*, Frances Power Cobbe cites the case of Mr. Martin Greener to illustrate how out of control wedding expenses had become. Mr. Greener was taken to bankruptcy court immediately following his daughter's wedding breakfast, for which he purchased lavish wedding favors, food, and gifts, including a grand piano, spending beyond his means and using the full extent of his credit. Cobbe concludes that "it is almost criminal, and entirely ridiculous, for people whose beverage through life will be beer to insist on thirty or forty guests to drink champagne and iced Burgundy." Fathers were not the only ones to overspend on weddings. In "On Some of the Impediments to Marriage," the "Bachelor" author claims that the bridegroom's expenses for a fashionable wedding had soared to a total of £500, whereas "the factory lad and lass, who have been keeping company, succeed in getting the knot fastened with the same fatal security and disastrous completeness for (I suppose) somewhere about 5s." According to *Chambers's*, the

> wedded pair often quickly repent of the needless expenditure that has taken place. However much the young wife may have been initiated into household affairs before her marriage, new knowledge comes on her surprisingly fast when she holds the domestic purse-strings herself. She begins to understand "what bills poor papa must have had to pay for that lovely breakfast, with its ices and confectionery, its choice of fruit and hot-house flowers." In her heart of hearts she feels now that she would like the money to spend very differently. . . . It is undoubtedly immoral to make marriage difficult and imprudent . . . but, this is really what ostentatious weddings often do. They give a false start to people with small incomes.[68]

Excessive honeymoon expenditures were also the frequent target of criticism. *Chambers's* uses the example of a couple in the professional class who, after an elaborate month-long wedding tour had spent almost all of the £200 they had to begin their lives and were left struggling to make ends meet for the rest of their days. The magazine favors the no-nonsense weddings among the working classes that reflect a "prudent looking forward to consequences" and an "absence of a pretentious false pride." Taking these modest practices as a model, the magazine recommends "dispensing with any wedding-tour, the newly-married pair taking up their abode at once in their appointed home. . . . And if people are afraid of being thrown on the monotony of each other's society without the preparatory distraction of new scenes, it would be well to hesitate before marrying at all. Probably a holiday trip when the pair have been married some little time and have fallen into each other's ways, is far more enjoyed than the so-called honeymoon." The criticism of outrageous wedding expenses reveals a fissure in the wedding fantasy that, by the end of the century, was at its height and already beginning to crumble as standards were becoming more and more unrealistic. Flanders argues that no one earning less than £300 a year could actually afford to follow all of the wedding recommendations made in guidebooks, and few of those could even do so.[69]

The decline of the fashionable wedding probably began as soon as it was deified in the press. In *Little Dorrit* (1857), Charles Dickens presents the contrasting weddings of two sisters, Fanny and Amy Dorrit, one terribly ostentatious and one beautifully simple. It is no question which sister and which wedding is supposed to be exemplary. Fanny Dorrit and Edmund Sparkler have a spectacular ceremony in Rome that includes the best guests "to grace the occasion. The best hotel, and all its culinary myrmidions . . . set to prepare the feast. The drafts of Mr Dorrit [to pay for the wedding] almost constituted a run on the Torlonia Bank. The British Consul hadn't seen such a marriage in the whole of his Consularity." An Italian cook, a Swiss confectioner, and a fancy carriage grace the scene. Despite all of this, the marriage is an unhappy one based on status alone. In contrast, Amy Dorrit's marriage to Arthur Clennam, just released from debtor's prison, is a modest affair much anticipated by the reader. The couple marched directly from the Marshalsea prison to "the neighboring Saint George's Church, and went up to the altar," where all of their friends were waiting. There, Amy and Arthur are married,

> with the sun shining on them through the painted figure of our Savior on the window. And they went . . . to sign the Marriage Register. And there, Mr Pancks . . . looked in at the door to see it done, with Flora gallantly supported on one arm and Maggy by the other, and background of John Chivery and father, and other turnkeys, who had run around for the moment, deserting the parent Marshalsea for its happy child. . . . They all gave place when the signing was done, and Little Dorrit and her husband walked out of the church alone. They paused for a moment on the steps of the portico, looking at the fresh perspective of the street in the autumn morning sun's rays, and then went down. Went down into a modest life of usefulness and happiness. . . . They went quietly down into the roaring streets, inseparable and blessed.[70]

Dickens, certainly, implied that a simple ceremony reflected a more virtuous and admirable marriage. Despite the myriad details provided in guidebooks for planning weddings and the elaborate examples of Society weddings featured in the press, a countervailing sentiment emerged in favor of the beauty and simplicity of modest events. The wedding and honeymoon were, in the end, ceremonies initiating couples into their new roles and families. Victorians expected love, companionship, and familial affection to be the hallmarks of marriage rather than wealth and status, even if these ideals ignored the fact that marriage was still, at its core, an economic venture. The final chapter will demonstrate the lasting power of the companionate ideal by examining how it inspired an assault on the institution of marriage itself. It will also consider how vexed such ideals were for the many who lived outside the bounds of traditional matrimony.

5

Bachelors, Old Maids, and Other Challenges to Marriage

What has become of the marrying man? Is he not becoming as extinct as the dodo? Will not future generations of geologists gloat over the infrequent discovery of his precious bones in rare rocks?

—*Temple Bar*, October 1888

In an unlegalised union the woman retains possession of all her natural rights; she is mistress of her own actions, of her body, of her property; she is able to legally defend herself against attack; all the Courts are open to protect her; she forfeits none of her rights as an Englishwoman; she keeps intact her liberty and her independence; she has no master.

—Annie Besant, *Marriage*, 1882

Diane Mapes opens *Single State of the Union* with a greeting from "Spinster Island," a location that illustrates the main premise of her book: that our supposedly advanced society still finds single women "unnatural" and "for whatever reason, single women just seem to drive people a little nuts." By hearkening back to the outmoded Victorian attitude toward old maids, Mapes drives home her point that public perceptions of women have not yet adjusted to the realities of 21st-century life. She characterizes the continuation of attitudes from the past in this way: "if you're not married, there's something *wrong* with you. You're too selfish. You're too picky. You're immature or commitment-phobic or maybe gay but you just won't admit it." Meanwhile, she observes, single women are having children without marrying, successfully climbing the corporate ladder, and purchasing their own homes. Despite—or perhaps because of—these successes,

> Conventional wisdom . . . holds that single women are nothing more than a bunch of lonely, troubled souls desperately trying to get *Hitched*—and fast. . . . Is it any wonder that our friends, families and coworkers paint our lives as so bleak and black and meaningless when practically every magazine, television show, and movie within spitting distance reaffirms the notion that a single woman's overarching need for love outweighs all other concerns (save that of her need to lose weight and create a kicky new holiday hair style)? . . . Whether single women like it or not, we're going to have our feet crammed into a pair of tiny glass slippers and sent stumbling off in the general direction of a ball.[1]

The idea of a modern women stumbling into a Victorian-style ball wearing uncomfortable shoes does not evoke nostalgia for the past, but rather a desire to shed its stodgy notions altogether. Yet, these lingering Victorian stereotypes about spinsters and old maids were actively challenged even then. Some 19th-century women and men also rejected the dominant culture's marital ideals. In fact, the Victorian era's obsession with love, marriage, and domesticity gave birth to marriage reformers, critics, and abstainers of both sexes who rejected their society's romantic notions to live unconventional love lives. Some chose or were forced to live, at least for a time, without amorous relationships, including bachelors and old maids, widows and widowers. Others formed unions that were outside of the bounds of legal marriage, including heterosexual cohabitation, romantic friendship, and same-sex partnership. Though Victorians often idealized the permanent companionate marriage, they also sought to transform it into a more egalitarian enterprise, perhaps even one based on contract law and dissolvable by mutual agreement. The critiques of Victorian attitudes Mapes employs, then, were already very familiar to the Victorians themselves.

BACHELORS

The *Temple Bar* quotation that opens this chapter epitomizes the problem posed by the seemingly ever-expanding population of bachelors who deliberately chose not to marry. If "the marrying man" had become "as extinct as the dodo," what was to become of the simultaneously increasing population of women seeking husbands?[2] By the end of the century, Victorians began to believe that marriage was falling out of favor among middle-class men who were increasingly avoiding marriage or putting it off until middle age. In 1874 Charles Ansell calculated the mean age of first marriage for men at 30.51; 16 years later W. J. Ogle determined that it had risen to 31.2 and that the number of unmarried professional men above the age of 50 was higher than that of any other class. Tosh argues that this was a result of the weakening of "the early Victorian model of domesticity" that "rested on an implied contract of master and protector in relation to dependant and subordinate." By the end of the century, "that contract no longer seemed to hold. The husband still had the undivided duty of maintaining and protecting the home, but his domestic power and prestige were wilting; the 'weaker' sex, it seemed, was discovering its own strength." Coinciding with this perceived loss of male power within the home was a shift in the conception of bachelorhood from a temporary stage in life to a character type or lifestyle.[3]

The culture of bachelorhood was spurred on by several factors that encouraged the delay of marriage. "On Some Impediments to Marriage," written "By a Bachelor" for *Fraser's Magazine* in 1867, explains why "as a rule, the young man of the period is not addicted to wedlock." The important impediments to marriage included the constricting rules of courtship that kept couples from really getting to know each other before marriage: "In the crowd of the ball-room one girl looks exactly like another—white muslin and false flowers being wonderful levelers—and even a clever girl cannot show that she has either heart or brains, when going at the rate of an express train." The public nature of standard courtship venues also contributed to the lack of opportunities for private conversations between young ladies and gentlemen. "In this country we have no pleasant habitual unambitious social intercourse like that which I have seen in some foreign cities. *There* when a man meets a girl who attracts him, he has no difficulty meeting her next day or the next, under circumstances which make it possible for him to ascertain what kind of girls she is." Furthermore, the author complains, when a man meets a marvelously decked out woman at a ball, it makes him wonder how he could ever hope to keep her in the style to which she seems accustomed. In addition to this financial consideration were the wedding expenses, which the author estimates had skyrocketed to an average of £500, "a huge slice out of the first year's income, and involving vast possibilities of debt, and of all the horrors which debt entails." This expense and relative lack of intimacy allowed to the middle and upper classes contrasted greatly with the "factory lad and lass, who have been keeping company" more closely and who could "succeed in getting the knot fastened" for a very small sum. However, the "Bachelor" acknowledges a recent Annual Report of the Registrar-General, indicating that "married men don't die as unmarried men do. Death knocks over bachelors like ninepins. . . . A wife may be an encumbrance in many ways, but if you wish to reach old age, she is worth any number of Parr's Life Pills." Regardless of this statistic in favor of marriage, the writer maintains that his £800 a year keeps him "in luxury as a bachelor" paying for his club, the opera, vacations, fancy dinners, and many bottles of claret. Marriage, he concludes, may be good for some men, but for others it is a permanent exile from a bachelor's "easy paradise."[4]

Such negative attitudes toward marriage were considered extremely selfish and career bachelors were often characterized as men with "the wish for luxury, the desire to evade responsibility, stinginess, love of comfort, the longing for glory." Bachelors were assumed to be channeling their money and their energies (sexual and otherwise) in the wrong—and implicitly immoral—direction. Some bachelors were assumed to be uninterested in women and, potentially, homosexual; others were considered to be rakes.[5] Plentifully available prostitutes in England and native women in the colonies provided an easy sexual outlet for single men, while more and more professions were the preserve of bachelors, particularly the armed services and the administration of colonial affairs. John Tosh claims that the "empire was run by bachelors; in the public mind it represented devotion to duty or profit (and sometimes pleasure) undistracted by feminine ties." Furthermore, Tosh observes that boarding school life, attendance at men's clubs with smoking rooms, billiard rooms, and dining facilities, and the increasing importance of organized sports may have contributed to making the Victorian upper-middle-class man "permanently disqualified from family life."[6]

On the other hand, Katherine Snyder argues that bachelorhood was more than merely an antidomestic state. Indeed, she points out that while bachelors "were often thought to be the antithesis of domesticity . . . they were also sometimes seen as its epitome." Their clubs and communal living spaces could be interpreted as alternative forms of domesticity right down to their "leather armchairs, blazing hearths, great windows, libraries full of books, morning papers, good food, and good wine." Some bachelors even argued that men's clubs prepared them for marriage rather than diverting them from it. Wilkie Collins takes this stance in his *Household Words* article "Bold Words by a Bachelor." Here Collins laments the separation from the community of men that marriage entails and urges women to allow their husbands to incorporate meaningful friendships into the home circle. He complains that "many a woman has snapped asunder all the finer ligaments which once connected her husband and his friend; and has thought it enough if she left the two still attached by the courser ties that are at the common disposal of all the world. Many a woman—delicate, affectionate, and kind within her own narrow limits— has committed that heavy social offense, and has never felt afterwards a single pang of pity or remorse." He declares the "general idea of the scope and purpose of the Institution of Marriage" to be a "miserably narrow one" that replaces true male friendships with domestic affection. Collins urges a broader view of marriage that integrates male friends into the fabric of domesticity so that "the light of its beauty" is not "shut up within the four walls which enclose the parents and the family, but must flow out into the world, and shine upon the childless and the solitary, because it has warmth enough . . . and because it may make them . . . happy too."[7] Collins's articulation of a new ideal of domesticity that welcomes bachelors into its fold is echoed by another bachelor's vision of communal family identity.

The author of "Why Men Do Not Marry" argues that home to him is only "a showy, ramshackle building; with water-pipes that burst; with kitchen boilers that leak; . . . with endless petty anxieties and constant worry." In contrast to this bleak view of domesticity, he imagines an alternative multi-family living arrangement patterned on college dormitories and men's clubs. He suggests a cooperative home in which each family has its own living space but comes together in common areas for meals and recreation. Under this plan, mothers would have other mothers with whom to consult, children would have a variety of playmates, dances could be held for those of courting age, a wide variety of reading material could be stocked for all, and a chef could be employed to cook quality meals for everyone. Such an arrangement, he claims, would provide "vastly more comfort and vastly less cost" than the traditional, isolated married life.[8] Whether a bachelor wanted to live in isolation from traditional domestic arrangements or to transform them altogether, his very existence was often seen as an affront to marriage.

Some bachelors, however, lamented the lack of traditional domestic ties and pined for female companionship—or at least household expertise. The poem "The Haunted Bachelor," published in the *Welcome Guest* in 1860, humorously explores the haunting of a lonely man who while sitting at his "cheerless chimney corner, / All grimy with years and smoke," sees "a tempting female vision." This enchanted creature impresses him with her domestic charms—which include making his breakfast, mending his shoes, and cleaning his messy abode (Figure 5.1). The bachelor yearns for this ideal woman who "will win me away from this gloomy life, / Away from this reckless self. / I will follow where she beckons—/ Through fire, o'er land or sea; / For never was fairy tempter / Like the spirit that beckons me!" A postscript attached to the poem brings the mysterious domestic goddess to life and proposes a practical solution to the bachelor's plight:

When her features—I mean the fairy's—
I calmly call to mind,
They resemble my cousin Mary's,
Who to me was always kind.
When a man can't grasp the first good
The next he had best seize on.
(Mem. Notice to quit at chambers,
And to call upon Uncle John).[9]

Conveniently, the haunted bachelor determines that all he needs to do to transform his dreary life is call on his uncle John so that he can propose to his devoted cousin.

chill, by way of improving the ventilation. As for the window, she never dreams of opening that. While we are writing this article, a lady sitting by informs us that, in a time incidental to wedded life, her nurse diligently fanned the room every morning by swinging the door at a brisk rate for some minutes together. She would, like a faithful nurse as she was, have died at her post sooner than open the window—except to throw something out of it.

The ordinary hygiene of houses; the management of the sick room down to the least detail; the great question, involving the many little questions, of diet; the necessity of observation in the nurse; the danger to that observation, arising from too tranquil a repose on "averages," which tell us that so many per cent. will die, but cannot instruct us how to perceive *which* of the hundred they are likely to be: all these things are soundly discussed in a reverential, earnest, not seldom humorous spirit. We suppose it is hardly necessary to explain that the "humour" of Miss Nightingale is something accordant with the highest, fullest, and deepest meaning ever given to that word.

An enormous error, indeed, would it be to put a vulgar and degenerate interpretation on the phrase in its application to these golden pages. Grave, solemn, tender, is the book throughout; and when we smile with the authoress, we love and honour her most.

You are a bad world, World. You have exalted knaves to the high seats, and have cast down the humble and meek. You have pitilessly entreated the poor and lowly—the true, the wise, the gentle, and the kind. You have sworn that X and Y are tall fellows of their hands, and will not be drunk, when you know that they are *no* tall fellows of their hands, and that they *will* be drunk. Yet you have sworn it. You have flattered and fêted the Pharisee, and have let the Samaritan want, full sore. Remember that! You have filled the rich with good things and the hungry you have sent empty away. You are a bad world, World; but God is merciful. Else would He never send to bless and comfort us such messengers of peace, and love, and trust, and healing tenderness, and mild, firm, radiant hope, as this crown of womanhood, FLORENCE NIGHTINGALE. T.

THE HAUNTED BACHELOR.

I SIT in a haunted chamber
  ('Tis one of a set of three),
In an old and gloomy Temple,
  Facing a huge plane-tree.
A seedy old tree, and dismal,
  Hung over with worsted balls,
That bob at my darkened window,
  Like tufts upon funeral palls.

'Tis a black look out on all sides,
  Wherever the gaze is met;
The fountain down in the courtyard
  Spirts with a ghostlike jet.
There are chimney-sweeping sparrows,
  With tails not worth their salt,
The very black wine I am drinking
  Was fetched from a neighb'ring vault!

Figure 5.1. "The Haunted Bachelor." *The Welcome Guest* 5.1 (1860): 431. Harry Ransom Humanities Research Center, University of Texas at Austin.

This bachelor, at least, is called away from his solitary life by the promise of a wife to fulfill his domestic needs, confirming Cobbe's opinion in "Celibacy *v.* Marriage" that "if a woman have but strength to make up her mind to a single life, she is enabled by nature to be far more independently happy therein than a man in the same position. A man, be he rich or poor, who returns at night to a home adorned by no woman's presence and domestic cares, is at best dreary and uncomfortable. But a woman makes her home for herself, surrounds herself with an atmosphere of taste and the little details of housewifely comforts." Regardless of Cobbe's confident pronouncements on behalf of the autonomy of single women, those who failed to marry by a certain age were often the target of scorn in a way that bachelors were not. As Cobbe notes, the press frequently commented on women's celibacy to "deplore it, abuse it, propose amazing remedies for it," while "no one scolds [bachelors] very seriously." Instead, "all the alarm, compassion, reprobation . . . are reserved for the poor old maids."[10] Indeed, old maids were often reviled figures, or at least pitiful ones, while bachelors seemed to have many legitimate excuses for refusing to marry.

SPINSTERS AND OLD MAIDS

Who was a spinster and when might she become an old maid? While these two terms were sometimes used interchangeably, a fine distinction was made between them. Technically, a spinster was a woman young enough to still expect to find a husband and an old maid was a woman presumed to be beyond marriageable age. While the ages were not set in stone, spinsters were likely to be under, and old maids to be over, 30. According to statistics reported in 1840, 52 percent of all married women were wed between the ages of 20 and 25, with 18 percent marrying between 25 and 30, and a mere 6.5 percent marrying between 30 and 35. Furthermore, the 1851 census revealed that as many as 30 percent of women between the ages of 20 and 40 were unmarried, with a surplus of half a million women over the population of men.[11] The realization that not all women would be able to find suitable husbands was startling to those who believed marriage was the only acceptable role for a middle-class woman. Many cultural commentators accordingly tried to come up with solutions to solve the problem.

W. R. Greg famously suggested that these "surplus women" be shipped to the colonies—where there was a corresponding surplus of men—to find husbands. In his essay "Why are Women Redundant?" Greg declares that the "enormous and increasing number of single women in the nation" is "quite disproportionate and quite abnormal" as well as "indicative of an unwholesome social state." His goal was to reduce the number of "redundant women" by shipping 500,000 of them to the United States and Australia where they would, presumably, be more likely to find husbands. He exempted working-class women from this plan since they were needed at home as domestic servants. According to Greg, these women were able to "fulfill both essentials of woman's being; *they are supported by, and they minister to men.* We could not possibly do without them." Under his plan, women who departed could perform their duty to society while those who stayed would "rise in value" and "be more sought" and "better rewarded" by men.[12] Greg's purely economic view of the matter ignored the fact that, as Rita Kranidis argues, emigration "could not prove an adequate solution, since the majority of spinsters were undesirable as colonial exports due to their age." Of course, these very women were also less desirable as wives.

Regardless of the flaws in Greg's reasoning, organizations such as the Female Middle Class Emigration Society and the British Ladies' Emigration Society offered loans and subsidies to those who chose to emigrate while also providing training, traveling companions, and security in ports and on arrival at their final destination. Between 1860 and 1900, about 90,000 single women emigrated to Australia with such organizational assistance, sometimes supplemented by packages including land and fare subsidies from colonial governments. Most of these women, however, went into domestic service and were therefore not the class of women to whom many of these programs were publicly marketed. Only about 300 emigrants were middle-class women who became governesses and perhaps later married.[13]

Single women who remained in England were encouraged to keep husband hunting, but to meanwhile make themselves useful. *The English Maiden* called on those "who are deprived of the domestic hearth" to recognize that "humanity has claims on you, to which you will do well to listen." While *The English Maiden* speaks of "the single state" as "one not to be enjoyed, but endured" by serving others through charitable works, single women could potentially bring honor to the "generally . . . despicable" term *old maid* by fruitfully employing themselves "amid scenes of sickness and affliction" or in professions such as teaching or governessing. Though some worried that resigning themselves to such a life might end their marriage prospects forever, the *Guide for Governesses* sought to encourage ladies not to give up hope of marriage:

> As a rule, governesses make excellent wives; they don't marry with the romantic ideas of love and bliss that girls who have never left home do. They have had opportunities of seeing in other families how much is required from a wife and mother. . . . Therefore a governess, whilst she should by no means enter the profession as some do, with the idea of entering a higher society than she would meet with at home, and making a good match, need not alarm herself with the idea of her being a governess preventing her making one in her own sphere.[14]

Single women had several acceptable ways to contribute to society, but most commentators felt that marriage should still be their ultimate goal and insisted that their activities prepare them for the eventuality of becoming good wives.

In "What Shall We Do with Our Old Maids?" Cobbe took a different approach from the emigration advocates and the wait and hope adherents. She argued that society at large should alter its expectations for women in response to a new reality: "The old assumption that marriage was the sole destiny of woman, and that it was the business of her husband to afford her support, is brought up short by the statement that one woman in four is certain not to marry, and that three millions of women earn their own living at this moment in England." She concludes that two options are possible. Either "we must frankly accept this new state of things, and educate women and modify trade in accordance therewith" or "we must set ourselves vigorously to stop the current which is leading men and women away from the natural order of Providence. We must do nothing whatever to render celibacy easy or attractive; and we must make the utmost efforts to promote marriage by emigration of women to the colonies, and all other means in our power." Cobbe advocates the first option more vigorously, though she does not overtly reject marriage as a goal. Instead, she maintains that "it is desirable that women should have other aims, pursuits, and interests in life beside matrimony, and that by possessing them they are guaranteed against being driven into unloving marriages, and rendered more fitting for loving ones; while their single life, whether in maidenhood or widowhood, is made useful and happy."[15] For Cobbe, the occupations of a single woman should be fulfilling in themselves and should not simply bide time or be aimed at increasing one's marketability as a wife.

Of course, there were women who remained unmarried by choice, especially toward the end of the century. Ruth Freeman and Patricia Klaus argue that between 1870 and 1920 a change in attitude toward spinsters was evident. "No longer reclusive, useless, and embittered, the new spinster led an outgoing, productive life. She traveled with friends and enjoyed herself. As a result of this change—an increase in self-confidence and an awareness of the advantages of spinsterhood and the disadvantages of married life—marriage came to be regarded as an option rather than an absolute necessity for women." Women increasingly had access to education, opportunities for mobility (trains, bicycles), and clubs that allowed a rich intellectual and social life.[16] White-collar professions for women also slowly expanded to include typewriting, secretarial work, and telegraphy, thus providing unmarried women with more varied means of self-support.

As Maud Wheeler argues in *Whom to Marry*, "this age recognizes the truth that woman's life and aims are not necessarily limited to any one sphere, that her life may be well and nobly spent, even though the crown of wifehood and motherhood are denied her, and the stigma that formerly attached itself to 'old maidenhood' is being rapidly effaced. The whole tendency of the age is for the development of women's faculties and possibilities." By 1909 Myrtle Reed could point out in *The Spinster Book* that married women should not pity unmarried women because unmarried woman might actually pity *them*: "When nearly all the married friends a spinster has have come to her with the same story, the variations being individual and of slight moment, she begins to have serious doubts of matrimony as a satisfactory career. . . . The chains of love may be sweet bondage, but freedom is hardly less dear. The spinster, like the wind, may go where she listeth, and there is no one to say her nay." An unmarried woman, Reed says, "is not asked what she did with the nickel which was given her the day before yesterday. . . . She is not subjected to the humiliation of asking a man for money to pay for his own food, his own service, and even his own laundry bill." An old maid depicted in the *London Reader* in 1880 confirms this view, stating that she has had opportunities to marry and passed them up deliberately:

> I ask myself with which one of the beautiful girls that I have seen take the marriage vow would I exchange today? Not one. Some are living apart from their husbands; some are divorced; some are wives of drunken men; some are hanging on the ragged edge of society, endeavoring to keep up appearances; some are toiling to support and educate their children. . . . A few there are who are loved and honoured wives, mothers with happy homes; but, alas, only a very few.[17]

Despite such progressive views, negative attitudes toward single women persisted.

Old maid stories that grappled with the challenge single women presented to societal ideals about marriage popped up everywhere, rivaling honeymoon stories for popularity in the periodical press. Elizabeth Gaskell's *Cranford* is perhaps the most famous, with its community of silly old maids. Gaskell describes them as "Amazons," a sly recognition of how out of proportion the fear of surplus women had become. The Amazons of Cranford are perhaps warriors for their own strict codes of conduct, the violation of which gives rise to many comic situations. In Cranford, the arrival of a married couple inevitably results in the disappearance of the gentleman who "is either fairly frightened to death by being the only man in the Cranford evening parties, or he is accounted for by being with his regiment, his ship, or closely engaged in business all the week in the great neighboring commercial town of Drumble. . . . Whatever does become of the gentlemen, they are not in Cranford."[18] The old maids may scare away the gentlemen, but they are remarkably domesticated and live by the rules of elegant economy that allow them to maintain their shabby genteel lifestyles. These single women are certainly less threatening than quaint and amiable. Their series of adventures and mishaps reveal that despite their unconventional community, single women can live productively alone if they have a network of mutual support.

George Gissing's *The Odd Women* is another famous account of a community of single women, which has a much more serious tone. Writing in the 1890s rather than the 1850s, Gissing addresses a world that he sees slipping into a kind of sexual anarchy marked by the questioning of both gender roles and the foundations of modern marriage.[19] Rhoda Nunn and Mary Barfoot, two of the "Odd Women" of the title, seek to educate women for a life independent of men, preparing them for the slate of new clerical jobs for women. Against this backdrop we see the dreadful consequences of old maidenhood for the sisters Alice and Virginia Madden and the disastrous marriage of their younger sibling Monica, who seeks to escape their lonely, impoverished fate. But the climax of the novel focuses on Rhoda's seduction by the irresponsible and self-centered Everard Barfoot, Mary's cousin. Rhoda agrees to take a private trip to the seashore with Everard during which he proposes to her. Both Rhoda and Everard are ambivalent about marriage but equally uncertain about the status of a free union. Though they claim to support alternative forms of marriage, their power struggle over who shall define their union and whether or not they can trust each other outside of the bonds of legal marriage ultimately results in the collapse of the relationship. In the end, Rhoda is disappointed in love, but it is clear she has dodged a bullet. Instead of marrying or cohabiting, she becomes more passionately devoted to the feminist cause of helping other women live independently.

The majority of old maid tales published in the popular press at the end of the century, however, were not focused on how unmarried women could create their own social networks or cultivate alternative lifestyles. They were often either tragic tales of lost love or uplifting narratives about happy late-life matches; indeed, marriage was preserved as the key to a woman's happiness. Two stories published in the *Argosy* in the 1890s form a matching set of doom and gloom scenarios for old maids. In Katherine Carr's "Miss Anne: A Sketch," published in 1893, the lead character has spent her entire adult life awaiting the return of her first love, John, from Australia where he has been seeking his fortune to provide a good home for her. On his return, he is disappointed with what he sees: "the miniature of a girl with round pink cheeks and shining eyes, in the very prime of her beauty and freshness" had become "a little faded woman with straight, neatly-brushed hair, whose sunken eyes told of ill health and perpetual dullness of life . . . girlhood dead; in its stead, a washed out womanhood." When she recognizes how he now sees her, Anne decides to "be brave and save him from herself" by continuing her now familiar life as a ghost of her former self, "a forlorn old maid staring into the dying embers."[20] This depressing ending is outdone by Mark Holland's 1896 story "Miss Penrose." Here, we are presented with the heart-wrenching tale of a 30-year-old spinster who falls in love with a man who is in love—or at least pursuing a marriage—with a younger, wealthier woman. When Miss Penrose braves a raging storm to meet her beloved on his return from a boating trip, she is shocked to see him with his arm and his coat around the shoulders of a young lady visitor from London. Though Miss Penrose calls out to him, he passes by without noticing her. As she desperately looks on, she is torn by the winds from the pier and thrown to her death in the thrashing sea below. These tales certainly paint a discouraging picture of the single woman's chances for happiness if happiness is defined solely by marriage.

Ellen Thorneycroft Fowler's "Miss Latimer's Lover," published a few years later in the same magazine, provides a kind of antidote to the previous old maid tales. Anne Latimer, a governess by trade,

> was an old maid according to the measure of that most merciless of critics, the young girl; she was tired and timid and faded, and ought to have found ample satisfaction for her spinster soul in clothing clubs, and sewing parties, and such-like old-maidenly dissipations; but alas! She did not. Though she was well on her way down the shady slope of forty, she was actually guilty of the anachronism of falling in love—and for the first time too in her grey uneventful life.[21]

The object of her affections is Harry Scott, the church organist. Though most find Harry "to be a disagreeable, fault-finding, cynical recluse" Anne sees in him something special. When it is discovered that Sir Henry Denham, who disappeared and was presumed murdered 20 years ago, was last seen in her town right about the same time that Harry arrived there, Anne fears that the object of her affections has become a prime murder suspect. Now that Denham is next in line for an inheritance, the case has been reopened and Anne offers Harry her entire life savings of £300 to aid his escape from the authorities. Harry admits that he "destroyed" Sir Henry Denham but asks her to run away with him to hear his story, which he insists will justify his actions. Anne hesitates at first but soon decides to follow her heart. After they have been officially married, Harry reveals that he is indeed Sir Henry Denham and explains that she is now "her ladyship." Despite Harry's deliberate escape from his old life to live simply and anonymously, he and his new wife are now wealthy heirs to his family's fortune. Anne's faith in him has reaped great rewards and an old maid finally triumphs within the pages of the *Argosy*.

Millie Greene's "A Cycling Courtship" is another hopeful view of the possibility of marrying as an old maid. Published in *Belgravia*, a rival magazine to the *Argosy*, this story follows Miss Janet Craven's obsession with cycling. Janet takes up the activity despite her advanced age (she is 40) and hefty size (she starts cycling because her doctor orders her to lose weight). She and Roy Parker, her cycling instructor—a "tall, fair, and very slim young man" half her age, strike up a friendly relationship while biking around town. As Janet falls "more and more in love with her machine" and with "the joy of motion, and her greater thinness, combined with the feeling of triumph in her own strength," she grows happier and happier with Roy. Despite her improving cycling skills, she keeps paying him to help her. They spend every day together going on picnics and pleasant rides until Janet is advised to leave town to escape the scandalous gossip that has spread about her new relationship. When Janet finally succumbs to the pressure to leave, Roy realizes he is madly in love with her and decides he must earn a better living so that he can marry her. He invents a brake lock for bicycles that provides him with an adequate income and Janet accepts his proposal "in spite of the difference in the ages." The couple "lived the ideal life of true comrades, in absolute sympathy on all important matters" and Janet "had to thank her cycle craze for the possession of the most devoted of husbands, and the truest friends."[22] Whatever progress single women made in the Victorian period—increasingly educated, entering professions, and advancing their own rights—the popular culture continued to fit them into the framework of marriage as the only possible happy ending. As Diane Mapes argues, not much has changed today.

WIDOWS AND WIDOWERS

Along with apprehensions about how bachelors and old maids impacted marital ideals, there was also a great deal of anxiety about what affect the remarriage of widows and widowers might have on the marriage market. These worries were perhaps valid since in 1850 19 percent of all marriages would end within 10 years due to the death of a spouse (usually the husband) and 47 percent would end this way within 25 years. Many felt that if marriage was supposed to be a sacred bond based on true love, then it should last beyond the grave. The argument for preserving a union after the death of a spouse was often linked to the religious idea that spouses would reunite in the afterlife. This belief made remarriage highly suspect if not unthinkable. Indeed, some equated remarriage with adultery. As *Hints on Husband-Catching* declared in 1846,

> A second marriage—on whichever side—is that worst of all sacrileges, a sacrilege of the heart; the being you have loved is no more; never shall that voice be heard again which once gladdened your heart with its melody; never more shall that hand which once pressed yours in affection, repose in your tender grasp; never shall those worshipped eyes meet yours again with a glance of ineffable sympathy. . . . We may be told of a happier meeting in realms above; we may be bid to look upon the bliss which has passed as a mere mortal dream, to be realized in ten thousandfold bliss during an eternity in heaven; but these consolations in the first agony of grief fall coldly upon the ear. . . . Cold and heartless, then, must that man—or woman—be, who throws off with the mourning the memory of the mourned, and fills that vacant seat with the form of a stranger.

Pat Jalland notes that this idea was particularly potent for women for whom "widowhood was a final destiny, an involuntary commitment to a form of social exile." The death of a spouse left women without their powerful positions as wives, without their husbands' incomes, and often without hope of regaining their status.[23] The passage of the 1857 Divorce Act helped curb such sentiments by allowing the dissolution of marital bonds in life and thus weakening the argument against such dissolution after death.

The reality was that both widowers and widows sometimes did remarry, often for purely practical considerations like providing for their children or securing economic stability. The *London Reader* noted in 1879 that men, in particular, were prone to remarrying: "Having once tasted the sweets of married life men cannot, it seems, remain single. It appears that of 1,000 single men of 25 to 35 years of age, 110 or 112 marry each year. On the other hand, the corresponding number for widowers is 356, or three times as many." Widows, on the other hand, had more difficulty or more reservations about remarrying. The threat of widows on the marriage market, however, was seen as greater than that of widowers. In her study of widows, Cynthia Curran points out that by the 19th century widows had actually become much less of a threat than they had been centuries earlier. While remarriage rates were as high as 30 percent in previous centuries, by the Victorian era widows were only remarrying at an average rate of 11–12 percent. Curran argues that this was most likely because Victorian widows "no longer had a business inventory or a property concern to offer an eligible suitor, and they were further handicapped in the marriage market by the existence of younger, childless, single females, as well as the much-lamented surplus of women." Jalland notes that "marriage prospects for spinsters depended on their wealth, youth, and beauty, but these assets were even more significant for widows."[24] An 1842 *Punch* Cartoon illustrates how important wealth could be when beauty and youth had faded (Figure 5.2). "Illustrations of Humbug.—No. 1" pokes fun at a man seeking to marry a rich (and unattractive) widow. The gold digger cynically courts the widow while sitting underneath a portrait of her departed husband, declaring that their age difference is meaningless in the face of true love.

In contrast to widows, the remarriage rate among widowers remained as high as 30 percent. There were fewer stigmas associated with men's remarriage, especially if they had children to care for. *Hints on Husband-Catching* recommends that its audience of spinsters "look upon [widowers] as licensed game" in the marriage hunt. The widow, on the other hand, should be seen as a formidable foe; "she has been once, at least, in her life, successful in her pursuit, and the experience she has gained is likely to prove far more valuable to her, in her pursuit of a second, third, or fourth victim, as the case may be, than any instructions of mine." Though few of them actually remarried, young spinsters were advised to "be on

PUNCH'S PENCILLINGS.—N°· LIV.

ILLUSTRATIONS OF HUMBUG.—N°· I.

"'Tis true there is a slight difference in our ages, but with hearts that love, such considerations become frivolous. The world ! Pshaw !
Did you but love as I do, you would care but little for its opinion. Oh ! say, beautiful being, will you be mine ? "

Vol. III.—1842.

Figure 5.2. "Illustrations of Humbug.—No. 1." *Punch* (July–December 1842): 213. Used by permission of the University of Missouri–Kansas City Libraries, Dr. Kenneth J. LaBudde Department of Special Collections.

their guard" against the "machinations" of widows. In *The Spinster Book*, Myrtle Reed mischievously states that "next to burglars, mice, and green worms, every normal girl fears a widow. Courtships have been upset and expected proposals have vanished into thin air, simply because a widow has come into the game. There is only one thing to do in such a case; retreat gracefully, and leave the field to her." Reed gets to the heart of why widows were seen as a threat to husband-seeking maidens: "A widow has all the freedom of a girl, combined with the liberty of a married woman.

She has the secure social position of a matron without the drawback of a husband. She is nearer absolute independence than other women are ever known to be."[25] Not only could she anticipate what men wanted but she knew how to provide it.

Press reports on marriage statistics reinforced the notion of widows as predators. For example, in September 1850, the *London Journal* claimed that widowers were more likely to marry older women than were bachelors but that widows preferred men younger than themselves. However, it reassuringly argued that widows more frequently remarried widowers than bachelors. Still, the perception was that widows and widowers each hunted younger innocents. As Reed puts it, "if widowers and widows would only mate with each other, instead of trespassing upon the hunting grounds of the unmarried! It is an exceptional case in which the bereaved are not mutually wary. They seem to prefer the unfair advantage gained by having all the experience on one side."[26]

Widowers did, however, get some share of the criticism for their higher propensity to remarry. Reed warns girls against being trapped into a marriage in which one is forced "to take the crumbs another woman has left, especially if a goodly portion of the man's heart is suspected to lie in the grave." The specter of marrying a man who only needs someone to take care of the house and children is one that haunts Reed who claims that no woman "in her wildest moments, ever dreams of marrying a widower with three or four children, yet, when she is well on in her thirties, with her heart still unsatisfied, she often does that very thing, and happily at that." Reed imagines a newlywed bride confronted by the portrait of the woman she's replaced, the deceased woman's eyes looking down upon her in "stern judgment." " 'You may die,' those pictured lips seem to say, 'and some other will take your place, as you have taken mine.' " In darker days, "when the tactlessness, bad temper, or general mulishness of man wrings unwilling tears" from his new wife's eyes, the portrait will be relentless in its response: " 'You should not have married him,' the picture seems to say, or; 'He treated me the same way, and I died.' "[27] The scenes Reed conjures depicting what life might be like married to a widower were certainly not encouraging to young spinsters, or even to those verging on old maidenhood.

Although it was natural for a widower with family responsibilities to turn to his former wife's single sister to help care for his children and himself, this was illegal for much of the century. Some considered such unions immoral since on marriage a husband and wife became one flesh, thereby making the remarriage to a sister-in-law a form of incest. There was significant religious opposition to such unions based on the laws of affinity and, after 1835, Lord Lyndhurst's Act prohibited marriage with a deceased wife's sister altogether. Prior to this outright prohibition, such marriages could be granted but they were vulnerable to challenge under the law. However, these partnerships kept families intact and were often the most comforting and least disruptive options for remarriage. Couples continued to form these unions regardless of the law, often citing the wishes of the deceased wife herself. These couples typically blamed the church or the state for their problems and saw themselves as making the morally right choice. Even some clergymen and Dissenting ministers (some of whom had married their deceased wife's sisters) advocated the repeal of the law. Mary Jean Corbett points out that "while advocates of the ban feared that lifting it would contaminate all sibling bonds by admitting the possibility of adulterous incest . . . into the Victorian home," advocates of repeal "denied the charge of incest and disputed the grounds on which it was based." Opponents of the law saw the incest charge as absurd because "'one flesh' was only a metaphor" and because marriage was, increasingly "understood as a contract between individuals rather than as a union of families."[28] The changing status of marriage thus contributed to the ultimate demise of this unpopular law just as it had to many elements of Lord Hardwicke's Marriage Act, though in both cases it was a long road to repeal.

In January 1847 the *London Journal* reprinted an article from the *Church of England Journal* calling for the repeal of the law based on the following:

1. Marrying one's deceased wife's sister is not explicitly forbidden in scripture.
2. Marrying one's deceased wife's sister is not a relationship based on blood relation and therefore poses no physical ground for prohibition.
3. Marrying one's deceased wife's sister would not encourage the seduction of the wife's sister prior to her death due to the stringent moral and social consequences of adultery.
4. The deceased wife's sister is the fittest person to take charge of the motherless children.
5. "Because marriage in all these cases is permitted . . . in almost every other Protestant, as well as Roman Catholic, country, without producing any ill effects."

In 1850 *Fraser's Magazine* praised the populace for systematically disregarding the law, since obeying it would do more harm than good: "many a man may say,—'I would gladly marry my sister-in-law, and I know she would consent, if the law allowed it; but as it does not, I must marry somebody else': and so the law is the cause of her being turned out of the house instead of keeping her in it." The idea that people were simply defying the law was bolstered in the 1848 *Report of the Royal Commission*, which claimed that 1,384 illegal marriages in five districts had been contracted during the three-month period of the study and 90 percent of those were to deceased wife's sisters. There was a significant continuation of the practice despite the law. According to Parker, it took "a plethora of pamphlets, countless petitions to Parliament, 46 sessions of debate, 18 successful second readings in the House of Commons, one Royal Commission report, annual leaders in *The Times*, and the formation of two pressure groups" before the act was finally repealed in 1907.[29]

IRREGULAR UNIONS

Throughout the 19th century, a wide variety of irregular unions were formed in place of traditional marriages. Ginger Frost argues, "the Victorian attitude to unmarried cohabitation was not one of blanket condemnation. Instead, it was complex and contingent on many factors." Indeed, in some cases, those involved in irregular unions may well have been more widely accepted than those who remained lifelong bachelors or old maids. Martha Vicinus and others have carefully documented many well-known instances of female same-sex couples involved in intense, sometimes romantic, friendships or who even lived together as if married. Jane Welsh Carlye and Geraldine Jewsbury, Frances Power Cobbe and Mary Lloyd, Sophia Jex-Blake and Octavia Hill are a few examples among the vast range of intense female friendships and partnerships. Vicinus argues that "both women and men idealized their same-sex friendships, making them simultaneously more and less important" than heterosexual unions. Women's same-sex relationships were sometimes considered superior to heterosexual relationships if interpreted as existing on a higher, more spiritual plane. On the other hand, they could also be downplayed as a passing phase or as mere practice for more permanent heterosexual unions. One thing is certain, such relationships were not always grounds for exclusion from society. Many same-sex couples, including those who lived together in female marriages, were integrated into mainstream society. Sharon Marcus has argued that eroticized female friendships "peaceably coexisted with heterosexual marriages and moreover, helped to promote them." In fact, she claims that "female marriage, gender mobility, and women's erotic fantasies about women" were not necessarily disruptive to the traditional ideals of marriage, but rather were central to the social construction of those institutions in part because women's relationships with other women—regardless of their sexual nature—were seen as a sort of training ground for a woman's emotional and sensual connection to her future or present husband.[30] Indeed, in an age when adultery was so harshly condemned, the freedom of same-sex romances may have been especially liberating for those who were already married.

Male same-sex relationships, on the other hand, were seen as more disruptive of marital felicity. As Sean Brady claims, marrying and providing for one's family largely defined masculinity. While manliness also required "freedom of movement between home [and] work, and the public association with men," the idea that "emotional, sexual, and domestic alternatives could exist outside the family" was a threat to the foundations of society. Male friendships could be intensely homoerotic and still acceptable, particularly within the contexts of the armed forces, boys' schools, men's clubs, and sporting communities where close male relationships were treated as the norm. However, with the passage of the 1885 Criminal Law Act, sexual relations of any kind between men were criminalized and attention to such relationships intensified. If men were publicly accused and subsequently convicted of having sexual relationships with other men (characterized as "Gross Indecency" in Labouchere's Amendment to the 1885 Act), they were punished under the law, but also "ostracized, vilified and cast as highly unusual aberrations, beyond the acceptable pale of masculinity."[31] Such was the case with Oscar Wilde who was sentenced to two years of hard labor in 1895 for committing "Gross Indecency" with Lord Alfred "Bosie" Douglas. While the possibilities for alternative unions were generally expanding by the end of the century, male homosexual relationships were one case in which the line was being drawn more strictly. The consequences of being accused or convicted could be devastating, as they were for Wilde who never reignited his writing career and died soon after his release from prison.

Unmarried heterosexual relationships were also common throughout the century, especially among the working classes. Common-law marriages (which were not officially recognized by the law at all) were especially popular in industrializing towns and areas that attracted itinerant workers, such as railway navies or miners. Frontier areas with mobile populations also gravitated toward irregular unions because of the flexibility that such relationships afforded. Among the working classes, there was less shame associated with living together unmarried. Indeed, some working-class women may have entered into free unions hoping to leverage themselves into more permanent bonds later. However, others preferred not to marry to preserve their freedom or their wages. Since a marriage license could cost up to a week's pay for the poorer artisan classes, some couples cohabited without marrying to avoid paying the fees. Others objected to the established church and preferred to avoid the publicity involved with the required reading of the banns.[32]

Perhaps the most common reason for cohabiting without legally marrying was that at least one member of the pair had previously been married and was unable to obtain a divorce. Most of these couples would likely have married if the law had not prevented them. According to Gillis, some rural communities even maintained the custom of wife sale. This was not, technically speaking, a sale, but rather a ritual that sanctioned a kind of informal divorce and remarriage. Typically, the wife was passed along to a man with whom she was already having an affair. Presumably, the wife had agreed to the sale, which sanctioned her new relationship, though there may have been cases where this ritual was intended to humiliate or punish her. However, if the wife did not consent, the sale was usually considered void as it "constituted a just and legal termination of mutual obligations . . . in the popular consciousness." Gillis explains that while there was often a public spectacle of bidding, the end result was prearranged and that this, along with the wife's removal of her wedding ring and in some cases her signature on an informal separation agreement, "was meant to symbolize the transference of the husband's responsibility" to the new man.[33] The ritual of wife sale, most famously depicted in Thomas Hardy's *The Mayor of Casterbridge* (1886), declined radically throughout the 1860s and 1870s and had become obsolete by the end of the century.

Probert contends that there were not as many people living outside the bounds of formal marriage as historians like Gillis imagine. She points out that marriage was for many women an important guarantee of financial support and protection for themselves and their children. Furthermore, she maintains that those who sought privacy and wanted to avoid the publication of the banns could easily evade the standards set forth in the 1753 Marriage Act. Once a wedding was performed, for example, it "could not be invalidated on the ground that the parties had not resided in the place where the banns were published or the marriage solemnized." Likewise, the marriage of an underage couple could not be invalidated on the grounds of lack of parental consent unless the parent had objected at the time of the reading of the banns or the exchange of vows. As a result, a couple could easily escape scrutiny by marrying in a distant parish. Indeed, Probert notes that "the law reports contain a number of examples of evasive practices of this kind, and contemporaries commented on the way that parishes surrounding London lost much of their marriage trade to the anonymous urban parishes."[34] Many couples were thus able to secure their privacy and freedom by exploiting loopholes in the marriage regulations.

Even when couples did cohabit instead of marrying formally, they often behaved as if they were married and insisted on being recognized as such. Many had lifelong commitments and most expected monogamous and stable partnerships. Though the law did not officially recognize irregular unions, the courts regularly dealt with such relationships and often applied practical solutions that revealed some level of acceptance of them, particularly among the working classes. Frost points out that cohabiters "believed their unions entailed financial and emotional obligations, and the courts tacitly agreed," often awarding female cohabitants and their children financial settlements when they claimed desertion by a common-law husband. Upholding the responsibilities of fathers—whether they were properly married or not—was more important to judges than morally condemning unwed mothers. The state also had a financial motive to protect unmarried women and their children since it would potentially have to foot the bill for those who were not supported by their male partners. Likewise, according to Probert, "the moral obligation on a man to marry a woman who was bearing his child remained" even among the working classes. Thus, community sentiment was often enough to urge men to marry.[35]

Most who chose not to marry were among the working classes, but some members of bohemian and artistic circles—such as painters and actors—also openly eschewed marriage. Even among these groups, however, irregular unions were typically quite conservative. The couples usually maintained traditional gender roles and behaved like husband and wife. Frost argues that "facing up to the failure of a free union was difficult, particularly for women, since they were often economically dependent. In addition, they were socially isolated already; being a deserted fallen woman was one of the few situations that was worse." Cross-class cohabitation was also widespread, particularly among upper-class men and working-class women. In many cases, the men saw these unions as temporary while the women used them to better their economic situations. Famous cases include novelist Wilkie Collins—who kept two servant mistresses, Catherine Graves and Martha Rudd, in separate households. Several members of the Pre-Raphaelite Brotherhood had extended relationships with their working-class models. Dante Gabriel Rossetti and Ford Maddox Brown married models Lizzie Siddall and Emma Hill, while William Holman Hunt had a relationship with—but never wed—Ann Miller. Friedrich Engels spent 20 years with Mary Burns, an Irish mill worker, and lived with her sister Lizzie for 10 years after Mary's death.[36] There were many legitimate reasons for couples to avoid marriage and the community sometimes accepted those reasons. However, when unmarried couples were not embraced by their friends and family their situations could become unbearable. Both growing sympathy for such shunned couples and continuing objections to married women's status under the law were largely responsible for the late-century assault on marriage.

THE CASE AGAINST MARRIAGE

Throughout the century, birth and marriage rates were slowly declining as a result of increasing awareness and acceptance of more effective birth control methods. A significant movement aimed at limiting population growth and improving the lives of working-class women emerged in the 1820s and 1830s. Francis Place, a radical tailor, argued that the poor should control reproduction rates to avoid glutting the labor market and to improve the economic stability of working families. He circulated tracts urging fellow workers to marry early for stability but to limit the number of children by using contraceptive sponges soaked in vinegar or lemon juice. Likewise, working-class advocate Richard Carlile's *Every Woman's Book, Or What is Love* (1826) provided information about birth control methods and urged women to actively control their own fertility. However, neither Place nor Carlile made much impact since, as Anna Clark puts it, their intended audience was often insulted by the suggestion "that laboring people should breed or not breed according to economic circumstances." They felt that such advice "reduced them to the level of animals." Birth control was also associated with prostitutes and met with much disapproval on religious and moral grounds.[37] While these early efforts did not produce significant results, it is clear that more effective birth control methods were gradually being adopted.

Mason argues that couples were increasingly using barrier methods such as condoms, sponges, and spermicides by the middle of the century. There was a distinct class division when it came to such practices, with those in the higher classes restricting birth rates earlier and more dramatically, especially in London where middle-class rates were significantly lower than those among the working classes. During the 1870s the advertising of birth control methods greatly increased and resistance to family limitation deteriorated. Annie Besant and Charles Bradlaugh's 1876 republication of Charles Knowlton's *Fruits of Philosophy, or the Private Companion of Young, Married People* (first published in the United States in 1832) drew a great deal of attention to the subject.[38] Knowlton's pamphlet outlined the physiology of sexual reproduction and recommended treatments for impotency as well as methods of birth control. Besant was legally separated from her husband Frank (whom she married at 19) and lived for a time with Bradlaugh who was also separated from his wife. Their reprinting of the notorious pamphlet led to a conviction on charges of obscenity in 1877, which was overturned on a technicality. By undermining the idea that the goal of marriage was solely to procreate, the birth control movement began to redefine marriage along more egalitarian lines as it attempted to free women from continuous cycles of pregnancy and childbirth.

As a result, in the 1880s married couples had an average of 3.5 children, down from an average of 6.4 at mid-century. In addition to increasing knowledge of birth control methods, the Social Purity movement of the 1880s encouraged abstinence from sex even for married couples. Elizabeth Wolstenholme Elmy campaigned for the legal acceptance of marital rape as a crime, but while this did not gain traction in Parliament, middle-class wives were increasingly asserting their right to withhold sex. As Tosh puts it, "the danger to life from childbirth and venereal infection" was so pressing "that feminists demanded that men conform to women's standards of purity, rather than that women should enjoy the same sexual privileges as men." Fear of the detrimental affects of sexual excess and a desire for self-control together encouraged abstinence.[39] Furthermore, the increasing cost of raising a family and the falling child mortality rate encouraged couples to have fewer children.

While the movement toward smaller families gained strength, other approaches to reforming married life were underway. A strong case against traditional marriage based on progressive social ideals was already in place at the beginning of the century. Taking their cues from earlier activists such as William Godwin and Mary Wollstonecraft, 19th-century radicals Robert Own and his son Robert Dale Owen advocated sexual freedom as well as dissolvable civil marriage bonds. Their followers, known as Owenites, founded a socialist commune in the United States and spread their ideas through trade unions and periodical publications. Clark argues that "Owenite sexual radicalism was . . . a political articulation of existing practice in working-class culture" since cohabitation was already widely accepted. Owenites Anna Wheeler and Richard Thompson published attacks on the gender inequality inherent in contemporary marriage and advocated political rights for women as a solution to marital unhappiness. Margaret Chappellsmith's lectures and Frances Morrison's writings insisted that new marital relationships would only be successful if men could control their animal passions to ensure fidelity. Both agreed that true marriages were based solely on love and not on law. They argued that such unions were morally superior, despite charges that they were based on licentious or illegal bonds.[40] The impulse to transform gender roles and marital expectations was as much rooted in the companionate ideal as it was in working-class political radicalism.

However, the passage of the 1834 Poor Law put a damper on the influence of this early radicalism. The law brought an end to outdoor relief (government food and charitable support) for poor families and demanded that those who could not afford to support themselves enter workhouses where wives, husbands, and children would be separated. It seemed that one goal of this harsh system, based on the economic principles of Thomas Malthus, was to prevent marriage and reproduction among the poor altogether. Clark concludes the new law forestalled "any possibility that the Owenite critique on marriage could gain a wider radical resonance, for opposing the New Poor Law required radicals to defend working-class morality rather than undermine its shaky foundations." Working-class opposition to the new law was based largely on the right of working people to marry and have children, which was achieved by characterizing working families as just as traditional and moral as middle-class families. Barbara Taylor explains that "the combined effect of pressure from above and a changed social environment below was to narrow women's options and increase their sexual vulnerability. Under these circumstances, women were usually more interested in enforcing the obligations of marriage than in abolishing them." Furthermore, the confusing messages of Owenites about women's status—they protested the status quo marital domination of women but offered little security for women who chose an alternative path—may have been the last nail in the coffin of the nascent marriage reform movement.[41] Nor did the actual conditions at experimental Owenite communities help the public relations of these groups.

Between 1821 and 1845 seven official Owenite communes were established in Britain, including Manea Fen in Cambridgeshire (1838–1841) and Queenwood in Hampshire (1839–1845). These communities were particularly disappointing to the women who joined them. The living conditions were harsh for women who were required to work ceaselessly without much power over decision-making processes. Participants were often focused on survival and did not accomplish much in the way of transforming gender roles: women typically worked in the kitchen and performed traditional domestic duties. These groups generally abided by Robert Owens's proposal that a marriage would be solemnized based on a declaration of intent from the couple followed by a ceremony. Couples would retain the possibility of dissolving their unions after a trial period of one year. However, most members arrived married and stayed married, so these experimental ideals did not come into much practical use.[42] The fact that any arrangements couples made under these regulations were not recognized as legal unions could not have made them very attractive to women seeking stable relationships.

The French socialist doctrines of Charles Fourier were also popularized in England in the 1830s. Fourier advocated more cooperative relationships between men and women and rejected the legal, social, and moral oppression of women; indeed, he believed that society could not progress without extending women's liberty. George Henry Lewes and his wife Agnes lived in a household based on Fourier's communal principles with three other couples, including the Thornton Hunts. Agnes and Hunt developed a sexual relationship, which led to the birth of three children between them. After the birth of the second child that was not his own, Lewes wanted to end his marriage, but having once condoned his wife's adultery he could not file for divorce. The couple therefore separated but remained legally married. Lewes later entered into a 24-year relationship with Marian Evans (later known as novelist George Eliot), who agreed to a monogamous unmarried partnership and willingly served as stepmother to his children. According to Rose, the couple redefined for themselves what marriage was: "She would call herself Mrs. Lewes. She would be his wife. Whether or not they uttered the ritual oaths of fidelity, they would stay together always. . . . It was to be a regular marriage in every way but one: it was validated only by personal commitment."[43] The idea that a personal statement of devotion could constitute a marriage hearkened back to the Book of Common Prayer rules governing marriage and the pre-Harwicke marriage reforms. Even in an era when divorce was more widely available, many felt that formal marriage was an encumbrance. Yet, the availability of divorce after 1857 may also have temporarily squelched much of the early enthusiasm for marriage reform.

The marriage reform movement regained its momentum as a part of the reenergized feminist movement in the latter half of the century. Along with fighting for expanded education and professional opportunities and for the right to vote, feminist groups began to conceive of alternative forms of marriage. Sharon Marcus argues that the late-century "demand to reform marriage began as a quest to make it more equal and flexible, then evolved into a demand to make it less obligatory. To change the quality of life for the unmarried would alter marriage itself." Single women were at the forefront of this new marriage reform activism. Writers like Cobbe based their arguments about marriage reform on the ideal of companionate marriage—which was indeed conceived of as a kind of intense romantic friendship—that they experienced in their same-sex relationships. Marcus claims that "because female marriage was not a marginal, secret practice confined to a subculture, but was integrated into far-flung, open networks, women like Cobbe could model their relationship on a contractual ideal of marriage and propose that legal marriage remodel itself in the image of their own unions."[44] Some activists were also forward-thinking men, like Mill, who wanted more egalitarian relationships with educated women with whom they could have meaningful conversations.

In the summer of 1885, socialist Karl Pearson founded "The Men's and Women's Club" to discuss the future of gender, sex, and marital relations. Members included a group of Pearson's Cambridge friends as well as Elizabeth Cobb (wife of an MP), Cobb's sisters Loetitia and Maria Sharp, and novelist Olive Schreiner. While the members were not particularly sexually radical, a cohort of more activist feminists and socialists, including Annie Besant and Eleanor Marx Aveling were associated with the group. After four years, the club ultimately ended over the failure of the members to communicate openly across gender lines, the inability of the men to see the women as equals, and the nature of the romantic relationships that developed and deteriorated among group members. As Judith Walkowitz explains, "Men in the club were not only more socially and politically powerful than the women; as rejected suitors, dominant romantic interests, tutors, and, in one case, consulting physician, they exercised a supervisory role over the women at the most personal level." Yet, the most frequent complaint among the women was "the tendency of the men to treat [them] as objects of study rather than as equal participants in a joint inquiry." While the club members made no definitive statements about the subjects they explored, their inquiries and the publicity surrounding them "stimulated a media extravaganza on marriage and its discontents." Mona Caird's articles on marriage published in the *Westminster Review* in 1888 drew on the group's historical and evolutionary explorations of marriage, though Caird had actually been rejected as a club member. Caird's articles were not particularly original, but, Walkowitz notes, they were remarkable for the response they evoked including an estimated 27,000 letters sent to the *Daily Telegraph* to discuss them.[45]

Caird, who was married but lived independently from her husband with his consent, was passionate about marriage reform. Following Pearson's account of the evolution of marital practices, Caird argues in "Marriage" that contemporary marriage was based on the ancient tradition of wife capture, during which tribal men would kidnap the women they wanted for wives thereby making them their property by conquest. Following the theme of entrapment, she likens married women to chained dogs whom "we deny . . . freedom, and in some cases, alas! even sufficient exercise to keep his limbs supple and his body in health . . . if by any chance he is let loose, he gets into mischief and runs away. He has not been used to liberty or happiness, and he cannot stand it. . . . So, the dog is punished by chaining for the misfortune of having been chained, till death releases him." To remedy the problems caused by the restraint of women under marriage, Caird calls for more egalitarian unions based on mutual respect and friendship and decries the prohibitions against friendship between men and women that "make the ideal marriage—that is, a union prompted by love, by affinity or attraction of nature and by friendship—almost beyond the reach of this generation." Caird's description of the stale state of modern marriage echoes the critique offered by Wilkie Collins in "Bold Words by a Bachelor." She argues:

> The man who marries finds that his liberty has gone, and the woman exchanges one set of restrictions for another. She thinks herself neglected if the husband does not always return to her in the evenings, and the husband and society think her undutiful, frivolous, and so forth if she does not stay at home alone, trying to sigh him back again. . . . [Thus,] the more admirable the wives, the more profoundly bored the husbands! . . . For husband and wife are then apt to forget everything in the absorbing but narrow interests of their home, to depend entirely upon one another, to steep themselves in the same ideas, till they become mere echoes, half creatures, useless to the world, because they have run into a groove and have let individuality die.

Caird suggested rational solutions that would make marriage more flexible and free, starting with the co-education of the sexes, which she hoped would facilitate "genuine attachments founded on friendship."[46]

After the *Daily Telegraph* featured reader responses to Caird's critique of marriage in its correspondence section, she followed up with another article in the *Westminster Review* called "Ideal Marriage." Here she claims that "our present marriage system is coercive; the marriage contract being the only contract which we have to submit to without having a voice in the framing of its conditions; the only contract, moreover, which lasts for life." As a remedy, she proposes "free marriage," or a union intended to be permanent but that would be dissolvable. This union would be entered into by a contract administered by the state, but the two marrying parties would determine its terms. She elaborates even further on this idea in "The Morality of Marriage," published in March 1890 in the *Fortnightly Review*. Here, Caird provides further details about how free marriage contracts might work. To begin, she advocates less rigid and more equitable divorce laws and the complete right of the mother to child custody.

With these measures of equality in place, she argues, "there remains no valid reason against the immediate adoption of contract-marriage" which would enable "man and woman to obtain divorce on the same grounds" and "permit them to agree upon these grounds, subject to certain restrictions which would guard against the selection of absurd or frivolous reasons." Hearkening back to the Owenite marriage contract, she argues that a couple should be able to draw up an agreement to live together on terms they determine with the understanding that "the breaking of any of these promises may or may not constitute a plea for separation or divorce—again according to agreement."[47] If the union proved unsuitable for either party, after a specified period of time, divorce would be possible.

The comic journal *Fun* responded to the Caird media frenzy in 1888 with two satirical pieces. "Is Marriage a Failure?" parodies the readers' letters printed in the *Daily Telegraph*. One mock letter is sent by a spinster from "Vinegar Gardens" who definitively proclaims, "Marriage is a failure. I have studied the question for thirty years, and I ought to know." Another is from a "Trigamist" who would "certainly consider marriage a failure" having "married three ladies, all of whom are living." These humorous letters undermine Caird's generalized critique of marriage by implying that marital failure was not something systematic that emanated from the restrictions of the institution itself, but rather something that was the fault of the individuals involved (or not involved, as in the case of the spinster). "Mrs. Mona Caird's Craze," on the other hand, focuses on the failures of Caird herself. The first stanza declares:

> There was a lady-writer once whose name began with C.,
> Who wrote an essay which supplied much stuff for the *D.T.*;
> Her essay sneered at the nuptial knot, "Let the sexes," she says,
>   "be free,"
> For she Caird for no mere married folk, and nobody Caird for she![48]

In March 1892 *Judy: The London Serio-Comic Journal* picked up on a similar theme in a cartoon depicting a lady asking a bachelor if he thinks marriage is a failure (Figure 5.3). The gentleman responds that he doesn't know from personal experience, but his friend "Dashwood 'ud tell you. He married a girl for money and then found she hadn't got any." In a backhanded way this makes Caird's point for her, since she argues that if a marriage is based solely on such superficial bonds as wealth and status, then it is not a relationship worth having. While much of the public response to the idea of marriage reform centered on Caird, there were many other outspoken advocates for reform at the end of the century.

Socialist firebrand Annie Besant discouraged women from marrying altogether until the laws could be changed to better serve their needs. Besant channeled her political activism toward marriage reform in her 1882 book

IS MARRIAGE A FAILURE?

She.—Is Marriage a Failure?

He.—I don't know from Experience. My Friend Dashwood 'ud Tell you. He Married a Girl for her Money, and then Found she Hadn't Got any.

Figure 5.3. "Is Marriage a Failure?" *Judy, or the London Serio-Comic Journal* 9 (March 9, 1892): 118. Image published with permission of ProQuest. Further reproduction is prohibited without permission.

Marriage, as It Was, as It Is, and as It Should Be: A Plea for Reform. In *Marriage* Besant argues that married women's appalling lack of rights—including the right to control their own bodies—was reason enough for women to resist legal unions until marriage was reformed: "In an unlegalised union the woman retains possession of all her natural rights; she is mistress of her own actions, of her body, of her property; she is able to legally defend herself against attack; all the Courts are open to protect her; she forfeits none of her rights as an Englishwoman; she keeps intact her liberty and her independence; she has no master; she owes obedience to the laws alone." Of course, the significant disadvantages of illegal unions—including social disgrace and the potential of having bastard children—remained potent impediments to most women. Still, Besant declares it a choice between two evils and considers the evil "overwhelmingly greater on the side of legal unions." Besant urged the establishment of a Marriage Reform League to agitate for an act of Parliament to change the laws governing marriage. Greater equality in marriage as well as divorce laws, she argued, would make marriages generally more happy since "half the unhappiness of married life arises from the too great feeling of security which grows out of the indissoluble character of the tie. . . . If divorce were the result of jarring at home, married life would very rapidly change."[49] While Caird and Besant sought to improve marriage for women, some activists went so far as to call for its abolition.

Cicely Hamilton, actress, novelist, playwright, and founder of the Women Writer's Suffrage League in 1908, conceives of marriage in purely economic terms. In *Marriage as a Trade* (1909) Hamilton argues that women are "a manufactured product" developed solely to become wives and existing "only for the purpose of obtaining completeness through" men. However, she notes that as a result of idealized notions of marriage, women are denied the ability to use "the freedom of bargaining to the best advantage, permitted as a matter of course to every other worker," including prostitutes. Women's poor bargaining position thus imperiled them individually and threatened the efficacy of marriage itself. For Hamilton, the hope for a brighter future was in the hands of the "independent woman with an income, earned or unearned, at her own disposal, with the right to turn her energies into whatever channel may seem good to her." It is this woman, she argues, who "is steadily destroying the prestige of marriage," which for Hamilton is a good thing.[50] With the imminent decline of the prestige of marriage, Hamilton predicts, women will increasingly reject marriage and choose independent lives.

With perhaps the exception of Hamilton, most challenges to Victorian marriage were, in fact, based on the companionate ideal that Mill so presciently argued would have to lead to greater equality between husbands and wives. Conceptualizing marital relationships as love matches that would provide mutual fulfillment inevitably culminated in louder and louder calls for both the government and society at large to initiate the legal and attitudinal changes required to make the ideal a reality. With the passage of the Divorce Act of 1857, many pronounced the beginning of the end of marriage. While marriage became a dissolvable contract, some demanded that it also be based on mutual terms of agreement that would equalize power relations between husbands and wives. However, it was not until 1928 when the Equal Franchise Act brought full legal equality for adult men and women.

In the 21st century marriage has continued to progress just as many Victorians imagined it would. "The Decline of Marriage and Rise of New Families," a 2010 Pew Research Center study conducted in the United States, indicates that many of our current marital attitudes and conditions have much in common with the Victorians. Like them, we face what many see as a decline in marriage rates and traditional values. Pew identifies a very Victorian-style marriage gap indicating that marriage is more successful and more common among the most educated and highest income groups. Furthermore, among those under 30, cohabitation has begun to outpace marriage, nearly doubling since 1990. According to Pew, 44 percent of all adults (and more than half of all adults ages 30–49) say they have cohabited at some point in their lives. A striking 39 percent say that marriage has become obsolete. While some consider legal marriage for same-sex couples a threat, most aren't worried about expanding marital privileges to all. Pew's recent study of marriage in the United States, seemingly far removed from Victorian England, serves as an apt conclusion to this book because it illustrates that despite the very obvious differences between us and the Victorians, their relationships and their attitudes toward them were much more diverse than we typically imagine, and were in many ways just like our own.

NOTES

CHAPTER 1

1. Swan, *Courtship and Marriage*, 9; "Marriage without Love," 135; Maynard, *Matrimony*, 37–38; "Love," 118; Hall, *Bliss of Marriage*, 26–27.

2. Coontz, *Marriage*, 177–78; quoted in Rose, *Parallel Lives*, 39; Coontz, *Marriage*, 178.

3. Hibbert, *Queen Victoria*, quoted on 123, 141, quoted on 153.

4. Houston, *Royalties*, 33, 37.

5. Patmore, "Angel," 135, 126.

6. Swan, *Courtship and Marriage*, 41, 19–42.

7. Tosh, *Man's Place*, 5; Swan, *Courtship and Marriage*, 31–32.

8. Tosh, *Man's Place*, 28; Hammerton, *Cruelty and Companionship*, 150.

9. Ellis, *Wives of England*, 106–7, 14.

10. Hammerton, *Cruelty and Companionship*, 78.

11. Ellis, *Wives of England*, 59–60, 61, 174.

12. Foyster, *Marital Violence*, 77; Hammerton, *Cruelty and Companionship*, 30–31; Clark, *Struggle for the Breeches*, 248.

13. *Working Man's Wife*, 133–34; Clark, *Struggle for the Breeches*, 249, 263.

14. Hammerton, *Cruelty and Companionship*, 80–81.

15. "St. Valentine's Day," 79–80.

16. "Marriage," 215; "Matrimony," 20; "Pleasures of Matrimony," 183.

17. *Working Man's Wife*, 37–39.

18. Brontë, *Wildfell Hall*, 132, 202.

19. "Marriage," 484; [Hardy], *Happy though Married*, 47, 38; "Motives to Matrimony," 364.

20. Jalland, *Women, Marriage, and Politics*, 75, 52.

21. Shanley, *Feminism, Marriage, and the Law*, 9.

22. Tosh, *Man's Place*, 12.

23. Branca, *Silent Sisterhood*, 40, 44.

24. Perkin, *Women and Marriage*, 30.

25. Gillis, *For Better, for Worse*, 174, 243–44.

26. Corelli, *Modern Marriage Market*, 20–21.

27. "Courtship and Matrimony," 52.

28. "Love Making in 1891," 273.

29. Hammerton, *Cruelty and Companionship*, 81.

30. Shanley, *Feminism, Marriage, and the Law*, 7–8.

31. Chase and Levenson, *Spectacle of Intimacy*, 27–28.

32. Horstman, *Victorian Divorce*, 4–5; Stone, *Road to Divorce*, 191–192, 236.

33. Shanley, *Feminism, Marriage, and the Law*, 36; Stone, *Road to Divorce*, 362.

34. Horstman, *Victorian Divorce*, 85–86; Stone, *Road to Divorce*, 387.

35. Stone, *Road to Divorce*, 387.

36. Quoted in Horstman, *Victorian Divorce*, 86.

37. Ibid., 86–87.

38. Ibid., 144.

39. Hammerton, *Cruelty and Companionship*, 103; Stone, *Road to Divorce*, 385; Hammerton, *Cruelty and Companionship*, 118.

40. Perkin, *Women and Marriage*, 115.

41. Behlmer, *Friends of the Family*, 190.

42. Horstman, *Victorian Divorce*, 101; Mitchell, *Daily Life*, 105.

43. Hammerton, *Cruelty and Companionship*, 53–54.

44. Behlmer, *Friends of the Family*, 194; Horstman, *Victorian Divorce*, 152; Hammerton, *Cruelty and Companionship*, 56; Foyster, *Marital Violence*, 251.

45. Shanley, *Feminism, Marriage, and the Law*, 46.

46. Perkin, *Women and Marriage*, 18; Jalland, *Women, Marriage, and Politics*, 59, 66–67.

47. Mitchell, *Daily Life*, 104.

48. Bodichon, *Laws Concerning Women*, 21.

49. Shanley, *Feminism, Marriage, and the Law*, 30.

50. Horstman, *Victorian Divorce*, 78.

51. Cobbe, "Women and Minors," 10, 19, 21.

52. Shanley, *Feminism, Marriage, and the Law*, 103.

53. Coontz, *Marriage*, 178.

54. Quoted in Tosh, *Man's Place*, 53.

55. Chase and Levenson, *Spectacle of Intimacy*, 85; Mill, *Letters*, 58–59; Rose, *Parallel Lives*, 136.

CHAPTER 2

1. "Courtship," 148.

2. Behrendt and Tucillo, *Not That into You*, 17, 18–19.

3. Armstrong, "Domestic Woman," 135.

4. Ellis, *Daughters of England*, 4; Beeton, *Household Management*, 7.

5. Morgan, *Manners, Morals, and Class*, 87, 91; Gorham, *Victorian Girl*, 8.

6. Arthur, *Advice to Young Ladies*, 128.

7. "Courtship," 561.

8. *Etiquette of Love*, 60; *Etiquette of Courtship*, 7–9.

9. *Etiquette of Love*, 14–15; *English Maiden*, 181; Wheeler, *Whom to Marry*, 39–40, 74.

10. *Etiquette of Love*, 44; *Etiquette of Courtship*, 11; Arthur, *Advice to Young Ladies*, 139; Wheeler, *Whom to Marry*, 48.

11. *Etiquette of Courtship*, 19–20.

12. Mitchell, *Daily Life*, 151–152.

13. Broughton, *Cometh Up*, 70–71.

14. *Etiquette of Marriage*, 5; Wheeler, *Whom to Marry*, xvii–xviii.

15. Gillis, *For Better, for Worse*, 135; Davidoff, *Best Circles*, 14–17, 25; Mitchell, *Daily Life*, 154–155.

16. Evans and Evans, *Victorian Season*, 52.

17. Beetham, *Magazine of Her Own*, 90; Mason, *Making of Victorian Sexuality*, 117.

18. "Matrimonial Monitor," 302–303.

19. Ibid., 303, 307.

20. Davidoff, *Best Circles*, 29.

21. Mitchell, *Daily Life*, 149.

22. *Glass of Fashion*, v–vi.

23. Bailey, *Front Porch to Back Seat*, 20–21.

24. Davidoff, *Best Circles*, 43.

25. *Glass of Fashion*, 81, 62, 79.

26. Davidoff, *Best Circles*, 44.

27. *Glass of Fashion*, 63.

28. Collins, *No Name*, 43–44; *Glass of Fashion*, 89.

29. Ibid., 94–95.

30. Ibid., 99.

31. Ibid., 101.

32. "The Romance of Croquet," 49.

33. *Glass of Fashion*, 103, 106.

34. Ibid., 151–153.

35. Ibid., 157, 195–196.

36. Armstrong, *Letters to a Dèbutante*, 5.

37. Ibid., 50–53.

38. Ibid., 64, 70–71.

39. Ibid., 93–101.

40. Halttunan, *Confidence Men*, 99, 121.

41. Golden, *Posting It*, 216, 223; *Etiquette of Love*, 72.

42. *Letter Writer for Lovers*, n.p.; *Lover's Letter Writer*, 50, 53, 8.

43. "On Love Letters," 236; Barret-Ducrocq, *Love in the Time*, 114; *Letter Writer for Lovers*, 10.

44. *Lover's Letter Writer*, 5–7.

45. Ibid., 14.

46. *Letter Writer for Lovers*, 17–19.

47. Ibid., 46.

48. Grand, "Is it Ever Justifiable," 1016; *Etiquette of Marriage*, 11–12, 21; *Etiquette of Courtship*, 35–37; *Etiquette of Marriage*, 22, 9.

49. *Letter Writer for Lovers*, n.p.

50. Kane, *Victorian Families*, 98; Gillis, *For Better, for Worse*, 115; Mason, *Making of Victorian Sexuality*, 72; Kane, *Victorian Families*, 98–99.

51. Mason, *Making of Victorian Sexuality*, 156–157; Barret-Ducrocq, *Love in the Time*, 19–20; Mason, *Making of Victorian Sexuality*, 157.

52. Gillis, *For Better, for Worse*, 121; Frost, *Promises Broken*, 9.

53. Kane, *Victorian Families*, 93; Gillis, *For Better, for Worse*, 165; Mason, *Making of Victorian Sexuality*, 70.

54. *Lover's Letter Writer*, 21–22, 59.

55. Gaskell, *Cranford*, 64–65.
56. "The Courtship of Female Servants," 248.
57. "Before and after Marriage," 44.
58. "Courtship and Marriage Etiquette," 270, 280, 390, 300, 406.
59. Ibid., 300, 366.
60. *How to Get Married!*, 8, 12.
61. *Courtship As It Is*, 56, 58, 82, 88.
62. Ibid., 166.

CHAPTER 3

1. Kent, *Aunt Agony Advises*, 1, 8–9, 12–13.
2. Mitchell, *Fallen Angel*, 1.
3. Ibid., 3.
4. "Notices to Correspondents," *Reynolds's*, 384.
5. "Notices to Correspondents," *London Journal*, 320, 239, 400.
6. Ward, "A Charm," 250.
7. Beetham, *Magazine of Her Own?*, 62–63.
8. Ibid., 69, 70, 67.
9. "Cupid's Letter-Bag," 94–95, 256, 187.
10. Ibid., 224.
11. Ibid., 62, 128.
12. Ibid., 126, 160, 192.
13. Ibid., 187; Shaw, "Reading the Social Text," 185.
14. Rubery, *Novelty of Newspapers*, 51; "Romance of the *Times*,"10; Rubery, *Novelty of Newspapers*, 60.
15. Clay, *Agony Column*, 33, 34, 137.
16. "Notice to Correspondents," *Bow Bells*, 419; "Notices to Correspondents," *Reynolds's*, 127.
17. King, *London Journal*, 112, 215.
18. "Notices to Correspondents," *London Journal*, 320, 40.
19. Mitchell, *Fallen Angels*, 3; "Notices to Correspondents," *London Journal*, 368; Kent, *Aunt Agony Advises*, 61.
20. "Notices to Correspondents," *London Journal*, 272, 415, 176.
21. Ibid., 224, 63.
22. King, *London Journal*, 67–68.
23. Ibid., 215.
24. Cobbe, "Matrimonial Advertisements," f.p.
25. "The Marriage Market," 353; "Miscellaneous Advertisements," n.p.
26. "Matrimonial Advertisements," *Examiner*, 1274; "The Marriage Market," 353; "Matrimonial Advertisements," *Examiner*, 1274.
27. *Marriage Post*, n.p.
28. "Matrimony by Advertisement," 753, 754; "Matrimony Made Easy," *Illustrated Review*, 242.
29. "Candidates for Matrimony," 296.
30. Rubery, *Novelty of Newspapers*, 61.
31. MacDonald, *Girls Who Answer Personals*, xiv, xii, vii.
32. Ibid., 135, 132, 135.
33. Ibid., 180.

34. "Matrimonial Advertisements," *Bentley's*, 497; "Marriage Brokers," 325; "Marriage Made Easy," 404–405.

35. "Marriage Clubs," 151.

36. Eccles, *Matrimonial Lottery*, 23, 89.

37. "Matrimony Made Easy," *Chambers's*, 114.

38. *How to Get a Husband*, 2–3, 4, 5–6.

39. Ibid., 8, 11, 14–15.

40. Quoted in Stead, "Much Needed Marriage Bureau," 369; Swan, "Should We Establish," 615.

41. Swan, "Should We Establish," 616.

42. Stead, "In the City of Dreadful Solitude," 154; Stead, "Much Needed Marriage Bureau," 369; Stead, "Wedding Ring Circular," xxii.

43. Stead, "Round-About," 178; Cocks, *Classified*, 17–18.

44. "The Man about Town," 786.

45. Stead, "Wedding-Ring Circle," 154.

46. Ibid., 48, 369.

47. Sussman, *Victorian Technology*, 127–128.

48. "Telephonic Love-Song," 153.

49. Otis, *Networking*, 162.

50. Standage, *Victorian Internet*, 206.

51. Stubbs, "Telegraphy's Corporeal Fictions," 92.

52. Jepsen, *My Sisters Telegraphic*, 136–137.

53. "Kate," 60, 62.

54. Thayer, *Wired Love*, 170, 195, 250–251.

55. Ibid., 57.

CHAPTER 4

1. *Etiquette of Love*, 75, 77, 78.

2. Flanders, *Victorian Home*, 234.

3. Stone, *Uncertain Unions*, 12, 15, 17.

4. Probert, *Marriage Law*, 21; Stone, *Uncertain Unions*, 18.

5. Parker, *Informal Marriage* 16; Gillis, *For Better, for Worse*, 145; Michie, *Victorian Honeymoons*, 32.

6. Brontë, *Jane Eyre*, 323–324.

7. Parker, *Informal Marriage*, 21; Probert, *Marriage Law*, 232–233.

8. Jeaffreson, *Brides and Bridals*, 2.128, 173; "Our Marriage-Laws," 54; Jeaffreson, *Brides and Bridals*, 2.135, 176–180.

9. Parker, *Informal Marriage*, 36, 43.

10. Probert, *Marriage Law*, 166; Probert, "Impact of the Marriage Act," 258.

11. Parker, *Informal Marriage*, 44–45.

12. Parker, *Informal Marriage*, 33; Gillis, *For Better, for Worse*, 141–142.

13. Jeaffreson, *Brides and Bridals*, 2.206–207.

14. Probert, *Marriage Law*, 338.

15. *Etiquette of Modern Society*, 38; *Etiquette of Courtship*, 55–56.

16. Parker, *Informal Marriage*, 23.

17. Mitchell, *Daily Life*, 101–102; *Etiquette of Modern Society*, 39; Parker, *Informal Marriage*, 77.

18. Parker, *Informal Marriage*, 49, 72; Michie, *Victorian Honeymoons*, 23.

19. Gaskell, *North and South*, 7, 9–10, 13.

20. *Etiquette of Modern Society*, 41.

21. *Etiquette of Marriage*, 75, 44; "Fashions—A Wedding Trousseau," 280.

22. *Etiquette of Marriage*, 47; Jeaffreson, *Brides and Bridals*, 1.288; Gillis, *For Better, for Worse*, 150, 187.

23. *Etiquette of Marriage*, 9–11, 24–26.

24. *Etiquette of Modern Society*, 39; *Etiquette of Marriage*, 28.

25. Jeaffreson, *Brides and Bridals*, 1.211; *Etiquette of Modern Society*, 40; *Etiquette of Marriage*, 84, 28–9; "Wedding Presents," 52–53.

26. *Etiquette of Marriage*, 11; "Wedding Breakfasts," 239.

27. *Etiquette of Modern Society*, 39, 36; *Etiquette of Courtship*, 30–31; *Etiquette of Marriage* 13–15.

28. "Wedding Ring," 312; Jeaffreson, *Brides and Bridals*, 1.140–141; "Wedding Finger," 286.

29. *Etiquette of Modern Society*, 39.

30. *Etiquette of Marriage*, 52; *Etiquette of Modern Society* 39.

31. *Etiquette of Marriage*, 49; *Etiquette of Courtship*, 62; *Etiquette of Marriage*, 57–58, 61.

32. *Etiquette of Courtship*, 62; Jeaffreson, *Brides and Bridals*, 1.207; *Etiquette of Marriage*, 76.

33. "How Wedding Cakes Are Made," 156; "Royal Wedding Cake," 130.

34. *Etiquette of Courtship*, 64; *Etiquette of Marriage*, 77.

35. *Etiquette of Courtship*, 65, 79; *Etiquette of Marriage*, 60, 63.

36. *Etiquette of Marriage*, 63, 65, 66.

37. Olian, *Wedding Fashions*, iv–v.

38. "Wedding Costume," 77.

39. Olian, *Wedding Fashions*, v; Flanders, *Victorian Home*, 236; "Wedding Extravagances," 303.

40. *Etiquette of Courtship*, 66; Jeaffreson, *Brides and Bridals*, 1.168.

41. *Etiquette of Marriage*, 45; Cunnington, *English Women's Clothing*, 341.

42. *Etiquette of Courtship*, 67; *Etiquette of Marriage*, 53.

43. *Etiquette of Marriage*, 49–50; *Etiquette of Courtship*, 68.

44. Quoted in Gillis, *For Better, for Worse*, 145; Ibid., 187.

45. *Etiquette of Courtship*, 63; *Etiquette of Modern Society*, 40.

46. *Etiquette of Marriage*, 56; Shannon, *Cut of His Coat*, 176.

47. *Etiquette of Courtship*, 67–8, 71–72; Probert, *Marriage Law*, 230.

48. Quoted in Gillis, *For Better, for Worse*, 145–146, 187–189.

49. Ibid., 146; *Etiquette of Marriage*, 70–71; *Etiquette, Politeness, and Good Breeding*, 32–33; *Etiquette of Courtship*, 61; *Etiquette, Politeness, and Good Breeding*, 33.

50. *Etiquette of Modern Society*, 41; *Etiquette, Politeness, and Good Breeding*, 32.

51. *Glass of Fashion*, 235; "Wedding Breakfasts," 241.

52. *Glass of Fashion*, 233; Jeaffreson, *Brides and Bridals*, 1.299–301.

53. *Etiquette of Courtship*, 84-86.

54. Ibid., 86; *Etiquette of Love*, 82.

55. Jeaffreson, *Brides and Bridals*, 2.273, 275.

56. Michie, *Victorian Honeymoons*, 48, 45.

57. *Etiquette of Love*, 80; Michie, *Victorian Honeymoons*, 21.

58. Hardy, *How to Be Happy*, 7, 83; "Honeymoon Reflections," 56.

59. "A Quiet Honeymoon," 562, 563, 564–566.

60. Michie, *Victorian Honeymoons*, 26; quoted in ibid., 6.
61. Rose, *Parallel Lives*, 57, 58–60, 235.
62. Michie, *Victorian Honeymoons*, 61, 151.
63. Collins, *Law and the Lady*, 12, 16.
64. "A Terrible Wedding-Trip," part 1, 50.
65. Ibid., part 2, 75–77.
66. Gissing, "Honeymoon," 895.
67. Ibid., 897.
68. *Etiquette of Marriage*, 76; Cobbe, "Cost of Weddings," f.p., "Impediments to Marriage," 780; "A Few Words upon Marriage Customs," 18.
69. "A Few Words upon Marriage Customs," 19; Flanders, *Victorian Home*, 234.
70. Dickens, *Little Dorrit*, 636, 859–860.

CHAPTER 5

1. Mapes, *Single State*, ix, xiii–xiv.
2. "Why Men Do Not Marry," 218.
3. Tosh, *Man's Place*, 172, 182; Snyder, *Bachelors*, 4.
4. "On Some Impediments to Marriage," 774, 775, 780, 772, 782.
5. Snyder, *Bachelors*, 30, 32–33.
6. Tosh, *Man's Place*, 175, 177.
7. Snyder, *Bachelors*, 19, 44, 45; "Bold Words by a Bachelor," 506, 507.
8. "Why Men Do Not Marry," 219, 220.
9. "Haunted Bachelor," 432.
10. Cobbe, "Celibacy *v.* Marriage," 233; Cobbe, "What Shall We Do," 598.
11. "Statistics of Marriage," 155; Perkin, *Women and Marriage*, 226.
12. Greg, "Why Are Women Redundant?," 161, 158, 161, 163.
13. Kranidis, *Victorian Spinster*, 24, 28; Gothard, *Blue China*, 2, 8.
14. *English Maiden*, 127, 128, 131; *Guide for Governesses*, 27–28.
15. Cobbe, "What Shall We Do with Our Old Maids?," 594, 598.
16. Freeman and Klaus, "Blessed or Not?," 396, 401.
17. Wheeler, *Whom to Marry*, 55; Reed, *Spinster Book*, 208, 211, 216; "An Old Maid's Opinion," 191.
18. Gaskell, *Cranford*, 39.
19. Showalter, "Introduction," vii.
20. Carr, "Miss Anne: A Sketch," 250, 254.
21. Fowler, "Miss Latimer's Lover," 749.
22. Greene, "A Cycling Courtship," 90, 100, 101.
23. Jalland, *Death*, 230; *Hints on Husband-Catching*, 131–134; Jalland, *Death*, 231.
24. "'Nuptiality,'" 499; Curran, "Private Women," 225–227; Jalland, *Death*, 253.
25. Jalland, *Death*, 253; *Hints on Husband-Catching*, 134, 137, 138; Reed, *Spinster Book*, 183, 184.
26. "Marriage Statistics," 56; Reed, *Spinster Book*, 186.
27. Reed, *Spinster Book*, 188, 190.
28. Parker, *Informal Marriage*, 80; Frost, *Living in Sin*, 54–55; Corbett, "Husband, Wife, and Sister," 7.
29. "Marriage Act," 312–313; "Marriage with a Deceased Wife's Sister," 133; Parker, *Informal Marriage*, 81.

30. Frost, *Living in Sin*, 1; Vicinus, *Intimate Friends*, xviii; Marcus, *Between Women*, 2, 13–15.

31. Brady, *Masculinity*, 1–2, 27.

32. Gillis, *For Better, for Worse*, 201–202; Frost, *Living in Sin*, 126–128; Taylor, *Eve and the New Jerusalem*, 193–194.

33. Gillis, *For Better, for Worse*, 217, 215.

34. Probert, "Impact of the Marriage Act," 254–255.

35. Frost, *Living in Sin*, 18, 22–23; Probert, "Impact of the Marriage Act," 255.

36. Frost, *Living in Sin*, 139, 142, 106, 156–161.

37. Clark, *Struggle for the Breeches*, 181–182, 184.

38. Mason, *Making of Victorian Sexuality*, 50–58, 63.

39. Tosh, *Man's Place*, 155–156.

40. Clark, *Struggle for the Breeches*, 186; Taylor, *Eve and the New Jerusalem*, 212–213.

41. Clark, *Struggle for the Breeches*, 188, 187; Taylor, *Eve and the New Jerusalem*, 205, 216.

42. Taylor, *Eve and the New Jerusalem*, 252–253.

43. Rose, *Parallel Lives*, 214.

44. Marcus, *Between Women*, 208, 211.

45. Walkowitz, *City of Dreadful Delight*, 139–141, 145–146, 167, 168.

46. Caird, "Marriage," 187–188, 196, 197, 199.

47. Caird, "Ideal Marriage," 619; Caird, "Morality of Marriage," 325.

48. "Is Marriage a Failure?," *Fun*, 78; "Mrs. Mona Caird's Craze," 78.

49. Besant, *Marriage*, 33, 49.

50. Hamilton, *Marriage as a Trade*, 202, 5, 38, 229.

BIBLIOGRAPHY

Armstrong, Lucie Heaton. *Letters to a Bride, Including Letters to a Dèbutante*. London: F. V. White, 1896.

Armstrong, Nancy. "The Rise of the Domestic Woman." In *The Ideology of Conduct: Essays on Literature and the History of Sexuality*, edited by Nancy Armstrong and Leonard Tennenhouse, 96–141. New York: Methuen, 1987.

Arthur, T. S. *Advice to Young Ladies on Their Duties and Conduct in Life*. London: J. S. Hodson, 1856. *The Nineteenth Century: General Collection* (Microfiche Collection published by Chadwyck Healy in association with the British Library).

Bailey, Beth L. *From Front Porch to Back Seat: Courtship in 20th Century America*. Baltimore: The Johns Hopkins University Press, 1988.

Barret-Ducrocq, Francoise. *Love in the Time of Victoria: Sexuality and Desire among Working-class Men and Women in Nineteenth-century London*. Translated by John Howe. New York: Penguin Books, 1992.

Beetham, Margaret. *A Magazine of Her Own? Domesticity and Desire in the Woman's Magazine, 1800–1914*. London: Routledge, 1996.

Beeton, Mrs. [Isabella]. *Mrs Beeton's Book of Household Management*. 1861. Edited by Nicola Humble. Oxford: Oxford University Press, 2008.

"Before and after Marriage." *London Journal* (July 15, 1871): 44.

Behlmer, George K. *Friends of the Family: The English Home and Its Guardians, 1850–1940*. Palo Alto, CA: Stanford University Press, 1998.

Behrendt, Greg, and Liz Tuccillo. *He's Just Not That into You: The No Excuses Truth to Understanding Guys*. New York: Simon Spotlight Entertainment, 2004.

Besant, Annie. *Marriage, As It Was, As It Is, and As It Should Be: A Plea for Reform*. London: Freethought, 1882.

Bodichon, Barbara. *A Brief Summary in Plain Language of the Most Important Laws in England Concerning Women*. London: Trübner, 1869.

Brady, Sean. *Masculinity and Male Homosexuality in Britain, 1861–1913*. Houndsmills, UK: Palgrave Macmillan, 2005.

Branca, Patricia. *Silent Sisterhood: Middle Class Women in the Victorian Home*. Pittsburgh, PA: Carnegie Mellon University Press, 1975.

Brontë, Ann. *The Tenant of Wildfell Hall*. 1848. Edited by Stevie Davies. New York: Penguin Books, 1996.

Brontë, Charlotte. *Jane Eyre*. 1847. Edited by Michael Mason. New York: Penguin, 2003.

Broughton, Rhoda. *Cometh Up as a Flower*. 1867. Edited by Pamela K. Gilbert. Peterborough, ON: Broadview Press, 2001.

Caird, Mona. "Ideal Marriage." *Westminster Review* (November 1888): 617–636.

Caird, Mona. "Marriage." *Westminster Review* (July 1888): 186–201.

Caird, Mona. "The Morality of Marriage." *Fortnightly Review* (March 1890): 310–330.

"Candidates for Matrimony." *All the Year Round* (July 26, 1873): 295–299.

Carr, Katherine. "Miss Anne: A Sketch." *Argosy* (September 1893): 242–254.

Chase, Karen, and Michael Levenson. *The Spectacle of Intimacy: A Public Life for the Victorian Family*. Princeton, NJ: Princeton University Press, 2000.

Clark, Anna. *The Struggle for the Breeches: Gender and the Making of the British Working Class*. Los Angeles: University of California Press, 1995.

Clay, Alice. *The Agony Column of the "Times," 1800–1870*. London: Chatto and Windus, 1881.

Cobbe, Frances Power. "Celibacy v. Marriage." *Fraser's Magazine for Town and Country* (February 1862): 228–235.

[Cobbe, Frances Power]. "The Cost of Weddings." *Echo* (September 4, 1869): f.p.

Cobbe, Frances Power. *Criminals, Idiots, Women, and Minors: Is the Classification Sound?* Manchester, UK: A. Ireland, 1869.

[Cobbe, Frances Power]. "Matrimonial Advertisements." *Echo* (June 8, 1869): f.p.

Cobbe, Frances Power. "What Shall We Do with Our Old Maids?" *Fraser's Magazine for Town and Country* (November 1862): 594–610.

Cocks, H.G. *Classified: The Secret History of the Personal Column*. London: Random House, 2009.

[Collins, Wilkie]. "Bold Words by a Bachelor." *Household Words* (December 13, 1856): 505–507.

Collins, Wilkie. *The Law and the Lady*. 1875. Edited by David Skilton. New York: Penguin Books, 1998.

Collins, Wilkie. *No Name*. 1862. Edited by Mark Ford. New York: Penguin Books, 1995.

Coontz, Stephanie. *Marriage, a History: From Obedience to Intimacy or How Love Conquered Marriage*. New York: Viking Penguin, 2005.

Corbett, Mary Jean. "Husband, Wife, and Sister: Making and Remaking the Early Victorian Family." *Victorian Literature and Culture* 35 (2007): 1–19.

Corelli, Marie, and Lady Jeune, Flora Annie Steel, and Susan, Countess of Malmesbury. *The Modern Marriage Market*. London: Hutchinson, 1898.

"Courtship." *Chambers's Journal* (September 8, 1883): 561–563.

"Courtship." *London Journal* (March 6, 1875): 148.

Courtship as It Is and as It Ought to Be; by "A Careful Observer of the First," and "A Practical Experimentalist in the Latter." Otley, UK: William Walker, 1877. *Women and Victorian Values, 1837–1910* (Microfilm Collection published by Adam Matthew Publications in association with the Bodleian Library, Oxford).

"Courtship and Matrimony." *Anti-Teapot Review* (August 1867): 52–54.

"The Courtship of Female Servants." *London Review* (March 14, 1868): 248–249.

Cunnington, C. Willett. *English Women's Clothing in the Nineteenth Century: A Comprehensive Guide with 1,117 Illustrations.* 1937. New York: Dover, 1990.

"Cupid's Letter-Bag." *Englishwoman's Domestic Magazine* (June 1852): 62–63; (July 1852): 94–95; (August 1852): 126–127; (October 1852): 186–187; (August 1853): 128; (November 1853): 224; (December 1853): 256; (September 1854): 160; (October 1854): 192.

Curran, Cynthia. "Private Women, Public Needs: Middle-class Widows in Victorian England." *Albion: A Quarterly Journal Concerned with British Studies* 25.2 (Summer 1993): 217–236.

Davidoff, Leonore. *The Best Circles: Society Etiquette and the Season.* London: Croom Helm, 1973.

Dickens, Charles. *Little Dorrit.* 1857. New York: Penguin Classics, 2003.

Eccles, Charlotte O'Connor. *The Matrimonial Lottery.* London: Eveleigh Nash, 1906.

Ellis, Mrs. [Sarah Stickney]. *The Daughters of England, Their Position in Society, Character and Responsibilities.* New York: D. Appleton, 1843.

Ellis, Mrs. [Sarah Stickney]. *The Wives of England, Their Relative Duties, Domestic Influence, and Social Obligations.* New York: D. Appleton, 1843.

The English Maiden: Her Moral and Domestic Duties. London: Talboys, Clarke, and Wilson, 1841.

The Etiquette of Courtship and Matrimony: With a Complete Guide to the Forms of a Wedding. London: Routledge, Warne, and Routledge, 1865. *The Nineteenth Century: General Collection* (Microfiche Collection published by Chadwyck Healy in association with the British Library).

The Etiquette of Love, Courtship, and Marriage. London: Simpkin and Marshall, 1847. *Women and Victorian Values, 1837–1910* (Microfilm Collection published by Adam Matthew Publications in association with the Bodleian Library, Oxford).

The Etiquette of Marriage. London: John MacQueen, 1902. *Women and Victorian Values, 1837–1910* (Microfilm Collection published by Adam Matthew Publications in association with the Bodleian Library, Oxford).

The Etiquette of Modern Society: A Guide to Good Manners in Every Possible Situation. London: Ward, Lock, 1881. *The Nineteenth Century: General Collection* (Microfiche Collection published by Chadwyck Healy in association with the British Library).

Etiquette, Politeness, and Good Breeding. London: Ward, Lock, and Tyler, 1870. *The Nineteenth Century: General Collection* (Microfiche Collection published by Chadwyck Healy in association with the British Library).

Evans, Hilary, and Mary Evans. *The Party That Lasted 100 Days, the Late Victorian Season: A Social Study.* London: Macdonald and Jane's, 1976.

"The Fashions—A Wedding Trousseau." *Illustrated London News* (September 13, 1856): 280.

"A Few Words upon Marriage Customs." *Chambers's Journal* (January 8, 1881): 17–20.

Flanders, Judith. *Inside the Victorian Home: A Portrait of Domestic Life in Victorian England.* New York: W. W. Norton, 2006.

Fowler, Ellen Thorneycroft. "Miss Latimer's Lover." *Argosy* (June 1898): 749–755.

Foyster, Elizabeth. *Marital Violence: An English Family History, 1660–1857.* Cambridge: Cambridge University Press, 2005.

Freeman, Ruth, and Patricia Klaus. "Blessed or Not? The New Spinster in England and the United States in the Late Nineteenth and Early Twentieth Centuries." *Journal of Family History* 9.4 (Winter 1984): 394–414.

Frost, Ginger S. *Living in Sin: Cohabiting as Husband and Wife in Nineteenth-century England.* Manchester, UK: Manchester University Press, 2008.

Frost, Ginger S. *Promises Broken: Courtship, Class, and Gender in Victorian England.* Charlottesville: University Press of Virginia, 1995.

Gaskell, Elizabeth. *Cranford/Cousin Phillis.* 1853. Edited by Peter Keating. New York: Penguin Books, 1986.

Gaskell, Elizabeth. *North and South.* 1855. Edited by Patricia Ingham. New York: Penguin Books, 1995.

Gillis, John. *For Better, for Worse: British Marriages, 1600 to the Present.* Oxford: Oxford University Press, 1985.

Gissing, George. "The Honeymoon." *English Illustrated Magazine* (June 1894): 895–904.

The Glass of Fashion: A Universal Handbook of Social Etiquette and Home Culture for Ladies and Gentlemen. London: John Hogg, 1881.

Golden, Catherine. *Posting It: The Victorian Revolution in Letter Writing.* Gainesville: University Press of Florida, 2009.

Gorham, Deborah. *The Victorian Girl and the Feminine Ideal.* Bloomington: Indiana University Press, 1982.

Gothard, Jan. *Blue China: Single Female Migration to Colonial Australia.* Melbourne: Melbourne University Press, 2001.

Grand, Sarah. "Is It Ever Justifiable to Break Off an Engagement?" *Woman at Home* (1896–1897): 1016.

Greene, Millie S. "A Cycling Courtship." *Belgravia* (September 1898): 86–101.

Greg, W. R. "Why Are Women Redundant?" *National Review* 28 (1862): 434–460.

Guide for Governesses: (English and Foreign) Nursery and Finishing by "The Ladies' Agent for Schools and Governesses." York: Johnson and Tessyman, 1875. *Women and Victorian Values, 1837–1910* (Microfilm Collection published by Adam Matthew Publications in association with the Bodleian Library, Oxford).

[Hall, J. Parsons]. "Courtship and Marriage Etiquette." *London Journal* (June 30, 1849): 269–270; (July 7, 1849): 279–280; (July 14, 1849): 300–301; (August 11, 1849): 365–366; (August 25, 1849): 389–391; (September 1, 1849): 406–407.

Hall, S. S. *Bliss of Marriage, or How to Get a Rich Wife.* New Orleans, LA: J. B. Steel, 1858.

Haltunnan, Karen. *Confidence Men and Painted Women: A Study of Middle-class Culture in America, 1830–1870.* New Haven, CT: Yale University Press, 1982.

Hamilton, Cicely. *Marriage as a Trade.* New York: Moffat, Yard, 1909.

Hammerton, A. James. *Cruelty and Companionship: Conflict in Nineteenth-century Married Life.* London: Routledge, 1992.

[Hardy, Edward John]. *How to Be Happy though Married, Being a Handbook to Marriage by a Graduate in the University of Matrimony.* London: T. Fisher Unwin, 1885. *The Nineteenth Century: General Collection* (Microfiche Collection published by Chadwyck Healy in association with the British Library).

"The Haunted Bachelor." *Welcome Guest* 1 (1860): 431–432.

Hibbert, Christopher. *Queen Victoria: A Personal History.* Cambridge, MA: De Capo Press, 2001.

Hints on Husband-Catching: Or, A Manual for Marriageable Misses. London: T.C. Newby, 1846. *The Nineteenth Century: General Collection* (Microfiche Collection published by Chadwyck Healy in association with the British Library).

Holland, Mark. "Miss Penrose." *Argosy* (June 1896): 671–682.

"Honeymoon Reflections." *London Society* (July 1876): 56.

Horstman, Allen. *Victorian Divorce.* London: Croom Helm, 1985.

Houston, Gail Turley. *Royalties: The Queen and Victorian Writers.* Charlottesville: University Press of Virginia, 1999.

How to Get a Husband and How to Get a Wife. Glasgow: Home and Colonial Matrimonial Agency, 1888. *Women and Victorian Values, 1837–1910* (Microfilm Collection published by Adam Matthew Publications in association with the Bodleian Library, Oxford).

"How Wedding Cakes Are Made." *Review of Reviews* (February 1897): 156.

"Is Marriage a Failure?" *Fun* (August 22, 1888): 78.

"Is Marriage a Failure?" *Judy: The London Serio-Comic Journal* (March 9, 1892): 118.

Jalland, Pat. *Death in the Victorian Family.* Oxford: Oxford University Press, 1996.

Jalland, Pat. *Women, Marriage, and Politics, 1860–1914.* Oxford: Clarendon Press, 1986.

Jeaffreson, John Cordy. *Brides and Bridals.* 2 vols. London: Hurst and Blackett, 1873.

Jepsen, Thomas C. *My Sisters Telegraphic: Women in the Telegraph Office, 1846–1950.* Athens: Ohio University Press, 2000.

Kane, Penny. *Victorian Families in Fact and Fiction.* New York: St. Martin's Press, 1995.

"Kate: An Electromagnetic Romance." *Lightning Flashes and Electric Dashes: A Volume of Choice Literature, Humor, Fun, Wit, and Wisdom.* New York: W. J. Johnston, 1877.

Kent, Robin. *Aunt Agony Advises: Problem Pages through the Ages.* London: W. H. Allen, 1979.

King, Andrew. *The London Journal, 1845–83: Periodicals, Production, and Gender.* Aldershot, UK: Ashgate Press, 2004.

Kranidis, Rita S. *The Victorian Spinster and Colonial Emigration: Contested Subjects.* New York: St. Martin's Press, 1999.

The Letter Writer for Lovers: A Complete Guide to Lovers' Correspondence, Suited to All Classes of Society. Ward, Lock, n.d. *Women and Victorian Values, 1837–1910* (Microfilm Collection published by Adam Matthew Publications in association with the Bodleian Library, Oxford).

"Love." *Reynolds's Miscellany* (August 15, 1863): 118.

"Love-Making in 1891." *Punch* (December 10, 1891): 273.

The Lover's Letter Writer for Ladies and Gentlemen. London: George Routledge, 1866. *Women and Victorian Values, 1837–1910* (Microfilm Collection published by Adam Matthew Publications in association with the Bodleian Library, Oxford).

MacDonald, Arthur. *Girls Who Answer Personals.* Washington, DC, 1897.

"The Man about Town." *Country Gentleman: Sporting Gazette, Agricultural Journal, and "The Man about Town"* (June 18, 1898): 786.

"The Manoeuvering Mamma's Matrimonial Monitor, and Belgravian Belle's Bridal Beacon, Containing Twelve Hints for Bewitching Bachelors into Benedicts." *The Queen* (December 21, 1861): 299–309.

Mapes, Diane. "Introduction: Greetings from Spinster Island." *Single State of the Union: Single Women Speak Out on Life, Love, and the Pursuit of Happiness*. Emeryville, CA: Seal Press, 2007.

Marcus, Sharon. *Between Women: Friendship, Desire, and Marriage in Victorian England*. Princeton, NJ: Princeton University Press, 2007.

"Marriage." *London Reader* (March 28, 1878): 484.

"Marriage." *Reynolds's Miscellany* (March 21, 1868): 215.

"Marriage Act." *London Journal* (January 1847): 312–313.

"Marriage Brokers." *Reynolds's Miscellany* (May 11, 1867): 325.

"Marriage Clubs." *London Journal* (November 7, 1857): 151.

"Marriage, Health, and Morals." *London Reader* (January 10, 1880): 262.

"Marriage Made Easy." *London Review* (April 25, 1868): 404–405.

"The Marriage Market." *Chambers's Journal of Popular Literature, Science, and Art* (June 7, 1873): 353–356.

The Marriage Post and Fashionable Marriage Adviser. (June 1907): n.p. *Women and Victorian Values, 1837–1910* (Microfilm Collection published by Adam Matthew Publications in association with the Bodleian Library, Oxford).

"Marriage Statistics." *London Journal* (September 1850): 55–56.

"Marriage with a Deceased Wife's Sister." *Fraser's Magazine for Town and Country* (January 1850): 112–134.

"Marriage without Love." *Reynolds's Miscellany* (September 9, 1848): 135.

Mason, Michael. *The Making of Victorian Sexuality*. Oxford: Oxford University Press, 1994.

"Matrimonial Advertisements." *Bentley's Miscellany* 63 (January 1868): 491–502.

"Matrimonial Advertisements." *Examiner* (November 13, 1875): 1274.

"Matrimony." *Mirror* (January 4, 1845): 20.

"Matrimony by Advertisement." *Chambers's Journal of Popular Literature, Science, and Art* (November 26, 1870): 753–756.

"Matrimony Made Easy." *Chambers' Edinburgh Journal* (February 22, 1851): 113–115.

"Matrimony Made Easy." *Illustrated Review* (January 1871): 241–242.

Maynard, John. *Matrimony: Or, What Marriage Life Is, and How to Make the Best of It*. London: George John Stevenson, 1866.

Michie, Helena. *Victorian Honeymoons: Journeys to the Conjugal*. Cambridge: Cambridge University Press, 2006.

Mill, John Stuart. *Letters*. Vol. 1. Edited by Hugh S.R. Eliot. London: Longman, 1910.

"Miscellaneous Advertisements." *Penny Illustrated Paper and Illustrated Times* (June 11, 1910): n.p.

Mitchell, Sally. *Daily Life in Victorian England*. Westport, CT: Greenwood Press, 1996.

Mitchell, Sally. *The Fallen Angel: Chastity, Class, and Women's Reading, 1835–1880*. Bowling Green, OH: Bowling Green University Popular Press, 1981.

Morgan, Marjorie. *Manners, Morals and Class in England, 1774–1858*. New York: St. Martin's Press, 1994.

"Motives to Matrimony." *Critic* (August 1, 1855): 364.

"Mrs. Mona Caird's Craze: Written in a Mona-Tone." *Fun* (August 22, 1888): 78.

"Notices to Correspondents." *Bow Bells* (November 29, 1865): 419.

"Notices to Correspondents." *London Journal* (December 7, 1850): 224; (December 14, 1850): 239; (December 28, 1850): 272; (March 1, 1851): 415; (March 29,

1851): 63; (May 17 1851): 176; (August 28, 1852): 400; (February 8, 1861): 368; (May 19, 1866): 320; (January 11, 1868): 40.

"Notices to Correspondents." *Reynolds's Miscellany* (September 14, 1850): 127; (December 1862): 384.

"'Nuptiality,' or Chance of Marriage." *London Reader* (March 22, 1879): 499.

"An Old Maid's Opinion." *London Reader* (June 19, 1880): 191.

Olian, JoAnne. *Wedding Fashions, 1862–1912: 380 Designs from "La Mode Illustrée."* New York: Dover, 1994.

"On Love Letters." *Punch* (December 11, 1869): 236.

"On Some of the Impediments to Marriage. By A Bachelor." *Fraser's Magazine for Town and Country* (December 1867): 772–782.

Otis, Laura. *Networking: Communicating with Bodies and Machines in the Nineteenth Century.* Ann Arbor: University of Michigan Press, 2001.

"Our Marriage-Laws." *Chambers's Journal* (January 23, 1875): 53–55.

Parker, Stephen. *Informal Marriage, Cohabitation and the Law 1750–1989.* New York: St. Martin's Press, 1990.

Patmore, Coventry. *The Angel in the House.* London: Macmillan, 1866.

Perkin, Joan. *Women and Marriage in Nineteenth-century England.* Chicago: Lyceum Books, 1989.

Pew Research Center. "The Decline of Marriage and Rise of New Families." Social and Demographic Trends Project. http://pewsocialtrends.org/ (accessed November 18, 2010).

"Pleasures of Matrimony." *London Reader* (June 18, 1864): 183.

Probert, Rebecca. "The Impact of the Marriage Act of 1753: Was it Really 'A Most Cruel Law for the Fair Sex'?" *Eighteenth-Century Studies* 38.2 (Winter 2005): 247–262.

Probert, Rebecca. *Marriage Law and Practice in the Long Eighteenth Century: A Reassessment.* Cambridge: Cambridge University Press, 2009.

"A Quiet Honeymoon." *All the Year Round* (January 19, 1878): 562–566.

Reed, Myrtle. *The Spinster Book.* New York: G. P. Putnam, 1906.

"The Romance of Croquet." *Punch* (August 4,1866): 49.

"The Romance of the Times." *Leader* (January 1856): 10.

Rose, Phyllis. *Parallel Lives: Five Victorian Marriages.* New York: Vintage Books, 1983.

"The Royal Wedding-Cake." *Illustrated London News* (February 6, 1858): 130.

Rubery, Matthew. *The Novelty of Newspapers: Victorian Fiction after the Invention of the News.* Oxford: Oxford University Press, 2009.

Shanley, Mary. *Feminism, Marriage, and the Law in Victorian England, 1859–1895.* Princeton, NJ: Princeton University Press, 1989.

Shannon, Brent. *The Cut of His Coat: Men, Dress, and Consumer Culture in Britain, 1860–1914.* Athens: Ohio University Press, 2006.

Shaw, Margaret. "Reading the Social Text: The Disciplinary Rhetorics of Sarah Ellis and Samuel Beeton." *Victorian Literature and Culture* 24 (1996): 175–192.

Showalter, Elaine. "Introduction." In *The Odd Women.* 1893. By George Gissing. New York: Penguin Classics, 1993.

Snyder, Katherine V. *Bachelors, Manhood, and the Novel, 1850–1925.* Cambridge: Cambridge University Press, 1999.

Standage, Tom. *The Victorian Internet: The Remarkable Story of the Telegraph and the Nineteenth Century's On-line Pioneers.* New York: Berkley Books, 1999.

"Statistics of Marriage." *Mirror* (September 5, 1840): 155.

[Stead, W. T.]. "In the City of Dreadful Solitude: A Plea for a Matrimonial Bureau." *Review of Reviews* (February 1897): 154.

[Stead, W. T.]. "The Much Needed Marriage Bureau: A Suggested Alternative." *Review of Reviews* (April 1897): 369.

[Stead, W. T.]. "The Round-About." *Review of Reviews* (August 1898): 178.

[Stead, W. T.]. "The Wedding-Ring Circle." *Review of Reviews* (February 1899): 154; (January 1900): 48; (October 1900): 374.

[Stead, W. T.]. "The Wedding Ring Circular." *Review of Reviews* (July 1897): xxii–xxiii.

Stone, Lawrence. *Road to Divorce: England, 1530–1987.* Oxford: Oxford University Press, 1990.

Stone, Lawrence. *Uncertain Unions: Marriage in England 1660–1753.* Oxford: Oxford University Press, 1992.

Stubbs, Katherine. "Telegraphy's Corporeal Fictions." In *New Media, 1740–1915,* edited by Lisa Gitelman and Geoffrey B. Pingree, 91–111. Cambridge, MA: MIT Press, 2003.

"St. Valentine's Day." *Ladies' Treasury* (February 1, 1866): 78–81.

Sussman, Herbert. *Victorian Technology: Invention, Innovation, and the Rise of the Machine.* Santa Barbara, CA: Praeger Press, 2010.

Swan, Annie S. *Courtship and Marriage and the Gentle Art of Home-Making.* London: Hutchinson, 1894.

Swan, Annie S. "Should We Establish a Matrimonial Bureau?" *Woman at Home* (April 1897): 614–616.

Taylor, Barbara. *Eve and the New Jerusalem: Socialism and Feminism in the Nineteenth-Century.* London: Virago, 1983.

"The Telephonic Love-Song." *Punch* (April 1, 1893): 153.

"A Terrible Wedding-Trip: Part 1." *Chambers's Journal* (January 23, 1875): 49–51.

"A Terrible Wedding-Trip: Part 2." *Chambers's Journal* (January 30, 1875): 75–78.

Thayer, Ella Cheever. *Wired Love: A Romance of Dots and Dashes.* New York: W. J. Johnston, 1880.

Tosh, John. *A Man's Place: Masculinity and the Middle-class Home in Victorian England.* New Haven, CT: Yale University Press, 1999.

Vicinus, Martha. *Intimate Friends: Women Who Loved Women, 1778–1928.* Chicago: University of Chicago Press, 2004.

Walkowitz, Judith R. *City of Dreadful Delight: Narratives of Sexual Danger in Late-Victorian London.* Chicago: University of Chicago Press, 1992.

Ward, Megan. "'A Charm in Those Fingers': Patterns, Taste, and the *Englishwoman's Domestic Magazine.*" *Victorian Periodicals Review* 41.3 (Fall 2008): 248–269.

"Wedding Breakfasts." *London Society* (March 1874): 236–242.

"Wedding Costume." *Home Circle* (February 1850): 77.

"Wedding Extravagances." *Chambers's Journal* (May 11, 1878): 303.

"The Wedding Finger." *London Reader* (July 19, 1873): 286.

"Wedding Presents." *London Journal* (January 25, 1879): 52–53.

"The Wedding Ring." *London Journal* (January 16, 1858): 312.

Wheeler, Maud. *Whom to Marry, or All about Love and Matrimony.* London: Roxburghe Press, 1894.

Whom to Marry and How to Get Married! Or, the Adventures of a Lady in Search of a Good Husband. By One Who Has Refused "Twenty Excellent Offers at Least." New York: Office of the "New World," 1848.

"Why Men Do Not Marry." *Temple Bar* (October 1888): 218–223.

The Working Man's Wife. London: Religious Tract Society, 1844. *Women and Victorian Values, 1837–1910* (Microfilm Collection published by Adam Matthew Publications in association with the Bodleian Library, Oxford).

Yonge, Charlotte Mary. *The Clever Woman of the Family*. 1865. Edited by Clare Simmons. Peterborough, ON: Broadview Press, 2001.

INDEX

About the Author

JENNIFER PHEGLEY is Professor of English at the University of Missouri–Kansas City, where she teaches Victorian literature. She is the author of *Educating the Proper Woman Reader: Victorian Family Literary Magazines and the Cultural Health of the Nation* (2004) and coeditor of *Reading Women: Literary Figures and Cultural Icons from the Victorian Age to the Present* (2005), *Teaching Nineteenth-Century Fiction* (2010), and *Transatlantic Sensations* (2012).

Ingram Content Group UK Ltd.
Milton Keynes UK
UKHW020026260723
425794UK00003B/124